Lecture Notes of the Institute for Computer Sciences, Social Informatics and Telecommunications Engineering 278

More information about this series at http://www.springer.com/series/8197

Victor C. M. Leung · Haijun Zhang ·
Xiping Hu · Qiang Liu ·
Zhi Liu (Eds.)

5G for Future Wireless Networks

Second EAI International Conference, 5GWN 2019
Changsha, China, February 23–24, 2019
Proceedings

 Springer

Editors
Victor C. M. Leung
Department of Electrical and Computer
Engineering
The University of British Columbia
Vancouver, BC, Canada

Xiping Hu
Shenzhen University
Shenzhen, China

Zhi Liu
Shizuoka University
Shizuoka, Japan

Haijun Zhang
University of Science and Technology
Beijing, China

Qiang Liu
National University of Defense Technology
Changsha, China

ISSN 1867-8211   ISSN 1867-822X (electronic)
Lecture Notes of the Institute for Computer Sciences, Social Informatics
and Telecommunications Engineering
ISBN 978-3-030-17512-2   ISBN 978-3-030-17513-9 (eBook)
https://doi.org/10.1007/978-3-030-17513-9

This Springer imprint is published by the registered company Springer Nature Switzerland AG
The registered company address is: Gewerbestrasse 11, 6330 Cham, Switzerland

Preface

We are delighted to introduce the proceedings of the second edition of the 2019 European Alliance for Innovation (EAI) International Conference on 5G for Future Wireless Networks (5GWN). This conference gathered research contributions that address the major opportunities and challenges in novel 5G air interfaces, 5G spectrum, 5G networking architectures and techniques, 5G-driven modern network systems, 5G security and privacy, etc., with an emphasis on new analytical outcomes and novel application scenarios alike.

The technical program of 5GWN 2019 consisted of 13 full papers, in four oral presentation sessions in the main conference tracks. The conference sessions were: Session 1: Optimization Theory and Applications; Session 2: Intelligent Computing Technology for 5G Applications; Session 3: Resource Allocation and Management; and Session 4: Security and Privacy in Emerging 5G Applications. Aside from the high-quality technical paper presentations, the technical program also featured two keynote speeches and one panel session. The two keynote speeches were Xitong Li from HEC Paris, France, and Xiaojiang Chen from Northwest University, China. The panel discussion was titled "Future Wireless Networking: Progress and Prospects" and chaired by Haijun Zhang, along with panelists Xitong Li, Xiaojiang Chen, Xiaofei Wang, and Deke Guo.

Coordination with the steering chair, Imrich Chlamtac, was essential for the success of the conference. We sincerely appreciate the constant support and guidance. It was also a great pleasure to work with such an excellent Organizing Committee, and we thank them for their hard work in organizing and supporting the conference. We also thank the Technical Program Committee, led by our TPC co-chairs, Prof. Qiang Liu, Deke Guo, Shui Yu, who completed the peer review of technical papers and compiled a high-quality technical program. We are grateful to the conference manager, Kristina Lappyova, for her support and all the authors who submitted their papers to the 5GWN 2019 conference.

We strongly believe that the 5GWN conference provides a good forum for all researchers, developers, and practitioners to discuss all scientific and technological aspects relevant to 5G wireless networks. We also expect that future 5GWN conferences will be as successful and stimulating as indicated by the contributions presented in this volume.

April 2019

Victor C. M. Leung
Haijun Zhang
Xiping Hu
Qiang Liu
Zhi Liu

Organization

Steering Committee

Imrich Chlamtac — Bruno Kessler Professor, University of Trento, Italy

Organizing Committee

General Chair

Victor C. M. Leung — The University of British Columbia, Canada

General Co-chairs

Haijun Zhang — University of Science and Technology Beijing, China

Xiping Hu — Shenzhen Institutes of Advanced Technology, Chinese Academy of Sciences, China

TPC Chair and Co-chairs

Qiang Liu — National University of Defense Technology, China

Deke Guo — National University of Defense Technology, China

Shui Yu — Deakin University, Australia

Sponsorship and Exhibit Chair

Han Hu — Nanyang Technological University, Singapore

Local Chairs

Guoming Tang — National University of Defense Technology, China

Pan Li — National University of Defense Technology, China

Yiqi Wang — National University of Defense Technology, China

Workshops Chair

Zhengguo Sheng — University of Sussex, UK

Publicity and Social Media Chair

Zehua Wang — The University of British Columbia, Canada

Publications Chair

Zhi Liu — Shizuoka University, Japan

Web Chair

Wei Cai   Kwantlen Polytechnic University, Canada

Technical Program Committee

Yanjie Dong   The University of British Columbia, Canada
Zhaolong Ning   Dalian University of Technology, China
Yanxiang Guo   The University of Hong Kong, Hong Kong,
                                     SAR China
Yilong Li   University of Wisconsin-Madison, USA
Xitong Li   HEC Paris, France
Zhiping Cai   National University of Defense Technology, China
Chengzhang Zhu   University of Technology Sydney, Australia
Wentao Zhao   National University of Defense Technology, China
Xianfu Chen   VTT Technical Research Centre of Finland
Wen Ji   Chinese Academy of Sciences, China
Renchao Xie   Beijing University of Posts and
                                     Telecommunications, China
Luoyi Fu   Shanghai Jiaotong University, China
Zhi Liu   Shizuoka University, Japan
Zehua Wang   The University of British Columbia, Canada
Yongyi Ran   Nanyang Technological University, Singapore

Contents

x   Contents

Security and Privacy in Emerging 5G Applications

Optimization Theory and Applications

Joint Scheduling and Trajectory Design for UAV-Aided Wireless Power Transfer System

Yi Wang[1](✉), Meng Hua[2], Zhi Liu[3], Di Zhang[4], Haibo Dai[5], and Ying Hu[6]

[1] School of Intelligent Engineering, Zhengzhou University of Aeronautics,
Zhengzhou 450046, China
yiwang@zua.edu.cn

[2] School of Information Science and Engineering, Southeast University,
Nanjing 210096, China
mhua@seu.edu.cn

[3] Department of Mathematical and Systems Engineering, Shizuoka University,
Shizuoka 432-8561, Japan
liu@shizuoka.ac.jp

[4] School of Information Engineering, Zhengzhou University,
Zhengzhou 450001, China
iedzhang@zzu.edu.cn

[5] School of Internet of Things, Nanjing University of Posts and Telecommunications,
Nanjing 210003, China
hbdai@njupt.edu.cn

[6] Institute of Electronics and Information,
Jiangsu University of Science and Technology, Zhenjiang 212003, China
zfhy116118@126.com

Abstract. In this paper, we focus on an unmanned aerial vehicle (UAV)-aided wireless power transfer (WPT) system, where an energy transmitter is deployed on UAV and sends wireless energy to multiple energy-limited sensor nodes (SNs) for energy supplement. How to exploit the UAV's mobility via trajectory design and adopt suitable scheduling scheme of SNs will directly influence the whole charging efficiency over a given charging period. From the perspective of fairness among SNs, our aim is to maximize the minimum energy received by all SNs by jointly optimizing the UAV's trajectory and SNs' scheduling scheme with the UAV's maximum speed constraint as well as the initial/final location

This work was supported in part by the National Natural Science Foundation of China under Grant 61801435, Grant 61801243 and Grant U1833203, in part by the Project funded by China Postdoctoral Science Foundation under Grant 2018M633733, in part by the Scientific and Technological Key Project of Henan Province under Grant 182102210449 and Grant 192102210246, in part by the Scientific Key Research Project of Henan Province for Colleges and Universities under Grand 19A510024, in part by Science and Technology Innovation Teams of Henan Province for Colleges and Universities (No. 17IRTSTHN014), in part by the Natural Science Research Project of Jiangsu Province for Colleges and Universities (No. 16KJB510008).

V. C. M. Leung et al. (Eds.): 5GWN 2019, LNICST 278, pp. 3–17, 2019.
https://doi.org/10.1007/978-3-030-17513-9_1

constraint. However, the established problem is in a non-convex mixed integer form, which is difficult to tackle. Therefore, we first decompose the original problem into two subproblems and then develop an efficient iterative algorithm by using the successive convex optimization technique, which leads to a suboptimal solution. Numerical results are provided to demonstrate the superiority of our proposed algorithm over the benchmarks.

Keywords: Unmanned aerial vehicle (UAV)
Wireless power transfer (WPT) · SNs scheduling
Trajectory optimization

1   Introduction

Wireless senor networks (WSNs) have been widely used in every aspect of society due to its low cost and convenient deployment on variety scenarios, such as environmental monitor, biomedical observation, data collection and so on [1,8]. However, the vast majority of sensor nodes (SNs) always have limited physical size, which leads to the lack of energy storage capacity. Therefore, how to charge the SNs plays on important role on prolonging the effective lifetime of the WSNs. Many attentions have paid to explore the natural energy for the SNs' energy harvesting, such as solar, thermoelectric or other physical phenomena [3,4,6,13]. Whereas, such schemes are usually subject to the weather and environment conditions to a large extent.

An emerging and promising solution is to utilize the radio-frequency (RF) transmission technique, namely wireless power transfer (WPT) system, whose advantage lies in that the SNs can directly harvest the energy from the energy transmitter (ET) via the RF signal. However, the RF signals will suffer from due serious path loss over long propagation distance, which results in severe performance loss in practical WPT systems in terms of the end-to-end WPT efficiency and the energy supply range. Consequently, in order to improve the WPT efficiency and provide ubiquitous wireless energy transmission to massive energy-constraint SNs, a large number of ETs should be deployed to shorten the distance between the SNs and ETs. Nevertheless, the corresponding deployment cost of ETs will increase dramatically and has a significant impact on the large-scale implementation of WPT systems.

Fortunately, the application of unmanned aerial vehicle (UAV) as mobile ET gives birth to a radically novel architecture for the WPT systems [12]. Exactly speaking, the ET is mounted on UAV for charging SNs and can rely on the UAV's flexible mobility to adjust its location arbitrarily in order to experience the favorable environment condition, which is more preponderant compared with the conventional ETs with fixed locations. Furthermore, low manufacturing cost of UAV as well as device miniaturization facilitate the implementations of the UAV-aided WPT system. In fact, low-altitude UAVs carrying communication transceiver has already been explored in recent studies [9,10,15], wherein UAVs are employed as aerial base stations or relays to boost the performance of terrestrial wireless communication systems. By optimizing the UAV's trajectory and use distance-based user scheduling, the communication link quality will be significantly improved by shortening the distance between the UAV and its served users, which makes the overall system throughput substantially promoted [9,10,15].

Inspired by aforesaid observations, we investigate a UAV-aided WPT system with multiple SNs. Precisely, a UAV is deployed as ET that flies over a specified area to help charge all the distributed ground SNs according to a proper scheduling manner, which is different from the previous work [12] focusing on a UAV-enabled WPT system with a special two users case. In this paper, our goal is to maximize the minimum total energy of SNs by jointly optimizing the UAV trajectory and designing the SN's wake-up schedule, with maximum speed, initial/final location, and energy conversion threshold constraints. Kindly note that with such a wake-up scheduling mechanism, a SN can remain in the sleep state without energy conversion device working until it receives the waking up beacon signal with good RF signal strength from the nearby UAV, at which time it will wake up and start harvesting the wireless energy from the UAV, and return to the sleep state after the transmission [7,16]. This is a useful technique to save the energy consumption of SNs and improve the charging efficiency by shutting down the energy conversion processing when the RF signal strength is not strong enough. This is different from the existing studies [10,11], which assumes that each SN keeps its energy conversion device running all the time as the UAV flies. As we know, the wireless channels between the SNs and the moving UAV fluctuate fast and drastically due to the UAV's flexible and high mobility. Thus, the received RF signal strength cannot always satisfy the energy conversion threshold, which will make the charging efficiency quiet low if the energy conversion device runs continuously. This is because the SN in waking-up state needs energy to maintain its normal operation.

Our design is formulated as a mixed-integer non-convex optimization problem, which is difficult to be optimally solved. By decomposing the original problem into two sum-problems and applying the successive convex optimization technique, an efficient iterative algorithm is proposed to find a suboptimal solution for our design. Numerical results show that the proposed scheme outperforms the benchmark schemes with static or simple straight trajectory of the UAV.

This paper is organized as follows. Section 2 introduces the system model. Section 3 proposes the iterative algorithm to solve the formulated problem. The numerical results and comparisons are presented in Sect. 4. Finally, the conclusion is given in Sect. 5.

2   System Model

As shown in Fig. 1, K single-antenna senor nodes (SNs) are distributed on the ground in a specific area with fixed locations and a single-antenna UAV broadcasts wireless energy to charge the nodes. The UAV travels along unidirectional trajectory with the practical maximum UAV speed constraint. It is assumed that

UAV flies at a fixed altitude H meters ('m' for short) and the maximum flying speed $V_{\max}$ meter/second ('m/s' for short). Meanwhile, the total flying time of UAV is denoted as time horizon T second ('s' for short).

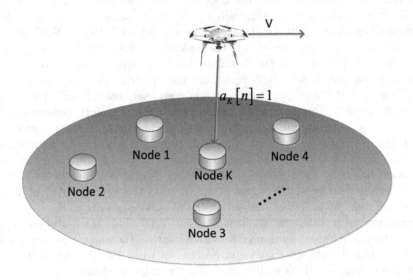

Fig. 1. UAV-aided WPT system with multiple SNs.

For the sake of mathematical description, we set up a three-dimensional Cartesian coordinate system, with all dimensions measured in meters, where the horizontal coordinate of node k is denoted by $\mathbf{w}_k = (x_k, y_k)^{\mathrm{T}} \in \mathbb{R}^{2 \times 1}$, $k = 1, \ldots, K$, and the horizontal coordinate of UAV over time instant t is denoted by $\mathbf{q}(t) = (x(t), y(t))^{\mathrm{T}} \in \mathbb{R}^{2 \times 1}$, $0 \leq t \leq T$. For ease of exposition, time horizon T is equally divided into N time slots with each slot duration δ. As such, the UAV trajectory $\mathbf{q}(t)$ over time T can be approximately denoted by N-length sequences $\{\mathbf{q}[n]\}_{n=1}^{N}$. Note that the slot duration δ should be sufficient small so that the UAV's location can be assumed to be unchanged within this slot [5,14].

Herein, we assume that the initial and landing locations of UAV are predefined as follows

$$\mathbf{q}[1] = \mathbf{q}_0, \ \mathbf{q}[N] = \mathbf{q}_F, \tag{1}$$

where $\mathbf{q}_0$ and $\mathbf{q}_F$ denote the UAV's initial and landing location coordinates, respectively. In practical, UAV usually has a maximum flying speed. Thus, in each time slot, UAV trajectory should be subject to the following constraint

$$\|\mathbf{q}[n+1] - \mathbf{q}[n]\|^2 \leq (V_{\max}\delta)^2, n = 1, \ldots, N-1 \tag{2}$$

where $\|.\|$ means 2-norm calculation. It indicates that the maximum distance of UAV traveled within a time slot cannot be exceeded $V_{\max}\delta$.

From [9,12,14], it can be found that the communication channel from UAV to each node is always dominated by line-of-sight (LoS) link due to the sufficient scattering environment around UAV in the air. Thus, the channel gain from UAV to node k at time slot n follows the free-space path loss model, which is given by

$$h_k[n] = \frac{\beta_0}{d_k^2[n]} = \frac{\beta_0}{\|\mathbf{q}[n] - \mathbf{w}_k\|^2 + H^2},$$ (3)

where $d_k[n]$ denotes the distance between UAV and node k at time slot n, and β_0 denotes the received power at the reference distance $d = 1\,\mathrm{m}$ for a transmission power of $1\,\mathrm{W}$.

2.1 Wake-Up Scheduling Criteria for Energy Harvesting

Herein, we adopt the sleep and wake-up mechanism, where indicates that the node can be waked up to connect with UAV at any time if and only if the received wireless signal strength satisfies the required energy conversion threshold [16].

Define time-varying wake-up scheduling variable $a_k[n]$, which indicates that node k is waked up at time slot n if $a_k[n] = 1$, and otherwise $a_k[n] = 0$. For notation simplicity, we define the UAV's trajectory set and wake-up scheduling set as $Q = \{\mathbf{q}[n], \forall n\}$ and $A = \{a_k[n], \forall k, n\}$, respectively. Assume that the transmit power of UAV is P, and then, the harvested power by node k at time slot n is given by

$$Q_k[n] = \eta_k P h_k[n] = \frac{\eta_k P \beta_0}{\|\mathbf{q}[n] - \mathbf{w}_k\|^2 + H^2},$$ (4)

where $\eta_k \in (0,1)$ denotes the energy harvesting efficiency at the receiver k.

Then, the total energy of node k during the duration time T can be expressed as

$$E_k = \underbrace{\delta \sum_{n=1}^{N} a_k[n] Q_k[n]}_{\text{harvested energy}} + \underbrace{\tilde{E}_k}_{\text{residual energy}},$$ (5)

where the first term denotes the harvested energy and $\tilde{E}_k$ means the residual energy of node k, which is assumed to follow independent Poisson distribution with expectation λ_k.

2.2 Problem Formulation

To achieve the fairness among SNs, we aim at maximizing the minimum harvested energy by jointly designing the SNs wake-up scheduling and UAV trajectory with UAV speed, initial/final locations and energy conversion threshold constraints over a finite horizon time T. The minimum harvested energy is defined as $\theta\left(Q, A\right) = \min\limits_{\forall k} E_k$. Hence, the involved problem can be established as

$$(\text{P1}): \quad \max\limits_{\{Q,A,\theta\}} \quad \theta$$

$$\text{s.t.} \quad E_k \geq \theta, \quad \forall k, \tag{6}$$

$$Q_k\left[n\right] \geq a_k[n]\xi, \quad \forall k, n, \tag{7}$$

$$a_k\left[n\right] \in \{0, 1\}, \quad \forall k, n, \tag{8}$$

$$\left\| \mathbf{q}\left[n+1\right] - \mathbf{q}\left[n\right] \right\|^2 \leq \left(V_{\max}\delta\right)^2,$$
$$n = 1, \ldots, N-1, \tag{9}$$

$$\mathbf{q}\left[1\right] = \mathbf{q}_0, \tag{10}$$

$$\mathbf{q}\left[N\right] = \mathbf{q}_{\mathrm{F}}, \tag{11}$$

Due to the coupled variables in (6) and the involved binary variables, problem (P1) is a non-convex mixed integer optimization problem, which cannot be directly solved by standard convex optimization techniques.

3 Suboptimal Solution to Problem (P1)

To solve problem (P1), we decompose it into two subproblems to optimize the UAV trajectory and SNs scheduling scheme separately. Then, an iterative algorithm is proposed via alternately optimizing the two suboptimal problems. Finally, the convergence of the proposed algorithm is analyzed.

3.1 Wake-Up Scheduling Optimization

In this section, we consider the subproblem of (P1) for optimizing wake-up scheduling A by assuming UAV's trajectory Q is fixed. As a result, the problem (P1) is relaxed to the following problem, which is given by

$$(\text{P1.1}): \quad \max\limits_{\{A,\theta\}} \quad \theta$$

$$\text{s.t.} \quad E_k \geq \theta, \quad \forall k, \tag{12}$$

$$Q_k\left[n\right] \geq a_k[n]\xi, \quad \forall k, n, \tag{13}$$

$$a_k\left[n\right] \in \{0, 1\}, \quad \forall k, n. \tag{14}$$

Note that problem (P1.1) is a classic linear 0-1 programming problem, which have a high complexity with the number of variables increasing. Thus, we first relax the binary variable $a_k[n]$ into continuous variable. That is, the constraint (14) is replaced by $0 \leq a_k\left[n\right] \leq 1$. Thus, the problem (P1.1) is recast into a linear programming problem, denoted as $(\bar{\text{P}}1.1)$. Furthermore, it can be proved that the optimal wake-up scheduling solution to problem $(\bar{P}1.1)$ is either 1 or 0, which indicates the problem $(\bar{P}1.1)$ and (P1.1) have same solutions. Then, we have the following Theorem.

Theorem 1. *Problem* $(\bar{P}1.1)$ *is equivalent to problem* (P1.1).

Proof. The corresponding partial lagrangian function of problem $(\bar{P}1.1)$ can be expressed as

$$
\begin{aligned}
&\mathcal{L}\left(a_k\left[n\right], \theta, \nu_k, \mu_{n,k}\right) \\
&= \theta + \sum_{n=1}^{N}\sum_{k=1}^{K} \mu_{n,k}\left(Q_k\left[n\right] - a_k[n]\xi\right) + \sum_{k=1}^{K} \nu_k\left(E_k - \theta\right) \\
&= \left(1 - \sum_{k=1}^{K}\nu_k\right)\theta + \sum_{k=1}^{K} \nu_k\tilde{E}_k \\
&\quad + \sum_{n=1}^{N}\sum_{k=1}^{K} \left[\mu_{n,k}\left(Q_k\left[n\right] - a_k[n]\xi\right) + \delta\nu_k a_k\left[n\right]Q_k\left[n\right]\right]
\end{aligned}
\tag{15}
$$

where the Lagrangian multipliers ν_k and μ_n are corresponding to the constraint (12) and (13) of problem $(\bar{P}1.1)$, respectively. Accordingly, the dual function for problem $(\bar{P}1.1)$ can be written as

$$
g\left(\nu_k, \mu_{n,k}\right) = \begin{cases} \max\limits_{a_k[n],\theta} \mathcal{L}\left(a_k\left[n\right], \theta, \nu_k, \mu_{n,k}\right) \\ \text{s.t. } 0 \le a_k\left[n\right] \le 1, \forall k, n \end{cases}
\tag{16}
$$

Next, we will prove $1 - \sum\limits_{k=1}^{K}\nu_k = 0$ with the method of reduction to absurdity. Suppose that $1 - \sum\limits_{k=1}^{K}\nu_k < 0$ (or $1 - \sum\limits_{k=1}^{K}\nu_k > 0$), and let $\theta \to -\infty$ (or $\theta \to \infty$) from (16). Then, the dual function $g\left(\nu_k, \mu_{n,k}\right)$ will tend to infinity, which is contradictory with the boundedness of $g\left(\nu_k, \mu_{n,k}\right)$. Thus, $1 - \sum\limits_{k=1}^{K}\nu_k = 0$ should be satisfied.

With the given dual variables ν_k and $\mu_{n,k}$, the dual function $g\left(\nu_k, \mu_{n,k}\right)$ can be solved to obtain the optimal solutions $a_k[n]$ and θ. Since $1 - \sum\limits_{k=1}^{K}\nu_k = 0$, the optimal value of θ can be chosen with any real value. Based on this, it is clear that if $\left(\delta\nu_k Q_k\left[n\right] - \xi\mu_{n,k}\right) \ge 0$, $a_k[n] = 1$ will make $\left(\delta\nu_k Q_k\left[n\right] - \xi\mu_{n,k}\right)a_k\left[n\right]$ maximized, otherwise, $a_k[n] = 0$. This completes the proof. ∎

3.2   UAV Trajectory Optimization

In this subsection, we consider the second subproblem of (P1), namely optimizing UAV trajectory Q with a given wake-up scheduling scheme. As such, the UAV trajectory optimization subproblem can be formulated as

$$\text{(P1.2)}: \max_{\{Q,\theta\}} \eta$$

$$\text{s.t.} \quad E_k \geq \eta, \quad \forall k, \tag{17}$$

$$Q_k[n] \geq a_k[n]\xi, \ \forall k,n, \tag{18}$$

$$\|\mathbf{q}[n+1] - \mathbf{q}[n]\|^2 \leq (V_{\max}\delta)^2,$$
$$n = 1,\ldots,N-1, \tag{19}$$

$$\mathbf{q}[1] = \mathbf{q}_0, \tag{20}$$

$$\mathbf{q}[N] = \mathbf{q}_F. \tag{21}$$

It is worth stressing that the problem (P1.2) is still non-convex owing to the common term $\|\mathbf{q}[n] - \mathbf{w}_k[n]\|^2$ in constraints (17) and (18), which is challenging to find its optimal solutions. However, since $Q_k[n]$ in (4) is convex with respect to (w.r.t.) $\|\mathbf{q}[n] - \mathbf{w}_k[n]\|^2$. Thus, based on successive convex optimization techniques, we can obtain an approximate solution to problem (P1.2). Specifically, the left-hand side (LHF) of (17) and (18) are replaced by their own lower bounds via successively optimizing the incremental of UAV's trajectory at each iteration.

To proceed, let $Q_l = \{\mathbf{q}_l[n], \forall n\}$ denote the UAV's trajectory at l-th iteration, and $\{\triangle\mathbf{q}_l[n]\}_{n=2}^{N-1}$ denote the UAV's displacement. Then, the UAV's trajectory at $(l+1)$-th iteration at time slot n can be expressed as

$$\mathbf{q}_{l+1}[n] = \mathbf{q}_l[n] + \triangle\mathbf{q}_l[n], \ n = 2, \ldots N-1, \tag{22}$$

With the resulting trajectory after the l-th iteration, the corresponding harvested power by node k at l-th iteration over time slot n can be written as $Q_{k,l}[n] = \frac{\eta_0 P \beta_0}{\|\mathbf{q}_l[n] - \mathbf{w}_k\|^2 + H^2}$. Then, we have the following Lemma.

Lemma 1. *For any given UAV trajectory incremental $\{\triangle\mathbf{q}_l[n]\}_{n=2}^{N-1}$, the following inequality holds*

$$Q_{k,l+1}[n] \geq Q_{k,l+1}^{\text{lb}}[n] = \frac{\eta_k P \beta_0}{d_{k,l}^2[n]} - \frac{\eta_k P \beta_0}{d_{k,l}^4[n]}\Delta, \tag{23}$$

where $d_{k,l}[n] = \sqrt{\|\mathbf{q}_l[n] - \mathbf{w}_k\|^2 + H^2}$, $\Delta = \|\triangle\mathbf{q}_l[n]\|^2 + 2(\triangle\mathbf{q}_l[n] - \mathbf{w}_k)^{\mathrm{T}}\mathbf{q}_l[n]$, $n = 2, \ldots, N-1$.

Proof. Define a function $f(x) = \frac{a}{b+x}$ with constants $a > 0$ and $b > 0$. Clearly, $f(x)$ is convex w.r.t. $x \in (-b, \infty]$. Recall that any convex function is globally lower-bounded by its first-order Taylor expansion at any feasible point [2], i.e., $f(x) \geq f(x_0) + f'(x_0)(x - x_0)$. By setting $x_0 = 0$, we have

$$\frac{a}{b+x} \geq \frac{a}{b} - \frac{a}{b^2}x, \tag{24}$$

Hence, the harvested power $Q_{k,l+1}[n]$ can be expressed as

$$
\begin{aligned}
Q_{k,l+1}[n] &= \frac{\eta_k P \beta_0}{\|\mathbf{q}_{l+1}[n] - \mathbf{w}_k\|^2 + H^2} \\
&= \frac{\eta_k P \beta_0}{d_{k,l}^2[n] + \Delta} \\
&\geq \frac{\eta_k P \beta_0}{d_{k,l}^2[n]} - \frac{\eta_k P \beta_0}{d_{k,l}^4[n]} \Delta = Q_{k,l+1}^{\text{lb}},
\end{aligned}
\tag{25}
$$

where $d_{k,l}[n] = \sqrt{\|\mathbf{q}_l[n] - \mathbf{w}_k\|^2 + H^2}$, $\Delta = \|\triangle\mathbf{q}_l[n]\|^2 + 2(\triangle\mathbf{q}_l[n] - \mathbf{w}_k)^{\mathsf{T}}\mathbf{q}_l[n]$ with $n = 2, \ldots, N - 1$. This completes the proof. ∎

Lemma 1 tells us that for given UAV trajectory Q_l and incremental $\{\triangle\mathbf{q}_l[n]\}_{n=2}^{N-1}$, the new iterated energy $E_{k,l+1}$ is lower-bounded by $E_{k,l+1}^{\text{lb}}$, which is concave w.r.t. $\{\triangle\mathbf{q}_l[n]\}_{n=2}^{N-1}$. Then, we have

$$
E_{k,l+1}^{\text{lb}} = \delta \sum_{n=1}^{N} a_k[n] Q_{k,l+1}^{\text{lb}}[n] + \tilde{E}_k.
\tag{26}
$$

By defining $\eta_{l+1}^{\text{lb}}(Q_{l+1}, A_{l+1}) = \min_{\forall k} E_{k,l+1}^{\text{lb}}$, problem (P1.2) can be reformulated as follows

$$
(\bar{\text{P}}1.2) : \max_{\{\{\triangle\mathbf{q}_l[n]\}_{n=2}^{N-1}, \eta_{l+1}^{\text{lb}}\}} \eta_{l+1}^{\text{lb}}
$$

$$
\text{s.t.} \quad E_{k,l+1}^{\text{lb}} \geq \eta_{l+1}^{\text{lb}}, \quad \forall k,
\tag{27}
$$

$$
Q_{k,l+1}^{\text{lb}}[n] \geq a_k[n]\xi, \quad \forall k, n,
\tag{28}
$$

$$
\|\mathbf{q}_l[n+1] + \triangle\mathbf{q}_l[n+1] - \mathbf{q}_l[n] - \triangle\mathbf{q}_l[n]\|^2
$$
$$
\leq (V_{\max}\delta)^2, n = 2, \ldots, N - 1,
\tag{29}
$$

$$
\|\mathbf{q}_l[2] + \triangle\mathbf{q}_l[2] - \mathbf{q}[1]\|^2 \leq (V_{\max}\delta)^2,
\tag{30}
$$

$$
\|\mathbf{q}[N] - \mathbf{q}_l[N-1] - \triangle\mathbf{q}_l[N-1]\|^2 \leq (V_{\max}\delta)^2,
$$

$$
\mathbf{q}[1] = \mathbf{q}_0,
\tag{31}
$$

$$
\mathbf{q}[N] = \mathbf{q}_F
\tag{32}
$$

Kindly note that the LHS of constraint (27) are concave w.r.t. $\{\triangle\mathbf{q}_l[n]\}_{n=2}^{N-1}$. Therefore, the problem $(\bar{\text{P}}1.2)$ is convex. As a result, we can resort to using standard convex technique to solve it, and the problem (P1.2) can be approximately solved by successively updating $\mathbf{q}_{l+1}[n]$ based on the optimal solution to $(\bar{\text{P}}1.2)$, which is summarized in Algorithm 1. Furthermore the optimal value of problem (P1.2) is lower bounded by the optimal solution in Algorithm 1.

Algorithm 1. Successive Trajectory Optimization with Fixed Wake Up Scheduling.

1: **Initialize** $\{\mathbf{q}_0[n]\}_{n=2}^{N-1}$, $\mathbf{q}[1] = \mathbf{q}_0$, $\mathbf{q}[N] = \mathbf{q}_F$, $l \leftarrow 0$, the tolerance $\varepsilon > 0$.
2: **Repeat**
3:    Obtain optimal solution $\{\triangle\mathbf{q}_l[n]\}_{n=2}^{N-1}$ of $(\bar{\text{P}}1.2)$.
4:    Update UAV's trajectory $\mathbf{q}_{l+1}[n] \leftarrow \mathbf{q}_l[n] + \triangle\mathbf{q}_l[n]$.
5:    $l \leftarrow l + 1$.
6: **Until** The fractional increase of the objective value of $(\bar{\text{P}}1.2)$ is less than tolerance ε.

3.3 Joint Wake-Up Scheduling and UAV Trajectory Optimization

In this subsection, with the solutions to problem (P1.1) and $(\bar{\text{P}}1.2)$, we propose an iterative algorithm for jointly optimizing wake-up scheduling and UAV trajectory, which is summarized in Algorithm 2. Note that since the subproblem (P1.2) for UAV trajectory optimization cannot be optimally solved by Algorithm 1, thus the optimality cannot be directly declared for Algorithm 2.

Algorithm 2. Block Coordinate Descent Method for Problem (P1).

1: **Initialize** the UAV's trajectory as $\{\mathbf{q}_0[n]\}_{n=2}^{N-1}$, $\mathbf{q}[1] = \mathbf{q}_0$, $\mathbf{q}[N] = \mathbf{q}_F$, and $l \leftarrow 0$ as well as tolerance $\varepsilon > 0$.
2: **repeat.**
3:    Obtain the optimal wake-up scheduling criteria
      $\{a_{k,l}[n]\}, \forall n = 1, \ldots, N$ and $\forall k = 1, \ldots, K$
      to problem $(\bar{\text{P}}1.1)$.
4:    Fix the wake-up scheduling criteria $\{a_{k,l}[n]\}$
      obtained from step 3, then obtain the optimal
      UAV trajectory $\{\mathbf{q}_{l+1}[n]\}$ using Algorithm 1.
5:    Update $l \leftarrow l + 1$.
6: **until** the fractional increase of the objective value of (P1) is less than tolerance ε.

3.4 Convergence Proof for Proposed Algorithm

In this subsection, the convergence properties of the proposed Algorithms 1 and 2 will be analyzed, respectively. First, for the given trajectory Q_l, the optimal solution to problem (P1.1) can be denoted as A_{l+1}. Thus, we have

$$\theta(Q_l, A_l) \le \theta(Q_l, A_{l+1}). \tag{33}$$

At each iteration in Algorithm 1, the objective function η_{l+1}^{lb} is non-decreasing over l as follows

$$\eta_l^{\text{lb}}(Q_l, A_{l+1}) \le \eta_{l+1}^{\text{lb}}(Q_{l+1}, A_{l+1}). \tag{34}$$

Based on the fact that problem (P1.2) is upper-bounded by a finite value, Algorithm 1 is guaranteed to converge. Due to the fact that $\theta(Q_l, A_{l+1}) = \eta_l^{\mathrm{lb}}(Q_l, A_{l+1})$, $\eta_{l+1}^{\mathrm{lb}}(Q_{l+1}, A_{l+1}) \leq \eta_{l+1}(Q_{l+1}, A_{l+1})$ and $\eta_{l+1}(Q_{l+1}, A_{l+1}) = \theta_{l+1}(Q_{l+1}, A_{l+1})$, it is readily to declare that $\theta(Q_l, A_l) \leq \theta_{l+1}(Q_{l+1}, A_{l+1})$, which indicates that Algorithm 2 is non-decreasing over each iteration l. Furthermore, since the objective value of (P1) is upper-bounded by a finite value, Algorithm 2 is also guaranteed to converge.

4 Numerical Results

In this section, numerical results are provided to evaluate the performance of our proposed UAV-aided WPT scheme. In our system, we consider $K = 4$ SNs randomly distributed within a geographic area of size $100 \times 100\,\mathrm{m}^2$. The involved parameters are set as follows: $V_{\max} = 10\,\mathrm{m/s}$, $H = 10\,\mathrm{m}$, $P = 10\,\mathrm{W}$, $\beta_0 = 1$, $\xi = 10^{-4}$. Furthermore, we choose the time slot duration as $\delta = 0.3\,\mathrm{s}$. Without loss of generality, the energy harvesting efficiency coefficient is same, i.e., $\eta_k = \eta_0 = 0.7, \forall k$. Moreover, the residual energy at each SN follows Poisson distribution with same expectation, i.e., $\lambda_k = \lambda = 0.4\,\mathrm{J}$.

We first consider the case $\tilde{E}_k = 0, \forall k$, which implies that all the SNs have no energy retained at initialization. Figure 2 plots the UAV trajectory with different horizon time T. Without loss of generality, the UAV's initial and final locations are fixed to $\mathbf{q}_0 = (-100, 0)^{\mathrm{T}}$ and $\mathbf{q}_{\mathrm{F}} = (100, 0)^{\mathrm{T}}$, respectively. It can be observed from Fig. 2 that as T increases, UAV moves closer to the ground nodes. This is attributed to the fact that the longer flying time allowed, the more distance

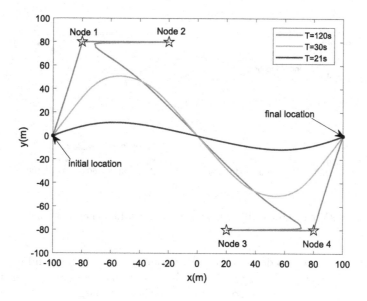

Fig. 2. UAV trajectory with different horizon time T.

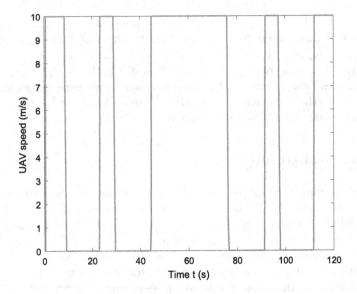

Fig. 3. UAV speed over time instant n at $T = 120$ s.

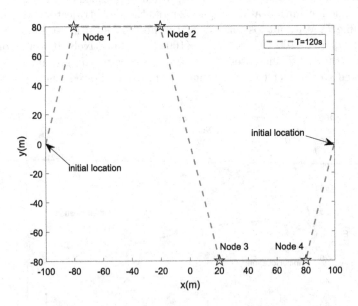

Fig. 4. UAV trajectory with different level of residual energy at each node.

can be traveled. Figure 3 depicts the UAV variation-speed corresponding to UAV trajectory in Fig. 2 at $T = 120$ s. It can be found that the equal dwell time is allocated to each node as horizon time T is sufficiently large.

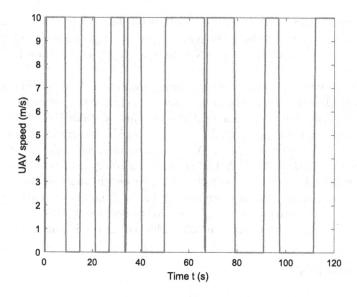

Fig. 5. UAV speed corresponding to UAV trajectory as shown in Fig. 4.

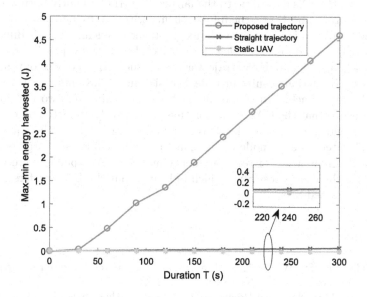

Fig. 6. Max-min energy harvested with different schemes.

Next, we consider that each SN has different levels of residual energy. The residual energy are respectively given by $\tilde{E}_1 = 0.8\,\text{J}$, $\tilde{E}_2 = 0.2\,\text{J}$, $\tilde{E}_3 = 0.6\,\text{J}$ and $\tilde{E}_4 = 0.3\,\text{J}$, which obtained by random realization with mean 0.4 J. It can be seen from Figs. 4 and 5 that UAV moves directly to node k with shortest distance, and different dwell time is allocated to each SN. Specifically, UAV spends a large mount of time to hover above the node which has less residual energy, and less time is allocated to hover above the node which has larger residual energy. This is attributed to the fact that the SN with less energy needs more time to be served by UAV.

At last, we compare our proposed scheme with static UAV scheme and traditional straight trajectory scheme for max-min energy harvested as shown in Fig. 6. It is reasonable to assume that the location of static UAV is located at the geometric center $\mathbf{q}_{\text{static}} = (0,0)^{\mathrm{T}} \in \mathbb{R}^{2 \times 1}$ and the straight trajectory is set as $\mathbf{q}[n] = \mathbf{q}_1 + \frac{\mathbf{q}_N - \mathbf{q}_1}{N-1} n, n = 0, \ldots, N - 1$. To process, the wake-up scheduling is optimized for both static UAV and straight trajectory schemes. One can find that the proposed scheme outperforms the two benchmark schemes. Furthermore, the performance gain is more remarkable as T increases. This is because UAV can move closer to or hover above SNs for power charge with better channel condition. As a result, the max-min total achieved energy is improved.

5   Conclusion

In this paper, we have investigated a novel UAV-aided WPT system, where the UAV charges the SNs according to the fairness criteria by jointly optimizing the UAV's trajectory and SNs' scheduling scheme with the flying constraints. The established problem is a non-convex mixed integer problem, which is difficult to tackle. Thus, we propose an efficient iterative algorithm by jointly optimizing wake-up scheduling and UAV trajectory with successive convex optimization techniques. Simulation results provide two significant insights. First, our proposed scheme has achieved significant performance gain over two benchmarks, which indicates that the UAV trajectory has significantly impacted on the WPT system. Second, for the same levels of residual energy at SNs, the equal dwell time is allocated to each node as horizon time T is sufficiently large. Furthermore, for different levels of residual energy at SNs, UAV spends more time to hover above the energy-less SNs, which indicates that the UAV prefers to serve the energy-drained SNs.

References

1. Akyildiz, I.F., Su, W., Sankarasubramaniam, Y., Cayirci, E.: Wireless sensor networks: a survey. Comput. Netw. **38**, 393–422 (2002)
2. Bertsekas, D.P.: Nonlinear Programming, 2nd edn. Athena Scientific, Belmont, MA (1999)
3. Bouabdallah, F., Bouabdallah, N., Boutaba, R.: Cross-layer design for energy conservation in wireless sensor networks. In: IEEE International Conference on Communications, pp. 1–6 (2009)
4. Fan, K.W., Zheng, Z., Sinha, P.: Steady and fair rate allocation for rechargeable sensors in perpetual sensor networks. In: ACM Conference on Embedded Network Sensor Systems, pp. 239–252 (2008)

5. Jeong, S., Simeone, O., Kang, J.: Mobile cloud computing with a UAV-mounted cloudlet: optimal bit allocation for communication and computation. IET Commun. **11**(7), 969–974 (2017)
6. Pang, Y., Zhang, Y., Gu, Y., Pan, M., Han, Z., Li, P.: Efficient data collection for wireless rechargeable sensor clusters in harsh terrains using UAVs. In: Global Communications Conference, pp. 234–239 (2015)
7. Say, S., Inata, H., Liu, J., Shimamoto, S.: Priority-based data gathering framework in UAV-assisted wireless sensor networks. IEEE Sens. J. **16**(14), 5785–5794 (2016). https://doi.org/10.1109/JSEN.2016.2568260
8. Shi, Y., Xie, L., Hou, Y.T., Sherali, H.D.: On renewable sensor networks with wireless energy transfer. In: 2011 Proceedings IEEE INFOCOM, pp. 1350–1358 (2012)
9. Wu, Q., Zeng, Y., Zhang, R.: Joint trajectory and communication design for UAV-enabled multiple access. In: 2017 IEEE Global Communications Conference, GLOBECOM 2017, pp. 1–6, December 2017. https://doi.org/10.1109/GLOCOM.2017.8254949
10. Wu, Q., Zhang, R.: Common throughput maximization in UAV-enabled OFDMA systems with delay consideration. IEEE Trans. Commun. 1 (2018). https://doi.org/10.1109/TCOMM.2018.2865922
11. Xu, J., Zeng, Y., Zhang, R.: UAV-enabled multiuser wireless power transfer: Trajectory design and energy optimization. In: 2017 23rd Asia-Pacific Conference on Communications, APCC, pp. 1–6, December 2017. https://doi.org/10.23919/APCC.2017.8304077
12. Xu, J., Zeng, Y., Zhang, R.: UAV-enabled wireless power transfer: Trajectory design and energy region characterization. In: 2017 IEEE Globecom Workshops, GC Wkshps, pp. 1–7, December 2017. https://doi.org/10.1109/GLOCOMW.2017.8269097
13. Xu, J., Zhang, R.: Throughput optimal policies for energy harvesting wireless transmitters with non-ideal circuit power. IEEE J. Sel. Areas Commun. **32**(2), 322–332 (2014)
14. Zeng, Y., Zhang, R., Lim, T.J.: Throughput maximization for UAV-enabled mobile relaying systems. IEEE Trans. Commun. **64**(12), 4983–4996 (2016)
15. Zeng, Y., Zhang, R., Teng, J.L.: Wireless communications with unmanned aerial vehicles: opportunities and challenges. IEEE Commun. Mag. **54**(5), 36–42 (2016)
16. Zhan, C., Zeng, Y., Zhang, R.: Energy-efficient data collection in UAV enabled wireless sensor network. IEEE Wirel. Commun. Lett. **7**(3), 328–331 (2018). https://doi.org/10.1109/LWC.2017.2776922

Deep Learning Based Antenna Muting and Beamforming Optimization in Distributed Massive MIMO Systems

Yu Chen[1,2(✉)], Kai Zhao[1], Jing-ya Zhao[1], Qing-hua Zhu[1], and Yong Liu[1]

[1] School of Telecommunication Engineering, Beijing Polytechnic,
Beijing 100176, People's Republic of China
buptchen@163.com
[2] School of Information and Communication Engineering,
Beijing University of Posts and Telecommunications,
Beijing 100876, People's Republic of China

Abstract. Inspired by the success of Deep Learning (DL) in solving complex control problems, a new DL-based approximation framework to solve the problems of antenna muting and beamforming optimization in distributed massive MIMO was proposed. The main purpose is to obtain a non-linear mapping from the raw observations of networks to the optimal antenna muting and beamforming pattern, using Deep Neural Network (DNN). Firstly, the antenna muting and beamforming optimization problem is modeled as a non-combination optimization problem, which is NP-hard. Then a DNN based framework is proposed to obtain the optimal solution to this complex optimization problem with low-complexity. Finally, the performance of the DNN-based framework is evaluated in detail. Simulation results show that the proposed DNN framework can achieve a fairly accurate approximation. Moreover, compared with the traditional algorithm, DNN can be reduced the computation time by several orders of magnitude.

Keywords: Deep learning · Distributed massive MIMO ·
Deep Neural Network · Antenna muting · Beamforming

1 Introduction

In recent years, with the increasing number of smart devices, various wireless services have been exploding, such as social networks, Internet of Things, high-quality radio video streams, etc. The resulting wireless data flow has also been increased by dozens of times. This has led to an increase in the cost of building, operating, and upgrading radio access network, while revenues have grown slowly. As a result, the massive multiple input multiple output (MIMO) technique [1], is proposed to handle the ever-increasing mobile traffic demands.

Characterized by the large number of antennas at the front-end of the radio frequency (RF) chains and the centralized signal processing, massive MIMO not only significantly improves the spectral efficiency, but also greatly reduces the energy

V. C. M. Leung et al. (Eds.): 5GWN 2019, LNICST 278, pp. 18–30, 2019.
https://doi.org/10.1007/978-3-030-17513-9_2

consumption. Hence the massive MIMO is deemed as one of the key techniques in the next generation mobile networks, i.e., 5G. The massive antennas are originally deployed on a single array in a centralized manner, which can achieve the channel harden and favorable propagation. However, recent studies [2] find that distributing the massive antennas not only inherent the advantage of centralized massive MIMO in terms of channel harden and favorable propagation, but also achieve the huge diversity gains through cooperative beamforming, which leads to superior capacity performance.

On the other hand, mobile traffic varies in the spatial and time domain. Always keeping all antennas of the distributed massive MIMO systems active is energy inefficient in the low traffic scenario. The large number of antennas would result in considerable energy consumption while contribute little to the QoS guarantee of users in such cases Hence, adaptively muting the transmission of some antennas according to the dynamic traffic demands seems to be a promising scheme to improve the energy efficiency.

Dynamically turning off the hardware of wireless networks, such as antennas, RF chains at the base stations (BSs), is a commonly used method to reduce the energy consumption, as can be seen in a survey [4]. Zhou et al. [5] proposed a traffic aware BS sleeping control scheme, which can achieve great energy efficiency gain. Alberto et al. [6] proposed cell wilting and blooming scheme to enable active BSs dynamically adjust the cell size to serve the users originally located in the coverage of sleeping BSs. In addition, cooperative beamforming based on the distributed antennas is well recognized to improve the performance of hardware sleeping. Niu et al. [7] proposed to utilize the cooperative beamforming technique to compensate the coverage hole caused by the BS sleeping. Whereas Shi et al. [8] focus a distributed massive MIMO network and proposed a group sparsity based joint cooperative beamforming and antenna muting algorithm. The results show that joint optimization of antenna muting allows more antennas stay in inactive states and hence achieves higher energy efficiency.

However, the previous works all solve the joint optimization problem of antenna muting and cooperative beamforming from the point of numerical optimization. Numerical optimization has played a key role in solving the problem of wireless resource management. In the literature, many kinds of handcrafted algorithms are developed to find a stable solution for the antenna muting and cooperative beamforming for certain scenarios. Nevertheless, Considering the NP hardness of the problem, such algorithms has high computing complexity and only suitable for certain scenarios. In addition, they also cause a serious gap between theoretical analysis design and practical application.

Deep learning has shown great potential and advantages in feature extraction and model fitting [9], thereby attracting a large number of scholars to study its theory and application, and it has developed rapidly in academia and industry. Inspired by its superior performance in solving complex control problems [9], in this paper, we aim to design low complex deep learning solution to find the optimal antenna muting and cooperative beamforming pattern in the distributed massive MIMO systems.

2 System Model

In this section, a typical distributed massive MIMO is considered. Then we formulate the signal model and power consumption model considering the antenna muting and cooperative beamforming.

2.1 Distributed Massive MIMO System

Consider a single cell of distributed massive MIMO system, as shown in Fig. 1. The single cell consisting of a large number of distributed antennas which jointly serve multiple users in the form of cooperative beamforming. Let $R : R = \{1, 2, ..., R\}$ denote the set of antennas and $U : U = \{1, 2, ..., U\}$ denote the set of user equipments (UEs). Each UE is assumed to be equipped with a single antenna. All the distributed antennas are connected to a centralized signal processing unit (denoted as the CPU), which is a cloudified processing pool. The CPU is able to collect and share the channel state information and user's requested data among the antennas in a centralized manner.

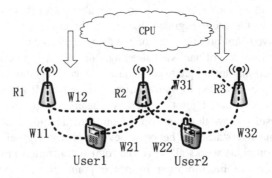

Fig. 1. The illustration of distributed massive MIMO

The channel between UEs and antennas are assumed to be block flat, i.e., the channel gain is constant during a certain time slot. At each time slot, the CPU is responsible for determining the antenna muting and cooperative beamforming pattern. The decision made is then distributed to the antennas. Upon received the muting and cooperative beamforming decision from the CPU, each antenna changes its state, namely keeping transmitting the data stream or enter the muting state. The transmitted symbols of UEs are assumed to be a Gaussian random variable with zero mean and unit variance. UEs receive the required data symbols from all the active antennas which performs cooperative beamforming. The corresponding signal-to-interference-plus-noise ratio (SINR) of each UE can be expressed as

$$SINR_u = \frac{\left|h_u^H w_u\right|^2}{\sum_{v \neq u} \left|h_u^H w_v\right|^2 + \sigma^2}, u \in U \tag{1}$$

where $h_u := [h_{1u}, h_{2u}, \ldots, h_{Ru}]^T$ represents the channel gain vector, and each element h_{ru} represents the channel gain from antenna r to UE u; similarity, the cooperative beamforming weights are stacked in a vector $w_u = [w_{1u}, w_{2u}, \ldots, w_{Ru}]^T$, wherein each element w_{ru} represents the beamforming weight from antenna r to UE u. Generally, the channel coefficients and the beamforming weights are all complex values, but in this study, in order to facilitate the algorithm, the modulus values of complex numbers were taken to work in the real-value domain, σ^2 is background noise during transmission.

By using the Shannon Hartley theorem, the maximum data transmission rate that each user u can achieve is given by:

$$R_u = B \log_2 \left(1 + \frac{SINR_u}{\Gamma_m} \right), u \in U \qquad (2)$$

Where, B is the channel bandwidth; Γ_m is SNR (Signal-to-Noise Ratio) interval, which depends on the specific modulation scheme.

When specifically considering a distributed massive MIMO network, the power consumption depends on the functionality splitting between the CPU and antennas. Herewith, we adopt a simple power consumption model similar to [10–12], which characterize the impact of the muting antenna on the total power consumption. This model is applicable to different types of base stations, i.e., there's basically a linear function relationship between the transmit power and the power consumption of the cell, and such a relationship is also applicable to the relationship between transmit power and the power consumption of the antennas. Therefore, an empirical linear functional relationship can be adopted for modeling each antenna:

$$P_r = \begin{cases} P_{r \in A, active} + \frac{1}{\eta_l} P_{r, trans} \\ P_{r \in S, sleep} \end{cases} \qquad (3)$$

Where, η_l is a constant, indicating the drain efficiency of the power amplifier, and it is a constant. $P_{r,active}$ is the power consumption of an antenna in active state, which is power consumption necessary for the basic operation of maintaining the antenna in the transmission working state. If an antenna does not have any information that can be transmitted and is not selected to be active for transmitting signals, then it will be in muting mode. In this mode, the power consumption of the antenna is $P_{r,sleep}$, in order to save energy, there's the need to transfer antenna into sleep mode as much as possible, thus to reduce the antenna in active state as much as possible. Antenna has two states, active and sleep, $A \subseteq R$ and $S \subseteq R$ represents respectively active set and sleep set of the antennas, and $A \cup S = R$. $P_{r,trans}$ is the transmit power of antenna and it satisfies the following relationship:

$$P_{r,trans} = \sum_{r \in A} \sum_{u \in U} |w_{r,u}|^2 \qquad (4)$$

Based on above analysis, the total transmission power consumption of the entire system in the current period can be expressed as:

$$P(A, S, G) = \sum_{r \in A} \sum_{u \in U} \frac{1}{\eta_l} |w_{r,u}|^2 + \sum_{r \in A} P_{r,active} + \sum_{r \in S} P_{r,sleep} \tag{5}$$

Where, the first term represents power consumption associated with the signal transmission process, while the second and third terms are the total power consumption of the antenna in active and sleep states respectively to maintain basic operation.

In order to minimize the total transmission power consumption, there are two strategies:

(1) Optimize the cooperative beamforming to reduce the transmit power;
(2) Reduce the number of active antennas and the corresponding transmission links.

However, the above two strategies are conflicting. In order to reduce the transmission power consumption, more antennas need to be activated to obtain the higher beamforming gain; but if more antennas are allowed to be activated, it will increase the power consumption of the transmission link. Therefore, in order to minimize network power consumption, joint optimization of the antenna (and corresponding transmission link) selection and transmit beamforming are required.

3   Problem Formulation

A very important part of transmission power model proposed in previous section is power consumption in the process of transmitting signals, which depends on the cooperative beamforming weights of each antenna. In order to minimize the total power consumption of the entire system based on meeting the user's needs, it's necessary to considering the joint antenna muting and cooperative beamforming design, and this problem can be expressed mathematically as follows:

$$\underset{A, \{w_{r,u}\}}{\text{minimize}} \sum_{r \in A} \sum_{u \in U} |w_{r,u}|^2 \tag{6}$$

In order to ensure that the needs of each user are met, the following constraints are required:

$$SINR_u \geq \gamma_u, u \in U \tag{7}$$

$$\gamma_u = \Gamma_m(2^{R_u/B} - 1) \tag{8}$$

Total transmit power sum of each antenna r is constrained by the following equation:

$$\sum_{u \in U} |w_{r,u}|^2 \leq P_r, r \in A \tag{9}$$

Where, R_u is the requirement of each user u, and P_r is the maximum allowed transmit power of all antennas. As can be seen, the optimization variables of the above combination optimization problem are the antenna muting decision A, and also the cooperative beamforming weights from each antenna to each UE $\{w_{r,u}\}$. The overall goal is to minimize total power consumption. It should be noted that the factor η_l in the power model (5) and other related parameters are ignored here because they are just constants. Herewith, the inequality (7) can also be rewritten as:

$$\sum_{v \in U} \left| h_u^H w_v \right|^2 + \sigma^2 \leq \frac{1 + \gamma_u}{\gamma_u} \left| h_u^H w_u \right|^2 \tag{10}$$

Given the need R_u of each user u, γ_u can be calculated according to Eq. (10) accordingly. Note that, if the antenna muting pattern A is known, this optimization problem can be transformed into a second-order cone programming (SOCP) problem, which can be efficiently solved by the convex optimization tools such as the CVX toolbox in the MATLAB. However, here the antenna muting pattern A and the cooperative beamforming weights need to be simultaneously solved. This makes this problem NP-hard and difficult to solve.

4 DNN Based Joint Antenna Muting and Beamforming Optimization

In this section, a brief introduction of DNN and DNN approximation theory is first present. Then a DNN approximate framework is constructed in order to establish a non-linear mapping between the network states and the optimal antenna muting and cooperative beamforming solution.

4.1 DNN Approximation Theory

For any deterministic algorithm that uses iteration to represent continuous mapping, its initial value can be used as an additional input variable, and then the trained neural network can be used to learn the given algorithm behavior [13]. If the potential optimization problem is a nonconvex problem with the multiple solutions, then it is necessary to use the initial value as one of the input variables, because if there is no initial value, the mapping cannot be well defined, that is, it may converge to multiple isolated solutions. Or one can learn the mapping relation well by fixing the initial value of the solution.

It can be verified that the iteration in each of the convex optimization problem solving processes represents a continuous mapping, and the optimization variables are in a compact set [14]. Therefore, if the channel implementation set $\{h_{ij}\}$ is assumed to be in a compact set, the solution can be arbitrarily approximated by the feedforward network with multiple hidden layers.

4.2 Construction of DNN Optimization System

DNN Structure Setting

The method proposed in this study uses a fully connected neural network with an input layer, multiple hidden layers and an output layer. The specific structure is shown in Fig. 2. The input of the neural network is a vector $h_u := [h_{1u}, h_{2u}, \ldots, h_{Ru}]^T$ of the magnitude of the channel coefficients. There are three network outputs, which are respectively beamforming matrix $w_u = [w_{1u}, w_{2u}, \ldots, w_{Ru}]^T$, the antenna state (even if each antenna in the network is on or off), and the optimal transmission power. In addition, the ReLU function is used as the activation function of the hidden layer.

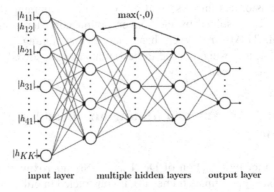

Fig. 2. Structure of DNN

Data Generation

The data is generated in the following manner. The modulus value $\{|h_{Ru}^{(i)}|\}$ of channel coefficients is first generated according to a particular distribution (described in more detail below), wherein superscript (i) is used to represent the index of training sample. For the sake of simplicity, the fixed maximum power P_{max} and ambient noise σ^2 for all the antennas were obtained. Then for each input tuple $(P_{max}, \{|h_{Ru}^{(i)}|\}, \sigma)$, there is a corresponding optimal control result. In other words, the state set of the optimal node antenna, the beamforming matrix and the power allocation vector. Using $v_k^0 = \sqrt{P_{max}}, \forall k$ as a fixed initial power value. Regarding the termination of the iteration, $obj_{new} - obj_{old} < 10^{-5}$ or iteration with times >500 can be chosen as the standard. The corresponding input-output relationship tuple $\left(\{|h_{Ru}^{(i)}|\}, \{|w_{Ru}^{(i)}|\}, P^{(i)}, A^{(i)} \subseteq R\right)$ is called as i^{th} training sample. Then is to repeat above process for multiple times, the entire training data set can be generated.

In the training phase of the neural network, the main function of verifying data set is to cross-validate the accuracy of generated network. Namely, randomly extracting a part from a set of measured data for modeling, and the rest of the data is used to verify the model to make the model selection. For the different models trained in the training set, their errors are counted, and the model with the smallest error is taken as the final model; and the network training should be terminated in time to avoid making the training depth too deep. In particular, the verification data set is relatively small compared to the amount of data in the training data set. In addition, T and V are respectively used to collect the index of the training set and data set.

Training Phase

In the training phase, the data set $\left(\left\{\left|h_{Ru}^{(i)}\right|\right\}, \left\{w_{Ru}^{(i)}\right\}, P^{(i)}, A^{(i)} \subseteq R\right)_{i \in T}$ generated by the above process is first used to optimize the weight of the neural network. The loss function used is mean-square error between the modulus values of each element corresponding to the algorithm of solving the convex optimization problem and the beamforming matrix of the neural network output. The loss function (or cost function) is used to measure the extent of fit to a function. The smaller the value of the loss function, the higher the fit of the model is. The optimization algorithm used is an effective implementation of the small batch stochastic gradient descent algorithm, which is known as the RMSprop algorithm [10], which is an adaptive learning rate method that divides the gradient by the running square value of its nearest corresponding amplitude. By introducing an attenuation coefficient, the gradient cumulant is attenuated by a certain ratio per turn. Specifically, it first randomly extracts a set of samples with the capacity of m from the training data set and its corresponding output. Then is to calculate the gradient and error, and update the gradient cumulant r, and update other variables according to r and the calculation parameters of the gradient at this time. The specific update steps are shown in Table 1. The algorithm can automatically change the learning rate and alleviate the rapid change of the learning rate. That is, if the gradient is too large, the learning rate should be attenuated faster, and if the gradient is smaller, the learning rate should be slower. Moreover, if the depth is deep in the learning process, the algorithm does not have the problem of learning to end prematurely, which is very suitable for dealing with non-stationary targets.

Specifically, the layer-by-layer training method should be used to initialize network weights in the training process. First is to train a network with only one hidden layer. Only after this layer of network training is finished, the training of a network with two hidden layers can be started, and so forth [11]. Through this method, the problem of data acquisition can be solved effectively, thus to obtain a better local extremum. Regarding the network construction, it is necessary to train the first self-encoder with the original input data and learn the first-order feature of the original input. The first-order feature is used as the input of the self-encoder to learn and obtain the second-order feature; then the second-order feature is used as the input of the classifier, thus to obtain a model of mapping the second-order feature through training. Finally, these three layers are combined to construct a self-coded deep neural network with the two hidden layers [12].

In this study, the attenuation rate was chosen to be 0.9 according to the recommendations in literature [9]. In addition, the appropriate maximum training number (max epoch) and L2 regularization coefficient were chosen through the cross-validation of the training set and the verification set, the verification data was used for multiple times to continuously adjust parameters. In order to further improve the network performance generated by the training, the truncated normal distribution generation variable is used to initialize the network weight. Namely, first is to generate a variable according to the standard normal distribution, and then is to judge its absolute value. If it is greater than 2, it will be discarded and regenerate the new variable. In addition, the weight of each neuron is divided by the square root of its input number, which is to normalize the variance of each neuron output.

Test Phase

In the test phase, the performance of the trained neural network will be tested, and the channel parameters will be generated as the test data set according to the same distribution as the training phase. The function is to detect constructed neural network and effectively measure the deviation of the algorithm to evaluate the model accuracy. This method can test the performance of the neural network, and evaluate the performance of the results obtained based on the robustness of the model obtained through the training phase.

During the test, the first is to make the generated test data set pass through the trained neural network, and the optimized power distribution and beamforming results are also collected. Followed by is to compare the similarities between the resource allocation results generated by the DNN and the results of the numerical optimization algorithm. The higher the similarity, the more accurate the DNN is constructed.

Table 1. RMSProp algorithm

algorithm
Selecting global learning rate ε, attenuation rate ρ, and initial parameters θ
Selecting the small constant δ, usually setting to 10^{-6}, which is used for fixing the value when it is divided by the decimal
Initialize cumulative variable r=0
While does not reach the stop criterion **do**
Collecting a small batch $\{x^{(1)},...,x^{(m)}\}$ containing m samples from the training set, and the corresponding target is $y^{(i)}$
Calculative gradient: $g \leftarrow \frac{1}{m}\nabla\theta\sum_i L(f(x^{(i)};\theta),y^{(i)})$
Cumulative squared gradient: $r \leftarrow \rho r+(1-\rho)g\odot g$
Calculation parameter update: $\Delta\theta=-\dfrac{\varepsilon}{\sqrt{\delta+r}}\odot g$ (element-by-element application $\dfrac{1}{\sqrt{\delta+r}}$)
Application update: $\theta \leftarrow \theta+\Delta\theta$
End while

5 Simulation and Performance Evaluation

5.1 Simulation Environment

Joint antenna muting and cooperative beamforming problem solving
   This problem belongs to a class of non-convex optimization problems. Hence to find an optimal solution, we use the greedy scheme, where each combinations of antenna states (on/off) are explored, and for each given antenna muting pattern, we transformed the cooperative beamforming problem into a convex problem and solved it using mature toolbox.

DNN model construction
The model constructed in this study is a neural network with multiple hidden layers, which can be used to solve the problem of processing complex data. The method of training the multilayer neural network is to train one layer at a time, and a special network type called Auto encoder for each hidden layer can be trained. An automatic encoder is a layer in a neural network, and the goal is to copy its input at the output of the neural network. When the number of neurons in the hidden layer is less than the size of its input, the auto-encoder compresses it to express its input. The auto-encoder uses regularizer to learn the sparse representations in the first layer of the network, which can control the effects of the regularizer by setting various parameters. After building a complete DNN using the training data, the network is optimized by using the validation set data, which performs the backpropagation over the entire multi-layer network to improve network performance and minimize the loss function. In this study, the mean-square error of the modulus value of each element in the beamforming matrix was chosen as the loss function.

5.2 Channel Models

Each channel coefficient is generated according to a standard normal distribution, that is, a Rayleigh fading distribution with the zero mean and unit variance. Rayleigh fading distribution is a reasonable channel model and is widely used to simulate the performance of various resource allocation algorithms [13]. In the simulation of this study, five different network scene settings were considered, the numbers of antenna and user were respectively (32,8), (64,8), (128,16). In these different scene settings, the calculation will be conducted, and the similarity of the traditional optimization algorithm, DNN power consumption and beamforming matrix will be compared to evaluate its performance. So as to verify whether the input-output relationship learned by DNN can accurately approximate to the optimization algorithm, that is, to minimize the power consumption while satisfying user requirements.

5.3 DNN Parameter Selection

This section selected the following parameters for the deep neural network: maximum number of training options was five parameters from 50 to 1000, and the selection of L2 regularization coefficient was five parameters from 0.5 to 0.001. For all simulation numerical results, the constructed DNN has one input layer, three hidden layers, and one output layer, each hidden layer is with 200 neurons. The network input is a set of channel coefficient matrices. The channel coefficient matrix is a complex matrix. However, in order to facilitate the training of network, the modulus value of the channel coefficients will be used as input, so that the DNN works in the real domain. The size of the matrix depends on the number of users, the number of antennas and the number of antennas. The output of the network is the result of node control, the optimal beamforming matrix and the optimal power consumption. The beamforming matrix is usually a complex matrix, but in order to uniformly process in the real domain, this study took modulus values of each element of the matrix.

5.4 DNN Performance Evaluation

The evaluation was made in following three aspects: (1) the fit of beamforming matrix w generated by the DNN method and the traditional optimal algorithm, and the mean-square error of modulus value of the elements of two w were taken. If the sum of the mean-square error is smaller, showing the constructed DNN is more compatible with the traditional optimal algorithm; (2) For the total power generated by the two methods, the two powers are compared, if two power are almost the same, it proves that the constructed DNN can achieve optimal nodes management and beamforming; (3) When the two methods are used to solve the same problem, if the time spent on the constructed DNN is significantly less, then it is meaningful to apply it to solve the practical problem.

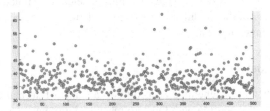

Fig. 3. Power scatter plot

Figure 3 shows the power consumption similarity obtained by the traditional algorithm and the DNN method when the number of antenna and UE are configured as (32,8). The x-axis is the channel realizations while the y-axis denotes the total consumed power. The circle and plus sign represent respectively total transmission power obtained from the traditional method and DNN method. It can be seen through 500 data points of the test set that the power consumption at each point can be well studied, and there are few points that have not been learned, indicating that the fit of the two methods is higher, and the compatible accuracy of the two is shown in Fig. 4.

In order to demonstrate the similarity of the two methods, the mean-square error and a joint scatter plot of the power consumption difference-beamforming matrix in Fig. 4 is used, where the configuration of antenna number and user number is set as (64,8), (128,16), respectively. It can be seen from the figure that accuracy of power

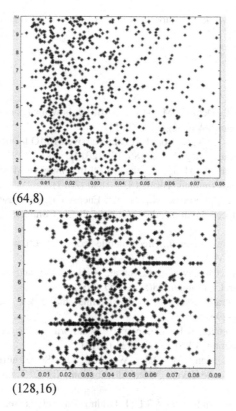

(64,8)

(128,16)

Fig. 4. Power difference and mean-square error joint scatter plot

consumption difference reaches the magnitude of 10^{-15} order, which can be completely coincident with almost every point learned; and the sum of the mean-square error of the elements of the beamforming matrix is at most 0.1, and the accuracy of most points is less than 0.05, proving every point can be learned very accurately.

6 Conclusion

In summary, DNN as a substitute for the traditional optimization algorithm which has a small amount of calculation and a short processing time. The DNN can precisely approximates the traditional algorithm, and the accuracy can reach the magnitude of 10^{-15}, achieving expected goal. This can well meet actual needs and significantly save energy consumption while satisfying user needs, thereby reducing operating costs to meet requirements of green communication. On the other hand, compared with the traditional numerical optimization method, the calculation process of DNN is low in complexity. This can significantly reduce calculation time, which is suitable for dealing with the complex combination optimization problems in dynamic scenes, thereby meeting needs of reality, having great guiding significance for solving real-time communication problems.

Acknowledgment. This work was supported by the Beijing City Board of education project (NO. KM201810858004).

References

1. Hoydis, J., Brink, S.T., Debbah, M.: Massive MIMO: how many antennas do we need? In: Communication, Control, & Computing (2011)
2. Larsson, E.G., Edfors, O., Tufvesson, F., et al.: Massive MIMO for next generation wireless systems. IEEE Commun. Mag. **52**(2), 186–195 (2014)
3. Ngo, H.Q., Ashikhmin, A., Hong, Y., et al.: Cell-free massive MIMO versus small cells. IEEE Trans. Wireless Commun. **16**(3), 1834–1850 (2017)
4. Wu, J., Zhang, Y., Zukerman, M., et al.: Energy-efficient base-stations sleep-mode techniques in green cellular networks: a survey. IEEE Commun. Surv. Tutorials **17**(2), 803–826 (2015)
5. Zhou, S., Gong, J., Yang, Z., et al.: Green mobile access network with dynamic base station energy saving. ACM MobiCom **9**(262), 10–12 (2009)
6. Conte, A., Feki, A., Chiaraviglio, L., et al.: Cell wilting and blossoming for energy efficiency. IEEE Wirel. Commun. **18**(5), 50–57 (2011)
7. Niu, Z.: TANGO: traffic-aware network planning and green operation. IEEE Wirel. Commun. **18**(5), 25–29 (2011)
8. Shi, Y., Zhang, J., Letaief, K.B.: Group sparse beamforming for green cloud-RAN. IEEE Trans. Wireless Commun. **13**(5), 2809–2823 (2014)
9. Dapeng, W., Yan, J., Wang, H., Dalei, W., Wang, R.: Social attribute aware incentive mechanism for device-to-device video distribution. IEEE Trans. Multimedia **19**(8), 1908–1920 (2017)
10. Zhang, H., et al.: Fronthauling for 5G LTE-U ultra dense cloud small cell networks. IEEE Wireless Commun. **23**(6), 48–53 (2017)
11. Zhang, H., et al.: Resource allocation for cognitive small cell networks: a cooperative bargaining game theoretic approach. IEEE Trans. Wireless Commun. **14**(6), 3481–3493 (2015)
12. Zhang, H., Huang, S., Jiang, C., et al.: Energy efficient user association and power allocation in millimeter wave based ultra dense networks with energy harvesting base stations. IEEE J. Sel. Areas Commun. **35**(9), 1936–1947 (2017)
13. Liang, S., Srikant, R.: Why deep neural networks for function approximation? In: ICLR, France Toulon, pp. 1–42 (2017)
14. Lecun, Y., Bengio, Y., Hinton, G.: Deep learning. Nature **521**(7553), 436 (2015)
15. Wu, D., et al.: Dynamic coding control in social intermittent connectivity wireless networks. IEEE Trans. Veh. Technol. **65**(9), 7634–7646 (2016)
16. Hornik, K., Stinchcombe, M., White, H.: Multilayer feedforward networks are universal approximators. Neural Netw. **2**(5), 359–366 (1989)

A Converged Network Architecture Oriented Towards NB-IoT

Weidong Fang[1,2], Wuxiong Zhang[1,2], Lianhai Shan[1(✉)],
Qianqian Zhao[1,2], and Wei Chen[3]

[1] Key Laboratory of Wireless Sensor Network and Communication,
Shanghai Institute of Microsystem and Information Technology,
Chinese Academy of Sciences, Shanghai 200051, China
LianhaiShan@163.com
[2] Shanghai Research Center for Wireless Communication,
Shanghai 201210, China
[3] School of Computer Science and Technology,
China University of Mining and Technology, Xuzhou 221116, Jiangsu, China

Abstract. Although NB-IoT's standardization gives us a future direction, we have to face some issues of existing networks converged, especially, the wireless sensor net-work (WSN) and cellular networks (CN) converged. On the other hand, the increase in number of sensor nodes and in the mobile devices is forcing the backhaul network architecture to undergo radical transformation. To meet the requirements of low latency and high quality of service (QoS), we put forward a novel converged network architecture. Meanwhile, we give three application scenarios. The analysis results show this architecture could facility the network design.

Keywords: 5G · Narrow-Band Internet of Things (NB-IoT) ·
Wireless sensor network · Network architecture · Heterogeneous network

1 Introduction

With the developments of the Internet of Things (IoT), the Internet of Everything is gradually from research to application [1–5]. However, the current 4G network is lack of capacity, which achieves to connect between the things and things. In fact, to compare to Bluetooth, ZigBee and other short-range communication technology, the mobile CN have some novel features, which involves the wide coverage, the mobility, the massive connectivity, as well as abundant application scenarios [6]. As the evolution of LTE (Long Term Evolution) technologies, 4.5 G has a peak rate of up to 1 Gbps, which means more connections based on the number of cellular networking. It supports mass M2M connectivity and lower latency. These characteristics will promote the rapid applications of HD video, VoLTE, as well as IoT. Fortunately, recognizing the importance, 3GPP has introduced a number of key features for IoT in its latest release, Rel-13. EC-GSM-IoT [7] and LTE-MTC [8]. Then, in the Third-Generation Partnership

© ICST Institute for Computer Sciences, Social Informatics and Telecommunications Engineering 2019
Published by Springer Nature Switzerland AG 2019. All Rights Reserved
V. C. M. Leung et al. (Eds.): 5GWN 2019, LNICST 278, pp. 31–39, 2019.
https://doi.org/10.1007/978-3-030-17513-9_3

Project's (3GPP's) Radio Access Network Plenary Meeting 69, the Narrow-Band Internet of Things (NB-IoT) is decided to standardize [9]. This standardization will focus on providing improved indoor coverage, supporting of a massive number of low-throughput devices, low latency sensitivity, ultra-ow device cost, low device energy consumption, and optimized network architecture.

Although NB-IoT's standardization gives us a future direction, we have to face some issues of existing networks converged, especially, the wireless sensor network (WSN) and cellular network (CN) converged. This is due to that, WSN have been generated an increasing interest from industry and research perspectives, and played a vital role in many fields, i.e. e-Health care [10], environment monitoring [11], industrial metering [12], surveillance systems [13] etc. WSN can be generally described as a network of nodes that cooperatively sense and may control the environment enabling interaction between persons or computers and the surrounding environment [14]. On the other hand, the convergence application of WSN and CN will become brighter and inevitable. Heterogeneous networks consisting of CN and WSN appear in many application areas. Many dedicated mobile phones are equipped with a WSN air - interface for technology testing, evaluation and demonstration purposes. These mobile phones can collect measurement data from a variety of sensor nodes and then forward this data to an information center of the CN. In such a case, CN is simply used as a backhaul infrastructure for WSN, i.e. there is no dynamic interaction between both networks.

To meet the requirements of WSN and CN converged, a novel converged network architecture of WSN and LTE-A is proposed in this paper. The rest of this paper is organized as follows. In Sect. 2, some related works are investigated and reviewed. In Sect. 3, our converged network architecture is proposed and analyzed. In Sect. 4, the future researches are described. At last, the conclusions are given.

2 Related Works

Modern technologies have been prepared for creating the convergent communications infrastructures of WSN and CN, which the WSN and CN have become a worldwide standard, with unprecedented levels of coverage, reliability and affordability. In this section, we discuss the research on the architecture and topology of WSN, cellular and the others.

In terms of the convergence of heterogeneous network, Deokhui et al. proposed a converged architecture for broadcast and multicast services in a heterogeneous network [15]. This architecture could efficiently support the broadcast/multicast services in LTE network. Malhan et al. presented the converged architecture, and analyze various services which are running on it along with the understanding of their characteristics [16]. Zhang and Liang proposed a new architecture for converged Internet of things based on Vector Network (VN) [17]. Tzanakaki et al. put forward a converged network architecture for energy efficient mobile cloud computing to satisfy the low-latency requirements of content-rich mobile applications [18]. Gercheva et al. summarized the benefits of converged next generation network architecture to meet the demands of latency and service quality requirements [19].

There had been a large amount of researches in creating WSN network structures (i.e. Flat or Hierarchical) [20]. In the hierarchical architecture, grouping sensor nodes into cluster had been widely pursued in order to achieve the WSN scalability objective. In each cluster, a sensor node was selected, termed as the Cluster Head (CH). Then, these cluster heads collected sensor data from other nodes in the vicinity and transmitted the aggregated data to the Gateway (GW). The CH was responsible for not only the general request but also receiving the sensed data of other sensor nodes in the same cluster and routing (transmitting) these data to the gateway. Thus, the CHs had higher energy cost because all of the transmitting data packet would pass through them and be sent to the gateway. And so, the CH selection was very important for WSN. In the next section, we will give a novel network architecture based on convergence of WSN and LTE-A.

3 Convergence of WSN and CN

In this section, we analyze the objectives of the integrations and three different application scenarios, and then propose the converged network architecture.

3.1 Objectives of Convergence

The primary objective of the project is to design a WSN fixed/mobile gateway including transmission path selection, mobility management and breakthrough access control signalling. In this research, we propose WSN-CN convergence strategies for connection-oriented, lifetime-oriented and hybrid deployment, where a mobile terminal used as a gateway for sensor nodes to transmit the detected data to backbone database under the help of 3GPP-LTE basic station (eNodeB). Therefore, this sensor network gateway is required to provide wireless interface(s) to other sensor nodes as well as the air interface of a mobile network system (e.g., 3G/3GPP/WiMAX) to the existing network infrastructures. The information from sensor network and CN will be merged autonomously. Therefore, the sensor networks cover the detecting area; while the CN will also cover this area and can help the sensor networks to acquire better transmission quality. The sensor networks MAC/Routing protocol design and some resource management algorithms/routing algorithms can be completed under the 3GPP-LTE eNodeB assistance. All the results from this research will provide a viable solution for the problem of optimizing provisioning of a large scale heterogeneous WSN and CN. The detailed objectives of the project are:

- Design a breakthrough control signaling between the gateway (including mobile and fixed gateway) and 3GPP-LTE eNodeB, gateway and common WSN nodes.
- MAC/Routing protocol design, including WSN fixed/mobile gateway selection and re-selection under 3GPP-LTE eNodeB assistance.

Research mobile management of gateway and resource allocation mechanism to guarantee the communication QoS.

3.2 Application Scenarios

Potential challenging of the Integration Potential impacts at high level to the LTE-A systems of signalling, protocol stacks etc. from a terminal point of view. This scenario considers a cellular system in which cellular UEs are under the control of the eNodeB.

In the coverage area, there exists a group of wireless sensor nodes constructing a WSN. In this area, it includes two types of gateways: fixed gateway (box in the figure) and mobile gateway (acting as cellular UE), which is shown in Fig. 1. All of the WSN gateway in the cell can provide the access for the WSN nodes, and all gateways are dual-mode and have WSN and CN interfaces. Then, the data from WSN can be directly forwarded to the eNodeB by the gateway. The normal mobile UE can also acquire the necessary information with the downlink data transmission from the eNodeB or from the other fixed/mobile gateway.

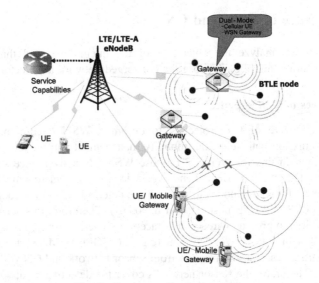

Fig. 1. System application scenarios

The application scenario is divided into three types:

UC1: UE overhears the WSN traffic and reports to eNodeB;

At the beginning, all the nodes are sleeping and BS doesn't have the detail information of these nodes. Then a UE will collect the information from these nodes. When the UE entries this zone, it begins to overhear the downlink control signalling, if it hears the control signalling, then it will wake up the nodes within its maximum communication range under the permission of the BS. After receiving the broadcast message from UE, the nodes wake up and send their reply to UE. Then the nodes will choose the optimal path to form the network. After the network is formed, UE sends the information of all the nodes in the network to BS. And it is ordered the sensor nodes collect data from them to BS in periodical or event-driven mode, which is shown in Fig. 2. After some time, UE maybe leave this zone, it cause the mobile gateway selection/reselection.

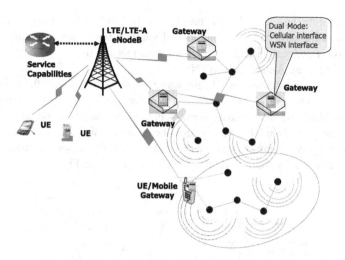

Fig. 2. UE overhears WSN application scenario

UC2: UE acts as mobile gateway of WSN (replacement/reselection or splitting);

After a UE acting as new mobile UE gateway enters the coverage of the WSN, it may cause the gateway (re)selection or even regrouping of the wireless sensor nodes, which is shown in Fig. 3. How to make a balanced trade-off between the complexity, performance gain and energy consumption etc. via a robust (re)selection and grouping algorithms is an essential issue for further study. Research the gateway (re)selection algorithms and sensor nodes grouping algorithms when certain UE gateways are arriving at the coverage of the WSN become the other important part.

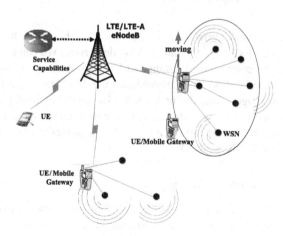

Fig. 3. Mobile UE gateway replacement

In the splitting task, we design load-balancing mechanism among different UE gateways and adjust the connected number of wireless sensor nodes in order to avoid the transmission congestion and decrease the transmission delay.

UC3: UE activates/deactivates WSN;

The mobility management of UE gateway is quite different with the conventional UE mobility in the 3GPP-LTE systems. This scenario is based on the mobile UE gateway providing the convergent access function for the WSN nodes. During the moving process of mobile UE gateway, it will enter/exit a WSN area, where the sensor nodes' convergence point is this gateway and the WSN sensor nodes will be activated/deactivated by the UE gateway, which is shown in Fig. 4.

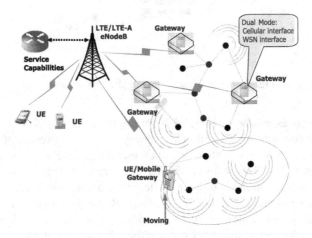

Fig. 4. UE activates/deactivates WSN

In fact, the BS doesn't know the exact position of the nodes but we know the general position of the nodes and the range of the dead zone. We can first select several positions, and the total communication range of UE should cover the range of the dead zone. After UE entries the dead zone, it will listen the downlink control signalling and set the broadcast message. Then the nodes will choose the optimal path to form the network. After the network is formed, UE sends the information of all the nodes in the network to BS. After collecting enough information, it moves to the next position and re-forms the topology of the network.

3.3   Converged Network Architecture

As WSN are being developed for a wide range of application fields of real-time monitoring and control, a design overview seems important so as to investigate alternative communication aspects while treating WSN as a whole system. As applications become more demanding the need to consider also deployment constraints and application particularities on top of the commonly used network factors, leads to new integrated design methodologies for addressing all complexity degrees of such systems.

The conventional network architecture of integrated CN and WSN is hierarchical, as shown in the left part of Fig. 5. All gateways are dual-mode and have both WSN and CN interfaces. A group of wireless sensor nodes constructs the data detecting plane, while the gateway and the base station (BS) comprised the system control plane. The WSN is controlled indirectly by the BS through the gateway. The gateway can just provide the access for the WSN nodes, and forward the detected data to the backhaul networks servers. Communications between WSN and CN use a data channel at the gateway, which however decreases the system efficiency. As shown in the right part of Fig. 5, in the network architecture, the sensor nodes may have the ability of hearing the downlink signaling from the UE gateway of CN. For the uplink, due to the limited transmission range of sensor nodes, the data is routed by the gateway.

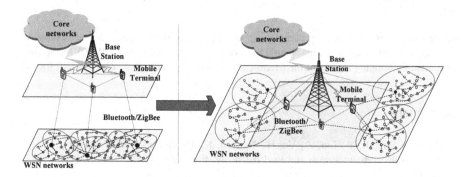

Fig. 5. Network architecture for CN and WSN

4 Future Directions

Considering the 3GPP-LTE eNodeB acting as database server, the routing table design including storage, updating and sharing between nodes needs to be further studied when considering the cellular and WSN convergence. The sensor networks transmission path database and topology information changing will become the other important part for the task of WSN gateway selection. We should research the transmission path and topology change with the mobile UE gateway entry/exit, and the routing table storage and maintenance methods. Research on the network and link layers of the WSN protocol stack has had as its main motivations the architecture and protocol design, energy conservation, and location. Although only a few studies concerning QoS in WSN have been performed, there are several very interesting works regarding QoS. An exact definition of QoS in the WSN context should be provided in the further study.

5 Conclusions

From this converged network architecture and other previous studies, we could think that the convergence of WSN and CN can benefit both of the two types of network. For WSN, the CN can enable higher layer control and optimization to prolong the network lifetime, improve the WSN system performance and provide QoS for WSN services. For CN, WSN can enable the cognitive and intelligent aspects of the cellular system. It is envisaged that converged network architecture of WSN and CN could enable better wireless services and more data-centric applications. On the other hand, the CN can control and manage attached WSN, thus making WSN more efficient in energy saving and performance improvement. Moreover, WSN can enrich mobile applications and provide real-time measurement data for network performance and service coverage optimization in CN. As for the telemetry and remote management of distributed assets, the convergence of WSN and CN can be used in the supervisory control and data acquisition system. WSN in these applications need to be managed and optimized with the aid of CN. Hence, enabling technologies needed to be researched and developed for interactive control and joint optimization of converged CN and WSN.

Acknowledgment. This work is partially supported by the National Natural Science Foundation of China (61571004), the Shanghai Natural Science Foundation (No. 17ZR1429100), the Scientific Instrument Developing Project of the Chinese Academy of Sciences (No. YJKYYQ20170074).

References

1. Nguyen, P.L., Ji, Y., Liu, Z., Vu, H., Nguyen, K.: Distributed hole-bypassing protocol in WSNs with constant stretch and load balancing. Elsevier Comput. Netw. **129**(1), 232–250 (2017)
2. Feng, J., Liu, Z., Wu, C., Ji, Y.: AVE: autonomous vehicular edge computing framework with ACO-based scheduling. IEEE Trans. Veh. Technol. **66**(12), 10660–10675 (2017)
3. Li, F., Ding, Z., Wang, Y., Li, J., Liu, Z.: BEM channel estimation for OFDM system in fast time-varying channel. IEICE Trans. Commun. E100-B(8) (2017)
4. Li, Q., Fan, H., Sun, W., Li, J., Chen, L., Liu, Z.: Fingerprints in the air: unique identification of wireless devices using RF RSS fingerprints. IEEE Sens. J. **17**(11), 3568–3579 (2017)
5. Liu, Z., Zhang, C., Gu, B., Dong, M., Ji, Y., Tanaka, Y.: Markov-decision-process-assisted consumer scheduling in a networked smart grid. IEEE Access **5**, 2448–2458 (2016)
6. Ratasuk, R., Vejlgaard, B., Mangalvedhe, N., Ghosh, A.: NB-IoT system for M2M communication. In: Proceedings of IEEE Wireless Communications and Networking Conference Workshops (WCNCW), pp. 428–432 (2016)
7. TR 45.820 v13.1.0. Cellular system support for ultra low complexity and low throughput internet of things, November 2015. http://www.3gpp.org/ftp/Specs/archive/45_series/45.820/45820-d10.zip
8. Ericsson and Nokia Networks. Further LTE physical layer enhancements for MTC. RP-141660, 3GPP TSG RAN Meeting #65, September 2014 (2016). http://www.3gpp.org/ftp/tsg_ran/tsg_ran/TSGR_65/Docs/RP-141660.zip
9. Gozalvez, J.: New 3GPP standard for IoT. IEEE Veh. Technol. Mag. **11**(1), 14–20 (2016)
10. Carvalho, L., Campos, R., Ricardo, M.: Context-aware low-energy Wi-Fi sensor networks for e-health. In: The 15th International Conference on e-Health Networking, Applications & Services (Healthcom), pp. 361–365. IEEE (2013)
11. Xu, G.B., Shen, W.M., Wang, X.B.: Marine environment monitoring using wireless sensor networks: a systematic review. In: International Conference on Systems, Man and Cybernetics (SMC), pp. 13–18. IEEE (2014)

12. Agajo, J., Theophilus, A.: Using wireless sensor networks for industrial monitoring. In: International Conference on Wireless Sensor Network IET-WSN, pp. 113–121. IET (2010)
13. Hilal, A.R., Khamis, A., Basir, O.: A holonic federated sensor management framework for pervasive surveillance systems. In: International Systems Conference, pp. 361–366. IEEE (2011)
14. Verdone, R., Dardari, D., Mazzini, G., Conti, A.: Wireless Sensor and Actuator Networks. Elsevier, London (2008)
15. Deokhui, L., Woosuk, K., Byungjun, B., Hyoungsoo, L., Jaewoo, S.: Converged architecture for broadcast and multicast services in heterogeneous network. In: 16th International Conference on Proceedings of the Advanced Communication Technology (ICACT), pp. 141–145 (2014)
16. Malhan, P., Shrote, N., Naik, K., Mathur, P.: Analysis of quality of services (QOS) on converged architecture. In: 2nd International Conference on Computer Science and Network Technology (ICCSNT), pp. 71–75 (2012)
17. Zhang, J., Liang, M.: A new architecture for converged internet of things. In: International Conference on Internet Technology and Applications, pp. 1–4 (2010)
18. Tzanakaki, A., Anastasopoulos, M.P., Peng, S., et al.: A converged network architecture for energy efficient mobile cloud computing. In: International Conference on Optical Network Design and Modeling, pp. 120–125 (2014)
19. Gercheva, R.S., Chitti, S.H., Prasad, N.R., Prasad, R.: Review on the benefits of converged next generation network architecture. In: 16th International Symposium on Wireless Personal Multimedia Communications (WPMC), pp. 1–5 (2013)
20. Lin, C., He, Y.X., Peng, C., Yang, L.T.: A distributed efficient architecture for wireless sensor networks. In: 21st International Conference on Advanced Information Networking and Applications Workshops AINAW 2007, pp. 428–434 (2007)

Intelligent Computing Technology for 5G Applications

Smartphone-Based Intelligent Sleep Monitoring

Pansheng Fang[1,2(✉)], Zhaolong Ning[3], and Xiping Hu[1]

[1] Shenzhen Institutes of Advanced Technology, Chinese Academy of Sciences,
Shenzhen 518055, China
{ps.fang,xp.hu}@siat.ac.cn
[2] School of Electronic and Information Engineering,
South China University of Technology, Guangzhou 510641, China
[3] School of Software, Dalian University of Technology, Dalian 116620, China
zhaolongning@dlut.edu.cn

Abstract. The sleeping quality is one of the most important factors to judge people's health status, and has drawn increasing attention of the public recently. However, the quantified results of sleeping quality can generally be achieved in labs with the help of high precision instrument, such as Actigraphy or professional graph like Polysomnography (PSG), and are thus not available for the general public. In this paper, we construct a novel way of sleep-scoring system implanted in the iSmile app. iSmile first collects the sounds recorded by smart phone recorder, then classifies the sound frames with a light weight decision tree algorithm. Based on the number and the average amplitude of sleep-related events, we score the users' sleeping quality in three aspects (respectively cough-score, snore-score and talk-score) using Pittsburgh Sleep Quality Index (PSQI) and Pediatric Sleep Questionnaire (PSQ). During users' sleeping period, iSmile also collects data from the accelerator sensor to predict the users' mood (presented in valence and arousal) and recommend smart alarm sounds to help improve their mood. For the experiment, we involved 5 participants (20 nights in total) and achieved high precision of predicting sleep events (above 89%), with the users' valence and arousal improved by 14.57%. From succinct chart of sleeping score on the App UI, users can see the visualized results of their sleeping quality.

Keywords: Sleep scoring · Sleep event detection · Microphone

1 Introduction

Sleeping plays a significant role in human's live for human beings spend up to one-third of their lifetime sleeping. The effect of sleep related problems is wide and profound. According to the statistic provided by the Institute of Medicine (US), about 50 to 70% of US citizens suffer from chronic sleep problems [1]. Moreover, insufficient sleep can result in fatigue and frequent sleepiness at daytime, such as nodding off while driving and accidentally falling asleep at work [1, 2]. Clinical studies also reveal that sleep has something to do with many severe diseases such as diabetes, obesity and

© ICST Institute for Computer Sciences, Social Informatics and Telecommunications Engineering 2019
Published by Springer Nature Switzerland AG 2019. All Rights Reserved
V. C. M. Leung et al. (Eds.): 5GWN 2019, LNICST 278, pp. 43–59, 2019.
https://doi.org/10.1007/978-3-030-17513-9_4

depression [2, 3]. Obviously, the sleeping-related problems deserves more attention from the society, and people need to view the visualized judgement of their sleeping quality.

People also need to know about the sleeping events that reducing their sleeping qualities. The research in [12] indicates that snoring loudly can be a signal of sleep apnea. Frequent Coughing and snoring can be the symptom of Chronic Obstructive Pulmonary Disease (COPD) [13], and sleep-talking is relevant to poor sleeping quality [14, 15].

Though the public have started to focus on their sleeping quality, and specific sleeping events, they are not accessible to visualized results of sleeping quality, which are only achievable in labs through high precision instruments to analyze electrical signals with Polysomnography (PSG) [5, 6, 9]. Normal citizens also lack robust self-judging standards. The Pittsburgh Sleep Quality Index (PSQI) [7] and Pediatric Sleep Questionnaire (PSQ) [8] provide workable self-scoring standards, but some of the items in the questionnaires (such as "How often have you had trouble because you cough or snore loudly during the past month?" and "Select the frequency of snoring") are actually not workable when users live alone. Even though the users have a sleeping partner, the self-judgement can be not accurate because people measure the loudness and the frequency. Moreover, wearable devices such as Actigraphy, are always utilized to detect the valence and arousal of users. However, these devices bring unnecessary costs and uncomfortable feelings to users wearing them [12].

The meteoric adoption of smartphones places a rich sensor platform in the pockets, purses, and backpacks of many people. Interestingly, many people choose to use their phones as an alarm clock, placing these sensors in proximity of the bed. A recent study by the Pew Internet and American Life project found that 44% of mobile phone owners (83% of teens) sleep with their phones on or near their beds [10]. This advance in technology and associated change in behavior offers the possibility of cheaply and effectively tracking people's daily sleep behaviors without the need for additional hardwares or for a significant change in behavior.

In this paper, we presented iSmile, a workable system to score people's sleeping quality automatically with the detection of sleeping events using smart phone microphones, and recommend a smart alarm to improve users' mood. The App is easy to use: users just need to set the alarming time when they go to bed, and place the mobile phone somewhere near their heads, and the App will start to collect data for scoring. The App records the sound from the built-in microphone of mobile phones, extracts the features, and detects sleeping-related events such as coughing, snoring and sleep-talking. Simultaneously, the App will collect data from the accelerator sensors of mobile phones to monitor the movement rate during the users' sleeping period. Before the alarm sounds, raw data can be uploaded to the cloud platform, and after the sever handles the raw data, a recommended alarm will be played at the mobile phones and a chart showing users' sleeping quality can be seen on the App UI.

When it comes to the designing of the system, a series of problems may occur. First of all, we need to distinguish different events correctly. Luckily, the work of [11] has proved that sleeping events of different people have similar features in variance, RMS (root mean square value) and energy spectrum distribution. Secondly, we need to find ways to eliminate the influence brought by the ambient noise. Lastly, we need to link the data collected with reliable scoring standards to finish the visualization of the score. The framework of the whole system will be introduced later in the third part.

2 Related Work

The system design is inspired by some existing sleeping monitor apps (such as Sleep miner [19]) and smart alarm app (such as Sleep cycle [16] and Snail sleep [17]). The system presented in EAST [20] gives a method to extract features from accelerator sensors of mobile phones to predict users' moods when they wake up. ISleep [11] presents long-term sleep scoring based on the PSQI (Pittsburgh Sleep Quality Index), which is a widely-used subjective sleep quality assessing questionnaire. It also provides short-time sleep quality scoring ways, but only with the help of Artigraphy.

In addition to the PSQI, PSQ (Pediatric Sleep Questionnaire) also provide ways to assess sleeping quality from the aspect of snore/cough loudness and rate. To classify the severity of snore and other sleeping events [21, 22]. Authors in [21] show that the snoring intensity is measured as low at 90 ± 4 dB at 500 Hz, and high at 96 ± 4 dB at 500 Hz. The authors in [22] use the mean maximum decibel level to classify snoring as mild (40–50 dB), moderate (50–60 dB), or severe (>60 dB), and concludes that louder snoring can be an indication of more severe Obstructive Sleep Apnea (OSA). To handle other sleeping events like coughing and sleep-talking, we can apply the same way according to their average intensity and numbers.

The accurate detection should be based on robust knowledge of the acoustics of sleeping events. Authors in [23] did a research on 16 subjects and found that snoring frequency ranges from 137 Hz to 1243 Hz according to 200 samples. The author in [24] provides theoretical possibilities to distinguish snoring sound according to its acoustics indicating that snoring frequency is below 2000 Hz with peak power usually below 500 Hz.

We construct the iSmile smart scoring system making good use of the acoustic features of sleeping events, and manage to classify sleeping events such as snoring, coughing and sleep talking with an accuracy above 90%. iSmile uses our original scoring standard based on PSQI and PSQ to score users' sleeping quality nightly in three aspects: snore, cough and sleep talks. We also deploy smart alarm sounds designs to improve the mood of users.

3 System Overview

iSmile has combined the microphone sensing data part with the acceleration data processing part in the previous version of iSmile app, which improves the performance in distinguishing body movements from other sleep-related events.

The overall architecture of iSmile is shown in Fig. 1. iSmile is divided into two parts: the newly-implemented acoustics processing part and the accelerator signal processing part, which is accomplished in previous versions of iSmile [20]. iSmile read continuous acoustic signals at 16 kHz from mobile phone built-in microphones, and senses the accelerator sensor to acquire acceleration in x, y z direction.

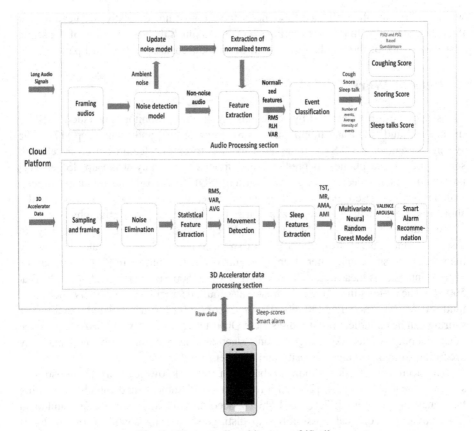

Fig. 1. The overall architecture of iSmile.

In the next step, raw data will be uploaded to the cloud platform. Then the audios are segmented into short pieces of about 5 s and sent to the acoustics part, the acceleration data will be processed in the other part.

In the acoustic processing part, the short audios are first fragmented into frames (20–50 ms for each). To reduce the energy loss of the edge of each frame, we apply a hamming window for each frame. They are fed to a noise detection fragment. Next, three features of the audio will be extracted from the non-noise frames to detect sleeping events. The noise audios will be used to update the noise detection model. After all the audios are processed, iSmile will score the users' sleeping quality according to the number and the average intensity of each sleeping event.

In the acceleration data processing part, four features will be extracted from the raw accelerator data. We apply an algorithm named neural random forest defined in [25] to predict the valence and arousal, representing the intrinsic attractiveness and measures how calming or exciting the information is respectively, of the users, and use a KNN-based algorithm to get recommended alarm sounds.

4 System Design

In this section, we introduce the structure of the audio processing part of iSmile in details. First of all, we present the method to detect ambient noise and the way to update the noise and the noise model. Then we introduce the features to classify different sleeping events. Afterwards we discuss the classification of sleeping events, and the measures to calculate normalized features terms. At last we will introduce the standard of scoring users' sleeping quality.

4.1 Ambient Noise Detection

Apparently, the ambient noise generated by various sources will affect the detection of sleeping events. At first, we need to distinguish the ambient noise from all the recorded audios. From our perspective, the ambient noise refers to the noise of the recording devices, the appliances that work continuously such as fans and air-conditioners, and other noise generated by outside environment such as rains, and winds.

The work of [11] indicates that ambient noises differentiate from sleeping events with relatively low variance of normalized standard deviation of each frame defined as follows:

$$\overline{std} = \frac{std_i - std_{mean}}{std_{mean} - std_{min}} \tag{1}$$

where std_i refers to the STD of ith frame of a noise audio piece which captures the stability of an acoustic signal frame, while std_{mean} and std_{min} denotes the mean and min standard deviation of a T-second acoustic signal window.

The authors in [11] also indicate that the value 0.5 can be set as the threshold to judge whether an audio piece is an ambient noise. However, our observation of more than 18,000 labeled noise audios shows that in extremely silent environment, even a very small fluctuation of recorded audio can cause the dramatical rise of variance (shown in Fig. 2). In this case, mis-classification of ambient noises will happen frequently. In order to fix this problem, we make some improvements in the noise detection model. Based on our observation of noise audios' features, we find that the intensity (shown by RMS) is much lower than sleeping events (shown in Fig. 3). So, we add RMS as another feature in noise detection model. From Fig. 3, we can see that more than 95% of the ambient noise frames have a RMS below 15.0, so 15.0 can be the threshold of judging whether audio pieces are ambient noises. In other words, if a 5-second frame is detected to have a $\overline{std}$ lower than 0.5 or RMS lower than 15.0, it will be recognized as ambient noise. With this method, we exclude the disturbance of slight fluctuation of sounds in silent environment.

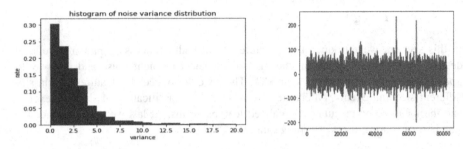

Fig. 2. a. Histogram of noise variance distribution. b. Noise waveform in silent environment

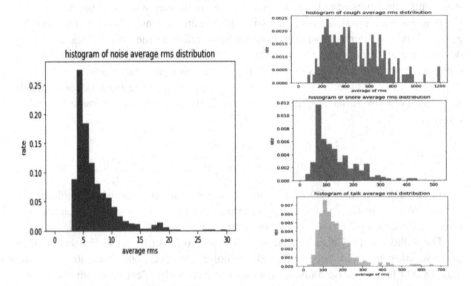

Fig. 3. The distribution of $\overline{\text{RMS}}$ of ambient noise (left) and sleep-related events (right).

4.2   Sleeping Event Features

- To classify the sleeping events, we choose three features to predict sleeping events based on the key characteristics of each sleep-related events.

The first one is root mean square (RMS), which presents the intensity of a non-noise audio piece. Suppose f is an acoustic piece that consists of n samples of acoustic amplitude $a_1, a_2, a_3, \ldots, a_n$. iSmile segments hours-long audios into 5-second-long frames, and each of them contains 80000 acoustic samples collected at 16 kHz. The RMS of the short audios frame f is given by:

$$\text{RMS}(f) = \sqrt{\frac{a_1^2 + a_2^2 + a_3^2 + \ldots + a_n^2}{n}} \tag{2}$$

The second feature is based on the observation of power spectrum of different sleeping events. Using the FFT algorithm [26], we can have a convenient observation of the energy distribution of an audio piece. The study in [27] indicates that snoring has scattered energy content in the higher spectral sub-bands (>500 Hz.), and we believe that sleep-related events such as coughing and sleep talking have their unique features in terms of spectrum. From Fig. 4, we can find that three kinds of sleeping events differ a lot from each other in their spectrum. To be specific, although all of their peak power at around 200 Hz, coughing has the highest peak energy of more than 1400, while the peak energy of snoring and sleep talking are respectively approximately 60 and 160. Moreover, snoring has the most scattered sub-peaks distribution ranging from 1200 Hz to around 5000 Hz in the spectrum, and in the spectrum of talking only several sub-peaks with small intensity appear. In terms of coughing's energy spectrum, sub-peaks appear at 3000 Hz and 3800 Hz with considerable intensity. In our implantation, we define the ratio of low-frequency energies to high-frequency energies (RLH) as the second feature. The RLH of a non-noise audio f can be calculated as follows:

$$\text{RLH}(f) = \frac{RMS(f_{low})}{RMS(f_{high})}, \tag{3}$$

where $RMS(f_{low})$ and $RMS(f_{high})$ denote the intensity of the energy of low frequency part and high frequency part of an audio frame respectively. We set 1200 Hz as the dividing point of high frequency and low frequency, and from Fig. 4 we can infer that snoring audios should have the lowest RLH while talking audios should have the highest one. In order words, the decreasing in RLH might be an indication of snoring events.

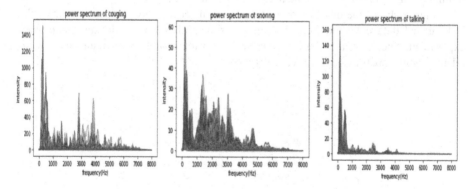

Fig. 4. The power spectrum of different sleep-related events

The third feature is variance (VAR), which reflects how far the amplitudes of acoustic signals within the frame are spread out. For instance, coughing is caused by the sudden and dramatic vibration of the vocal cord, so coughing audios should have higher variance than those of snoring and talking, which are both produced by relatively periodic vocal cord vibration.

4.3   Normalizing Measures

After an audio piece is detected as ambient noises, iSmile calculates three features for each of the frames. In order to estimate the current noise, iSmile computes the mean and standard deviation (*mean(RMS), std(RMS), mean(RLH), std(RLH), mean(VAR)* and *std(VAR)*) for each feature as the normalized terms. Then, each newly calculated distribution feature (*Feature$_{new}$*) will be used to update the current corresponding feature (*Feature$_{current}$*) according to an Exponential Moving Average (EMA) algorithm as follows:

$$Feature_{current} = Feature_{cureent} + \beta \times (Feature_{new} - Feature_{current}) \qquad (4)$$

In iSmile, the parameter βis set to be 0.4. The EMA algorithm makes sure that the normalized terms can adapt itself automatically in different environments.

4.4   Classification of Sleeping Events

In Sect. 4.2, we defined RMS, RLH, VAR as three features to distinguish different sleep-related events. To improve the robustness of the classification and reduce the influence of different external environments, we will normalize the three features with the Feature terms defined in Sect. 4.3 to acquire the features vectors (FV: $(\overline{RMS}, \overline{RLH}, \overline{VAR})$) for classification. For example, $\overline{rms}$ of a non-noise audio is calculated in the following way:

$$\overline{RMS}(f) = \frac{RMS(f) - std(f)}{mean(f)} \qquad (5)$$

Similarly, $\overline{RLH}$, and $\overline{VAR}$ are calculated in the same way.

Figure 5 shows the distribution of three normalized features. It is plotted from the 761 labeled data collected from 5 subjects using Meizu Note 5 during a one-week experiment. Specially, the class "*others*" refers to the sounds other than three sleep-related events, such as body moving (Fig. 6).

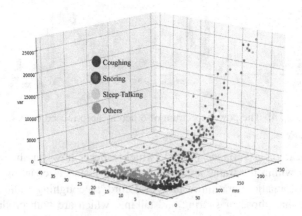

Fig. 5. The sound feature vectors of different events in feature space.

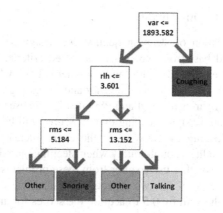

Fig. 6. The decision tree for event detection.

We apply a decision tree algorithm [28] as the classification model to detect sleeping events. The dotted rectangles indicate the splitting features, and the leaf nodes denote the classification results. The splitting features and thresholds are determined based on the information gain calculated by entropy. Specifically, the entropy of a node T is given by

$$\text{Entropy}(T) = - \sum_j p(j) \cdot \log(p(j)), \tag{5}$$

where $p(j)$ is the relative rate of class j at node T. In iSmile's case, $j = 3$. After splitting node T into k nodes $(T_1, T_2, \ldots T_k)$, we can calculate the information gain by

$$G = \text{Entropy}(T) - \left[\sum_{j=1}^{k} \frac{n_j}{n} \text{Entropy}(T_j) \right], \tag{6}$$

where n_j denotes the number of samples in node T_j. For each splitting, the system chooses the split that maximizes the information gain.

Next, we will describe the classification process in details. First, the non-noise audios are split into two groups according to $\overline{VAR}$, which reflects the extent of stability of acoustic signal. As a result, apparently audios with high $\overline{VAR}$ can be detected as coughing.

Then, the audios in the low $\overline{VAR}$ group are further split into two groups based on $\overline{RLH}$. As introduced in Sect. 4.2, low $\overline{RLH}$ reflects high dominant frequency, so low $\overline{RLH}$ audios are mostly classified as snoring and only a small number of audios in this group are classified as other noises because they have low $\overline{RMS}$. On the other hand, audios in high $\overline{RLH}$ group can be further categorized into two groups according to $\overline{RMS}$. While the low $\overline{RMS}$ audios are detected as other noise, the high $\overline{rms}$ audios are judged to be sleep-talking.

4.5 Scoring Users' Sleeping Quality

To realize the quantification of sleeping quality, we design a light-weight sleeping quality scoring standard based on two widely accepted criteria, one is PSQI, which provides the items of sleep-related events, and the other is PSQ, which gives the idea to scoring the quality from the angle of the intensity and appearing frequency of sleeping events. Table 1 lists the metrics in PSQI and PSQ that iSmile uses to calculate the score of sleeping quality. In our design, sleeping quality scores will be calculated from two aspects for different sleeping events. One is the event-intensity part, which shows whether the users snore, talk or cough loudly when sleeping, and the other is the event-rate part, which indicate whether users suffer from these problems frequently at nights. After the calculation of each of the two aspects is finished, we will add the scores of two parts and multiply the sum by 0.5 to acquire the scores for an event. Table 2 lists the items in iSmile's scoring items in details.

Table 1. Metrics from PSQI and PSQ iSmile uses

PSQI B4	Cough or snore loudly
PSQI B3	Cannot breathe comfortably
PSQ A2-a3	Usually/always snores
PSQ A4	Snore loudly

Table 2. The scoring criteria of iSmile

Scoring aspects	Detailed aspect	Rate
Coughing	The intensity of coughing	50%
	The frequency of coughing	50%
Snoring	The intensity of snoring	50%
	The frequency of snoring	50%
Sleep taking	The intensity of sleep talking	50%
	The frequency of sleep talking	50%

In terms of the event-intensity part, from 761 labeled sleeping events collected from 5 subjects, we can see the distribution of average RMS of each sleeping events. The results shown in Fig. 4 indicates that the average RMS of more than 95% of coughing is above 200, and less than 5% of that is above 800. If the average intensity of a coughing event is below 200, it will be scored as 100, which means the user snores slightly, while the ones whose intensity is between 200 to 800 receive score at 66.7, the remaining received only 33.3 points because it means users are coughing very loudly. Similarly, for snoring events, the average RMS below 50 will be scored at 100, and the remaining at 50. For talking, the average RMS below 120 and the remaining will be scored at 100 and 50, respectively.

For event appearing frequency scoring, if a 5-second-long audio pieces is detected as sleeping events, users will receive 50 points for the relative event items. If no events are detected, users will be scored at 100.

In our implementation, the system will record the numbers of audios detected to be sleep-related events (let it be *num*), and before the alarm sounds, all of the sleeping quality scores will be summed together and divided by *num* as the final results.

5 Implementation and Evaluation

5.1 Implement on Android Devices

ISmile is facilitated by an emotion-aware cognitive system [20], to demonstrate the system performance. Since iSmile needs to collect raw data from the built-in microphone and accelerator sensor continuously. But for some reasons, nearly all of the Android devices manufactures will shutdown the process to save the battery life. We have tried hard to address this problem, including setting the Developer Mode and adding iSmile to the device whitelist. We even try the Doze model of the Android operating system [29], a new feature for Android 6.0, which reduces battery consumption by deferring background CPU and network activity for apps when the device is unused for long periods of time. Eventually we select Meizu Note 5 to conduct the experiments. The UI of iSmile is shown in Fig. 7.

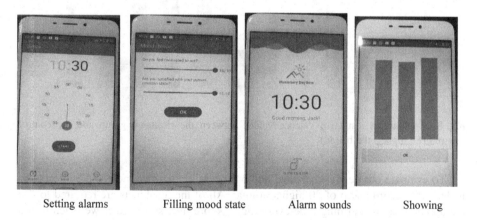

Setting alarms   Filling mood state   Alarm sounds   Showing

Fig. 7. Android UI of iSmile

The iSmile app takes up around 14 MB to install. When users run the iSmile app, they first enter the time setting page, where they can set the alarming time. After they press the *start* button, the system will start to collect record audios and acceleration data continuously. Before the alarm sounds, the raw data will be uploaded to the cloud platform, where the backend process will calculate the raw data to get the recommended music and the users' sleeping scores. Then on the Android side, recommended music will be played and users can see a chart showing their sleeping scores of coughing, snoring and sleep-talking. Users can record their current mood states, which will be uploaded to the backend process for later evaluations.

5.2 Experiments and Evaluation

In the previous version of iSmile, we have finished the design of smart-alarm recommendation. In that part, 8 subjects (three females and five males) were involved for ten days. 4 of the 8 subjects, labeled as control group, were given random alarms, and the other four, set as test group, were given the recommended alarms. Their self judgements of moods will be recorded every day, when they wake up. The results (shown in Figs. 8 and 9) reveals that the valence and arousal of the second group is raised by $\sqrt{10.33\% \times 10.33\% + 10.27\% \times 10.27\%} = 14.57\%$ compared with the first group.

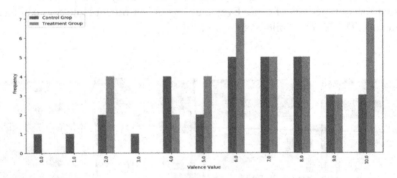

Fig. 8. Comparison results of valence values between the treatment group and the control group. (The higher, the better.)

To evaluate our newly-implanted audio processing part, we include 5 subjects (all males) and record audio of 20 nights in total. All of the 5 subjects are required to run the app and set an alarming time every night before they sleep. Later we listen to the audios recorded, and manually judge whether the system make the right detection of sleeping events. Table 3 shows the event detection results of data collected in the form of Audio Detection Accuracy (ADA).

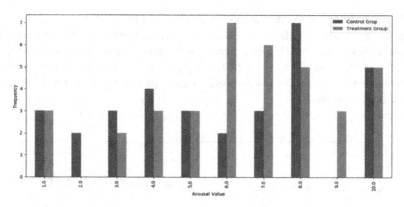

Fig. 9. Comparison results of arousal values between the treatment group and the control group. (The higher, the better.)

Table 3. The detection accuracy in the experiment

Subject	Coughing (ADA)	Snoring (ADA)	Sleep-talking (ADA)
1	6/6 (100%)	7/7 (100%)	17/28 (60.7%)
2	5/5 (100%)	5/5 (100%)	12/17 (70.6%)
3	8/8 (100%)	6/6 (100%)	4/6 (66.7%)
4	5/5 (100%)	4/5 (80%)	6/6 (100%)
5	3/3 (100%)	6/6 (100%)	3/3 (100%)
Total	27/27 (100%)	28/29 (96.6%)	42/60 (70%)

As shown in Table 3, over 20 nights of sleeping, iSmile has achieved high accuracy detection of over 95% in terms of coughing and snoring. Only 1 snoring audio is misclassified as other sleeping events. The relatively low detection accuracy of sleep-talking is explainable, since people can't really control themselves when they are sleep-talking. Audio signals of sleep-talking differ a lot from each other even though they are all produced by the same individual. Given more time, we could collect more audio data of sleep talking in order to increase its detection accuracy. If the forth class (other sounds) are included in the calculation of ADA, iSmile actually achieved an accuracy of 89.19% (132/148).

The scores of 5 subjects in 4 nights are presented in Figs. 10, 11 and 12. From the results, we can infer that all of the 5 subjects have different sleeping problems. For example, subject 5 coughs a bit more than the other four subjects. Except subject 2, the other four participants all have slight snoring problems. From the degree of sleep-talking, subject 1 receives the lowest scores, indicating that his brain seems to behave more actively at nights.

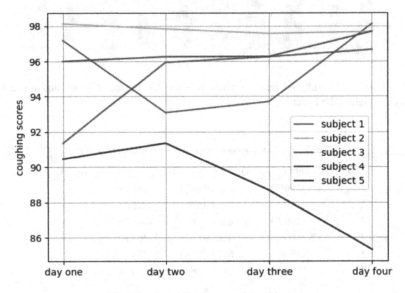

Fig. 10. Coughing scores of 5 subjects.

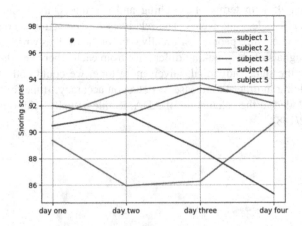

Fig. 11. Snoring scores of 5 subjects

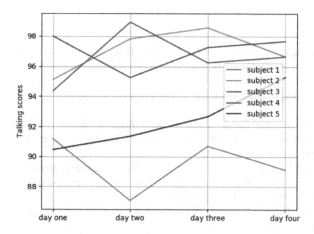

Fig. 12. Sleep-talking scores of 5 subjects

6 Conclusions and Future Work

In this paper, we introduce an original sleeping quality scoring app, named iSmile, which samples audios at 16 kHz from the smart phone built-in microphones to detect sleep-related events and scoring. ISmile also collect the data from smart alarm recommendations. To use this app, users just simply set the alarming time before they sleep, and the system will start to work. Before the alarm sounds, the raw data will be uploaded to the cloud platform. The backend program will calculate the sleeping scores and the recommended alarm sounds to improve the users' mood when they wake up. In the previous version of iSmile, we have achieved a 14.57% increase in users' mood in the form of valence and arousal. For the newly-deployed audio processing part, we have achieved a high accuracy detection of sleeping events for 5 subjects in 20 nights in total, and given the sleeping scores to show each individual's sleeping quality related to coughing, snoring as well as sleep-talking.

However, there are still some problems for us to handle. On one hand, due to the fact that backend program is deployed at the cloud platform, we need to upload all the raw data to the cloud site for later processing. In that case, there can be a huge data flow using this app. In other words, iSmile is not recommended for users without WI-FI currently. On the other hand, although we have achieved nearly 100% accuracy in detecting coughing and snoring, the ADA of sleep talking are much lower, which does great harm to the reliability of the final results of sleeping scores. What's more, the iSmile app has not been tested in many Android devices, but its stability still remains unknown. In the future, we will put much effort to address these problems and increase the system robustness. For example, we can deploy the processing part on the Android site to reduce the data flow, and we should collect more data of sleep talking to increase the judging accuracy. Last but not least, iSmile should be tested on different Android devices so that its performance can be judged in a more appropriate way.

References

1. Institute of Medicine, Colten, H.R., Altevogt, B.M. (eds.): Sleep Disorders and Sleep Deprivation: An Unmet Public Health Problem. The National Academies Press, Washington, DC (2006)
2. Parish, J.M.: Sleep-related problems in common medical conditions. Chest J. **135**(2), 563–572 (2009)
3. Foley, D., Ancoli-Israel, S., Britz, P., Walsh, J.: Sleep disturbances and chronic disease in older adults: results of the 2003 national sleep foundation sleep in America survey. J. Psychosom. Res. **56**, 497 (2004)
4. Gu, Y., Zhan, J., Liu, Z., Li, J., Ji, Y., Wang, X.: Sleepy: adaptive sleep monitoring from afar with commodity WiFi infrastructures. In: IEEE Wireless Communications and Networking Conference (WCNC), 15–18 April 2018
5. Douglas, N.J., Thomas, S., Jan, M.A.: Clinical value of polysomnography. Lancet **339** (8789), 347–350 (1992)
6. Divo, C.M., Selivanova, O., Mewes, T., Gosepath, J., Lippold, R., et al.: Polysomnography and ApneaGraph in patients with sleep-related breathing disorders. ORL J. Otorhinolaryngol. Relat. Spec. **71**, 27–31 (2009)
7. Buysse, D., Reynolds, C., Monk, T., Berman, S., Kupfer, D.: The Pittsburgh sleep quality index (PSQI): a new instrument for psychiatric research and practice. Psychiatry Res. **28**, 193–213 (1989)
8. Chervin, R.D., Hedger, K.M., Dillon, J.E., Pituch, K.J.: Pediatric Sleep Questionnaire (PSQ): validity and reliability of scales for sleep-disordered breathing, snoring, sleepiness, and behavioral problems. Sleep Med. **1**, 21–32 (2000)
9. Chesson, A., et al.: Practice parameters for the indications for polysomnography and related procedures. Sleep **20**, 406–422 (1997)
10. Pew Internet and American Life Project. http://pewinternet.org. Accessed 5 Dec 2018
11. Hao, T., Xing, G., Zhou, G.: iSleep: unobtrusive sleep quality monitoring using smartphones. In: Proceedings of the 11th ACM Conference on Embedded Networked Sensor Systems, Roma, 11–15 November 2013
12. Maimon, N., Hanly, P.J.: Does snoring intensity correlate with the severity of obstructive sleep apnea? J. Clin. Sleep Med. **6**, 475–478 (2010). [PubMed]
13. Scharf, S.M., Maimon, N., Simon-Tuval, T., et al.: Sleep quality predicts quality of life in chronic obstructive pulmonary disease. Int. J. Chron. Obstruct. Pulmon. Dis. **6**, 1–12 (2010)
14. Veldi, M., Aluoja, A., Vasar, V.: Sleep quality and more common sleep-related problems in medical students. Sleep Med. **6**, 269–275 (2005)
15. Manni, R., et al.: Poor sleep in adolescents: a study of 869, 17-year old Italian secondary school students. J. Sleep Res. **6**, 44–49 (1997)
16. Northcube: Sleep cycle alarm clock (2017). https://www.sleepcycle.com/. Accessed 5 Dec 2018
17. Seblong: Snail sleep (2016). http://www.seblong.com. Accessed 5 Dec 2018
18. Rofouei, M., et al.: A non-invasive wearable neck-cuff system for real-time sleep monitoring. In: BSN (2011)
19. Bai, Y., Xu, B., Ma, Y., Sun, G., Zhao, Y.: Will you have a good sleep tonight? Sleep quality prediction with mobile phone. In: BodyNets (2012)
20. Hu, X., et al.: Emotion-aware cognitive system in multi-channel cognitive radio ad hoc networks. IEEE Commun. Mag. **56**(4), 180–187 (2018)

21. Lamont, J., Baldwin, D.R., Hay, K.D., Veale, A.G.: Effect of two types of mandibular advancement splints on snoring and obstructive sleep apnoea. Eur. J. Orthod. **20**, 293–297 (1998)
22. Maimon, N., Hanly, P.J.: Does snoring intensity correlate with the severity of obstructive sleep apnea? J. Clin. Sleep Med. **6**(5), 475–478 (2010)
23. Agrawal, S., Stone, P., McGuinness, K., Morris, J., Camilleri, A.E.: Sound frequency analysis and the site of snoring in natural and induced sleep. Clin. Otolaryngol. Allied Sci. **27**(3), 162–166 (2002)
24. Perez-Padilla, J.R., Slawinski, E., Difrancesco, L.M., Feige, R.R., Remmers, J.E., Whitelaw, W.A.: Characteristics of the snoring noise in patients with and without occlusive sleep apnea. Am. Rev. Respir. Dis. **147**, 635–644 (1993)
25. Welbl, J.: Casting random forests as artificial neural networks (and profiting from it). In: Jiang, X., Hornegger, J., Koch, R. (eds.) GCPR 2014. LNCS, vol. 8753, pp. 765–771. Springer, Cham (2014). https://doi.org/10.1007/978-3-319-11752-2_66
26. Ganapathiraju, A., Hamaker, J., Picone, J., Skjellum, A.: A comparative analysis of FFT algorithms
27. Pevernagie, D., Aarts, R.M., De Meyer, M.: The acoustics of snoring. Sleep Med. Rev. **14**, 131–144 (2010)
28. Mitchell, T.: Machine Learning. McGraw-Hill, Boston (1997)
29. Sohil, A., Rastogi, S., Chawla, R.: Analysis for performance optimization of android applications. Int. J. Comput. Sci. Eng. Technol. **8**(3), 65–71 (2017)

Cluster Routing Protocol for Coal Mine Wireless Sensor Network Based on 5G

Wei Chen[1], Xiao Yang[1], Weidong Fang[2(✉)], Wuxiong Zhang[2],
and Xiaorong Jiang[1]

[1] School of Computer Science and Technology,
Mine Digitization Engineering Research Center of the Ministry of Education,
China University of Mining and Technology, Xuzhou 221116, Jiangsu, China
[2] Shanghai Institute of Microsystem and Information Technology,
Chinese Academy of Sciences, Shanghai 201899, China
weidong.fang@mail.sim.ac.cn

Abstract. In coal mine, the routing protocol in Wireless Sensor Network (WSN) based on fog computing can effectively achieve combination the monitoring task with the computing task, and provide the correct data forwarding path to meet the requirements of the aggregation and transmission of sensed information. However, the energy efficiency is still taken into account, especially, the unbalance of energy consumption. 5G is a technical system of high frequency and low frequency mixing, with characteristics of large capacity, low energy consumption and low cost. With the formal freeze on 5G NSA standards, 5G networks are one step closer to our lives. In this paper, a centralized non-uniform clustering routing protocol based on the residual energy and communication cost. The protocol considers all nodes as candidate cluster heads in the clustering stage and defines a weight matrix P. The value of the matrix elements takes into account the residual energy of nodes and the cost of communication between nodes and cluster heads, selected as the basis for the cluster head. When selecting a cluster head, each time a node with the largest weight is selected from a set of candidate cluster heads, other candidate cluster heads within the competition range abandon competition, and then updates the candidate cluster head set. Experimental results show that the protocol optimized in this paper can effectively extend the network life cycle.

Keywords: Wireless sensor network · Cluster-based routing protocol ·
Non-uniform clustering · Multi-cluster-head cluster · 5G

1 Introduction

The deployment of wireless sensor network does not require basic infrastructure, Nodes can form a network in a self-organized manner instead of using linear circuits. which gives the wireless sensor network in mine monitoring a broad application space.

Wireless sensor network is a network that deployed by a large number of sensor nodes deployed in a certain area in an ad-hoc manner. The energy in the sensor node is provided by the battery. The wireless sensor network is generally deployed in the

V. C. M. Leung et al. (Eds.): 5GWN 2019, LNICST 278, pp. 60–67, 2019.
https://doi.org/10.1007/978-3-030-17513-9_5

unreachable area, so the sensor node cannot be replenished by replacing the battery. This makes the energy factor determine the life cycle of the wireless sensor network.

This paper proposes a centralized non-uniform clustering routing protocol based on the residual energy and communication cost based on the protocol proposed by Professor Li et al. [1]. This paper defines the weight matrix P, its element P[i, j] represents the node i as the weight of the cluster head node j. This paper also defines the weight of the node i is the sum of the row of the matrix P. When the nodes compete for the final cluster head, the node with the largest weight is selected as the optimal. The other nodes within the competition radius abandon the competition as ordinary nodes. This method has improved the life cycle of the network and reduced the residual energy variance of the nodes in the network.

2   Related Works

A Wireless Sensor Network (WSN) consists of enormous amount of sensor nodes. These sensor nodes sense the changes in physical parameters from the sensing range and forward the information to the sink nodes or the base station [2, 3]. Fog computing (FC) has received a great deal of attention in current period [4, 5]. FC can be viewed as an extension of cloud computing that services the edges of networks. Current research trends from areas [6–8], such as from Internet of Things and fog computing use sensors as the source of data [9–11]. Sharma, Suraj et al. [12] proposed a method which builds a routing path using each active grid head which leads to the sink. Data packets generated at any source node are routed directly through the data disseminating grid head nodes on the routing path to the sink. Li et al. [13] proposed a cooperative-based model for smart phone tasks. The rewards to each user with a smart sensor are distributed according to the region density. Lee et al. [14] presented a gateway based fog computing architecture for WSANs and argue that the key requirements of this architecture. This architecture mainly consists of master nodes and slave nodes, and manages virtual gateway functions, flows, and resources. Chakraborty et al. [15] presented the dynamic Fog, a high level programming model for time-sensitive applications that are geospatially distributed, large-scale, and latency sensitive. They analyzed the fog model with healthcare datum, more specifically with heart rate datum that is one of the most time-sensitive medical data which deals with life and death situations. Nunes et al. [16] anticipated the future by discussing a new generation of security and privacy mechanisms targeting specifically.

3   Clustering Routing Protocol

In this paper, the centralized unequal clustering routing protocol based on energy of node left and communication cost is an improvement of the protocol, which mainly improves in cluster head competition algorithm. The protocol considered the energy of node left when selecting the final cluster head, but the selection of the candidate cluster heads was random. While if candidate cluster heads selected do not contain higher residual energy, it is impossible to guarantee that the final cluster head has a higher residual energy, thus affecting the balance of energy consumption of the network. The Cluster Head Competition Algorithm proposed in this paper has made two improvements to the algorithm: ① all nodes were treated as candidate cluster heads. ② When selecting the final cluster head consider energy of node left and communication cost between member nodes and cluster heads. Multi-hop routing in clusters is the same as EEUC.

3.1 Cluster Head Competition Algorithm

The algorithm assumes that the node knows its own location. In the initialization phase after network deployment, all nodes and sink nodes communicate at once, and the nodes report their location and residual energy to the sink node. Cluster Head Selection Algorithm is performed by the sink node.

The Cluster Head Selection Algorithm proposed in this paper makes the following assumptions about wireless sensor networks:

(1) Each sensor node has unique ID, and all nodes are randomly distributed in the test area;
(2) After the node is deployed, it is location no longer changes and the energy cannot be replenished again. The location of the sink node has been fixed, with strong computing power and infinite energy.
(3) All nodes are homogeneous, that is to say, all nodes share the same computing power and communication capacity, and have the probability to be cluster head nodes or member nodes.
(4) The node has the ability to perceive position;
(5) Each node in the network collects data periodically and always has to send data;

The paper assumes that each node has data to send in each round, and the length of each data packet is constant. As a result, if the initial energy of sensor node is known the residual energy of sensor nodes based on clustering situation can be estimated.

Cluster Header Selection Algorithm is performed by the sink node. In Cluster Building Phase, sink node send clustering information to all the nodes in the network, clustering information includes whether the node is cluster head, and should also include the next-hop routing information of the node if it is, include it's cluster head nodes if not.

In Communication Phase, member nodes report the finish of data collection to cluster head node. The cluster head communicates with the sink node in a multi-hop method. The selection of the next hop routing node of the cluster head node is the same as that of propose protocol.

3.2 C-EEUC Protocol

Firstly, the paper analyzes the energy consumption of nodes in the protocol theoretically. The sensor node consists of four parts: sensor module, processor module, wireless communication module and energy supply module. Sensor modules and processor modules consume only a small amount of energy [17, 18]. The paper only considers the energy consumption of communication modules.

When the sensor node is sending data, the relation between energy consumption and communication distance of wireless communication is [19]:

$$E = kd^n \tag{1}$$

Where, d is the distance between the transmitting node and the receiving node, and the parameter n is the signal reduction factor, which generally is the real number ranges from 2 to 4.

Assuming that the model of free-space path consumption is adopted when the distance between two nodes is less than d_0, the model of multi-path fading is adopted when the distance is greater than d_0 [20], and d_0 is the distance, which is a constant variable, $d_0 = \sqrt{\varepsilon fs/\varepsilon mp}$, εfs is the energy consumption coefficient of power amplifier in the model of free-space path consumption, εmp is the energy consumption coefficient of power amplifier in the multi-path fading model.

When the sensor node is receiving data, the energy consumed by receiving data of k bit is as follows:

$$E = Eelec \times k \tag{2}$$

Where, $Eelec$ is the energy consumed by accepting one digit of data in the receiver circuit.

4 Experimental Simulation

4.1 Network Model

In order to compare the EEUC protocol with the protocol proposed in this paper, two sets of experiments are carried out in this paper. In the first experiment, 100 wireless sensor nodes are randomly deployed in the region. Suppose the coordinates of the lower left corner of the region are (0, 0) and the coordinates of the sink node are (150, 50). In the second experiment, 200 wireless sensor nodes are randomly deployed in the 200 * 200 region. Suppose the coordinates of the lower left corner of the region are (0, 0) and the coordinates of the sink node are (250, 100). In reference [1], the network performance is optimal when $T = 0.4$, $R_c^0 = 90$ and $c = 0.5$. Therefore, we initiate the parameters in the same way. The value of p in the LEACH protocol is 0.03. The influence of R_c^0 and c on the network performance in C-EEUC protocol is the next research goal of this topic. In this paper, the experimental parameters are chosen as the experimental contrast. We use MATLAB as the experiment platform.

4.2   Simulation Experimental Parameters

The experimental parameters of first group are shown in Table 1.

Table 1. Parameters in the first group experiments

Network parameters	Value
Range	(0, 0) to (100, 100)
Number of sensor nodes	100
Coordinates of sink node	(150, 50)
Node initial energy	0.5 J
Packet length	4000 bit
Eelec	50 nJ/bit
EDA	5 nJ/bit
Efs	10 pJ/(bit * m^2)
Emp	0.0013 pJ(bit * m^4)

The experimental parameters of second group are shown in Table 2.

Table 2. Parameters in the second group experiments

Network parameters	Value
Range	(0, 0) to (200, 200)
Number of sensor nodes	200
Coordinates of sink node	(250, 100)
Node initial energy	0.5 J
Packet length	4000 bit
Eelec	50 nJ/bit
EDA	5 nJ/bit
Efs	10 pJ/(bit * m^2)
Emp	0.0013 pJ(bit * m^4)

4.3   Experiment Results

In this paper, we compare LEACH protocol, EEUC and C-EEUC from three aspects: network life cycle, network energy consumption and node residual energy variance. Experiment results show that the proposed C-EEUC protocol is better than LEACH and EEUC in these three aspects. Define the time when the first sensor node is dead as the life time of the network.

Figure 1 shows the LEACH, EEUC and the number of rounds-remaining nodes of the algorithm proposed in this paper under the condition that 100 nodes are randomly arranged in the network coverage of 100 m * 100 m.

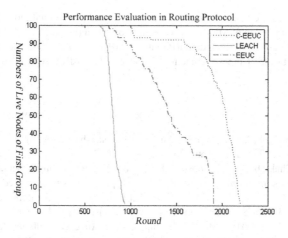

Fig. 1. Round-numbers of live nodes in first group

5   Conclusions

In a coal mine monitoring system, a clustering routing protocol could reduce the volume of data transmitted and the energy consumption in communication that cluster head nodes in WSN based on fog computing framework coalesce the data from cluster members before forwarding. However, cluster head nodes have to manage too many tasks in clustering routing protocols including cluster establishment, communication control in clusters, data coalescence, exchange data with sink nodes, and so on, which causes the imbalance of the energy consumption. In addition, if cluster head nodes communicate with the sink node in a multi-hop routing mechanism, head nodes near the sink node have to forward the data frequently, which makes the energy consumption even more imbalanced. Therefore, clustering routing protocol reduces the energy consumption of the network, but also contributes the imbalance to the network energy consumption. In EEUC protocol, the radius of the cluster close to the sink node is smaller, which reduces the size and increases the number of the clusters, so that more cluster heads could join the forwarding. Besides, the reduction of cluster members also reduces the energy consumption of the cluster heads. The uneven clustering routing protocol proposed in this paper, takes all nodes as candidate cluster head node. The weight matrix P is defined to calculate the residual energy of nodes and the communication cost between the nodes and the cluster head. Experiment results show that the routing protocol is better than LEACH and EEUC in the performance of prolonging network lifetime, reducing network energy consumption and balancing energy consumption.

Acknowledgment. The research is supported by National Natural Science Foundation of China (Grant No. 51874300), the National Natural Science Foundation of China and Shanxi Provincial People's Government Jointly Funded Project of China for Coal Base and Low Carbon (Grant No. U1510115), National Natural Science Foundation of China (Grant Nos. 51874299, 51104157), the Qing Lan Project, the China Postdoctoral Science Foundation (Grant No. 2013T60574), the Ph.D. Programs Foundation of Ministry of Education of China (Grant No. 20110095120008) and the China Postdoctoral Science Foundation (Grant No. 20100481181) and the Scientific Instrument Developing Project of the Chinese Academy of Sciences (No. YJKYYQ20170074).

References

1. Li, C.F., Chen, G.H., Ye, M., Wu, J.: An uneven cluster-based routing protocol for wireless sensor networks. Chin. J. Comput. **30**(1), 27–36 (2007)
2. Jamthe, A., Chakraborty, S., Ghosh, S.K., Agrawal, D.P.: An implementation of wireless sensor networks in monitoring of Parkinson's patients using received signal strength indicator. In: O'Conner, L. (ed.) 2013 9th IEEE International Conference on Distributed Computing in Sensor Systems, Cambridge, Massachusetts, pp. 442–447. IEEE (2013)
3. Suto, K., Nishiyama, H., Kato, N., Huang, C.-W.: An energy-efficient and delay-aware wireless computing system for industrial wireless sensor networks. IEEE Access **3**, 1026–1035 (2015)
4. Bhargava, K., Ivanov, S., Kulatunga, C., Donnelly, W.: Fog-enabled WSN system for animal behavior analysis in precision dairy. In: Yang, L.Q., Muller, P. (eds.) 2017 International Conference on Computing, Networking and Communications, pp. 504–510 (2016)
5. Vaquero, L.M., Rodero-Merino, L.: Finding your way in the definition fog: towards a comprehensive of fog computing. ACM SIGCOMM Comput. Commun. Rev. **44**(5), 27–32 (2014)
6. Zeng, J., Wang, T., Lai, Y., Liang, J., Chen, H.: Data delivery from WSNs to cloud based on a fog structure. In: Tarek, E.G., Christophe, C., Bing, G. (eds.) 2016 Fourth International Conference on Advanced Cloud and Big Data, Chengdu, Sichuan, China, pp. 104–109. IEEE (2016)
7. Zhu, Z., Zhuo, L., Qu, P., Zhou, K., Zhang, J.: Extreme weather recognition using convolutional neural networks. In: Mohan, S.K., Phillip, C.-Y.S., Mei-Ling, S. (eds.) 2016 IEEE International Symposium on Multimedia, San Jose, California, pp. 621–625 (2016)
8. Teerapittayanon, S., McDanel, B., Kung, H.T.: Distributed deep neural networks over the cloud, the edge and end devices. In: Lee, K., Liu, L. (eds.) 2017 IEEE 37th International Conference on Distributed Computing Systems, Atlanta, Georgia, pp. 328–339 (2017)
9. Eriksson, E., Dan, G., Fodor, V.: Radio and computational resource management for fog computing enabled wireless camera networks. In: Cui, S.R., Secci, S. (eds.) 2016 IEEE Globecom Workshops, Washington, DC, USA, pp. 1–6 (2016)
10. Majd, A., Sahebi, G., Daneshtalab, M., Plosila, J., Tenhunen, H.: Placement of smart mobile access points in wireless sensor networks and cyber-physical systems using fog computing. In: Didier, E.B., Julien, B. (eds.) UIC-ATC-ScalCom-CBDCom-IoP-SmartWorld, Toulouse, France, pp. 680–689 (2016)
11. Feng, J., Liu, Z., Wu, C., Ji, Y.: Mobile edge computing for the internet of vehicles: offloading framework and job scheduling. IEEE Veh. Technol. Mag. **14**(1), 28–36 (2019)
12. Sharma, S., Puthal, D., Tazeen, S., Prasad, M., Zomaya, A.Y.: MSGR: a mode-switched grid-based sustainable routing protocol for wireless sensor networks. IEEE Access **5**, 19864–19875 (2017)
13. Li, T., Liu, Y., Gao, L., Liu, A.: A cooperative-based model for smart-sensing tasks in fog computing. IEEE Access **5**, 21296–21311 (2017)

14. Lee, W., Nam, K., Roh, H.-G., Kim, S.-H.: A gateway based fog computing architecture for wireless sensors and actuator networks. In: Chang, M., Chen, N.-S., Huang, R., Kinshuk, M.K., Murthy, S., Sampson, D.G. (eds.) 2016 18th International Conference on Advanced Communications Technology, Bombay, India, pp. 210–213 (2016)
15. Chakraborty, S., Bhowmick, S., Talaga, P., Agrawal, D.P.: Fog networks in healthcare application. In: Cao, J., Carvalho, M.M. (eds.) Proceedings 2016 IEEE 13th International Conference on Mobile Ad Hoc and Sensor Systems, Brasília, Brazil, pp. 386–387 (2016)
16. Nunes, D., et al.: FoTSeC - human security in Fog of Things. In: Ali, A.B.M.S., Yang, X., Albert, Z. (eds.) 2016 IEEE International Conference on Computer and Information Technology (Cit), Nadi, Fiji, pp. 743–749 (2016)
17. Sun, L.M., Li, J.Z., Chen, Y., Zhu, H.S.: Wireless Sensor Networks. Tsinghua University Press, Peiking (2005)
18. Wang, X., Liu, Z., Gao, Y., Zheng, X., Chen, X., Wu, C.: Near-optimal data structure for approximate range emptiness problem in information-centric Internet of Things. IEEE Access 7, 21857–21869 (2019)
19. Liu, A.F., He, H., Wu, X.Y., Chen, Z.G.: Optimization of parameter selection for wireless sensor network with mobile base station. J. Central South Univ. (Sci. Technol.) 40(5), 1336–1344 (2009)
20. Heinzelman, W.R., Chandrakasan, A., Balakrishnan, H.: Energy-efficient communication protocol for wireless microsensor networks. In: Jay Jr., F.N., Robert, B. (eds.) Proceedings of the 33rd Annual Hawaii International Conference on System Sciences, vol. 2, p. 8020 (2000). https://doi.org/10.1109/hicss.2000.926982

Distributed Multiple-Service User-Experience Energy Saving Algorithm for Base Station

Yuanyuan Zeng[ID], Yu Zhang, Hao Jiang[(✉)], and Xian Zhou

School of Electronic Information, Wuhan University, Wuhan, Hubei, China
{zengyy,zyzhangyu,jh,zhouxianzx}@whu.edu.cn

Abstract. The issue about energy consumption of wireless network attracts more and more attention and becomes one of three energy efficiency features in 5G. The user associated base station switching on-off strategy can effectively reduce energy consumptions. The existing strategies mainly focus on Quality of Service for users, without fully considering the influence of user experience for specific applications and the problem of high time complexity of implementing the energy-saving strategy caused by the large scale of the 5G mobile network. This paper proposes Distributed Multiple-service User-experience Energy Saving Algorithm for base station (DMUES). Nonlinear integer programming is utilized to model the above problem, which achieves the tradeoff between user experience and energy consumption. By comparing with other relative energy saving strategy, the results show that DMUES achieves good performance on user experience and energy savings. Furthermore, the time complexity of energy saving strategy is reduced due to community partition.

Keywords: 5G · Base energy saving · Quality of Experience · Energy efficiency · Multi-service user experience

1 Introduction

With the advent of the 5G era, the demand for service applications and user experience has forced network operators to find new technologies to reduce operating costs and increase data transmission rate, thereby improving the quality of user experience. The exponential growth of data services has dramatically increased the demand for network facilities and has also caused large energy consumption. And the 5G communication network has been moving towards the deployment of very large-scale and dense base stations (BSs) [3]. Dense BS deployment results in excessive energy consumptions and carbon emissions, which causes hard burden on electrical energy facilities and affects the ecosystem greatly. Green communication, as one of the important requirements of 5G, requires that the total

© ICST Institute for Computer Sciences, Social Informatics and Telecommunications Engineering 2019
Published by Springer Nature Switzerland AG 2019. All Rights Reserved
V. C. M. Leung et al. (Eds.): 5GWN 2019, LNICST 278, pp. 68–85, 2019.
https://doi.org/10.1007/978-3-030-17513-9_6

energy consumption of the network will not increase when the user data traffic increases by a thousand times. It is expected that by 2020, the end-to-end energy consumption per bit in the future 5G network will need to be reduced to 1/1000. The IMT-2020 proposes that the future 5G will also work to improve the operational energy consumption and cost efficiency of network construction [1]. Therefore, in the future, 5G communication will be necessary to reduce energy consumption while maintaining various types of business growth. The increase in energy consumption costs has also led people to pay more and more attention to ways to reduce energy consumption.

Due to people's living habits and mobility characteristics, the traffic patterns of BSs in cities show tidal phenomena and spatial differences, that is, traffic loads of base stations experience significant peak and trough periods, and there may also be significant differences in the traffic loads of different base stations at the same time. According to the dense deployment of cellular base stations in cities, it is energy efficient that can effectively improve BS utilization by appropriately turning off some BSs and offload users to nearby BSs during non-peak times.

The important difference compared to the 4G research idea is that 5G is considered to be the first important user experience as a research core. In other words, in the upcoming 5G era, the most important thing is not speed, but more application and user experience, and a more adaptive business model. However, experience of users who are offloaded to other base stations may be affected to some extent. Traditional BS energy-saving strategy ensures the quality of service (QoS) of users as a prerequisite, mainly concludes service-related indicators such as delay, throughput, jitter, and packet loss while ignoring the influence of business characteristics on user experience. Quality of Experience (QoE) is a measure of acceptability based on user acceptance, Zhao et al. [18] pointed out that QoE can reflect user's satisfaction degree towards the network services based on quantitative modeling of QoS. In the multi-service oriented application architecture, accurate assessment of user experience toward different services according to service characteristics and demands for transmission resources are helpful to the optimization of system resources. To solve the problem, Gómez et al. [5] provided a detailed introduction to the QoE evaluation methods of services such as voice, video streaming and Web browsing, Khan et al. [9] used the Utility Function from Economics to evaluate the specific business services.

QoE overcomes the deficiencies of QoS metrics that ignore service features, it can better describe users' satisfaction with applications or services. Furthermore, considering that the time complexity of solving the problem is growing exponentially with the number of base stations, in this paper we propose a Distributed Multiple-service User-experience Energy Saving Algorithm for base station (DMUES) adopting QoE utility function to evaluate the multi-service user experience, and nonlinear integer programming is utilized to model the energy-saving strategy. And the community is divided into base stations in the city, and the base station energy-saving strategy is implemented separately in each community. Through experiments, it is proved that the proposed DMUES achieve good user experience and energy saving. Furthermore, it greatly reduces the computational complexity and time complexity.

2   Related Work

In the urgent need to achieve energy saving, the green cellular network has become a hot topic for researchers. The traditional energy-saving measures of cellular networks are mainly divided into four categories, namely, improving the energy efficiency of hardware components, optimizing the energy efficiency of the wireless transmission process, base station hibernation/cell zooming, and deploying heterogeneous units [17]. The way to improve the energy efficiency of hardware components requires network operators to replace cellular network system components on a large scale with high implementation costs. Improving energy efficiency by optimizing the wireless transmission process requires a compromise between energy saving and network performance. The method of deploying heterogeneous units is to reduce energy consumption through the use of plug-and-play small cell base stations in the middle of cellular networks (including microcells, picocells etc.) [7].

Cell Zooming is a cell-like breathing concept that changes the base station's coverage area by adjusting the state of the BS. It includes measures such as adjusting base station height, power, sleep, and full shutdown. When a base station is in a low-load state, it can serve users under neighboring base stations by increasing its coverage area and reduce the load on neighboring base stations. Even if all the base stations are under low load, even partial base stations can be completely turned off to achieve energy saving. The BS consumes the largest proportion of energy in the cellular network. By monitoring the traffic of the base station, selectively shutting down some base station transmitting units and cooling equipment (air conditioners, etc.) during off-peak hours, the energy saving effect is very considerable. In 5G heterogeneous networks, the deployment of dense cellular network base stations makes the coverage area of a single base station smaller. The base station's business model is more random, which makes the strategy of shutting down the base station more desirable. Combining 5G heterogeneous network deployment with the base station's sleep mode will yield significant benefits in terms of energy savings [10].

The base station closure policy usually determines the state of the communication unit (base station) of the cellular network by monitoring the traffic load in the network. It is mainly divided into three categories, which are strategies based on traffic load, strategies based on user association and strategies combining traffic load and user association respectively. Han et al. [6] proposed base switching strategy based on traffic load, and solving the problem by centralized greedy decision-making and decentralized autonomous decision-making respectively. Zhu et al. [19] proposed a QoS-aware user association scheme to reconfigure the cell association for energy saving. Oh et al. [13] proposed a practically implementable switching-on/off base energy-saving algorithm considering base load and user association both, and the algorithm can be operated in a distributed manner with low computational complexity. Jiang et al. [8] estimated the aggregate traffic demands of the BS communities and proposed a switch-off strategy while guaranteeing minimal service requirements. Son et al. [16] developed a theoretical (and also practical) framework for BS energy saving that encompasses both dynamic BS operation and user association.

The load based BS on-off switching strategy pays more attention to energy efficiency other than the association status of users. The user association switching strategy needs to switch the BS on-off state frequently according to user association, which brings extra energy consumptions. The hybrid method of joint load and user association based switching strategy avoids frequent status switching with more balanced energy consumptions and better user experience.

For multi-service application architectures, different services have different characteristics and requirements for network transmission quality. The models of users' perceptions of different services are different and need to be evaluated using corresponding models. This will help optimize the resources of the system. The cellular network is a multi-service application architecture. For the characteristics of the business and the demand for network transmission resources, accurate assessment and modeling of different services can help optimize system resources. The European Telecommunications Standards Institute introduced the concept of QoE, and provided a mapping analysis between QoE and network performance indicators for different services. [15] The literature [4] proposes a general formula that links QoE and QoS parameters through an exponential relationship.

3   System Model

In order to describe the energy consumption of the BSs, this section gives the energy consumption model. A BS usually consists of several cells with different radiation azimuths, and cells share the base architecture like cooling system of the BS. Energy consumption of a cell is divided into static consumption (consumption from transmission antenna and power amplifier) and dynamic consumption (consumption related with load/utilization, which varies with cell load), and cells of a BS share the consumption of base architecture.

For the measurement of user experience for specific service types in mobile cellular networks, this paper introduces QoE utility function to model user experience for multi-services.

3.1   Cell Affinity Relationship

To get users' association state to cells, we should first get the coverage area of each cell. Each BS has multiple cells, and the cells belonging to the same BS have the same geographical coordinate. The coverage is different. The coordinate of a point closer to the BS on the center line of the covered cell area with the sector as the position coordinate of the cell is the azimuth, and is a very small positive value. Then we adopt Voronoi tessellation to divide the areas based on the location (latitude and longitude) and antenna radiation azimuth of cells. Cell division example from a typical city of Zhejiang province, China is showed in Fig. 1.

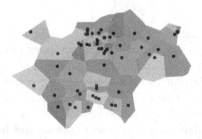

Fig. 1. Coverage areas division of cells

Whether a user can access to a cell depends on user's distance and direction relative to the cell, that is, user-cell affinity relationship. We can construct the affinity graph G_A of users and cells. G_A can be described as a bipartite graph consisting of users and cells. If a user is within the coverage area of a cell, then we can add an edge between them.

In this paper, user association strategy proposed in [2] is adopted. It is assumed that the inter-cell interference and environmental interference are both Gaussian white noises, and the received signal strength of user is only related to the distance. On this condition, users will associate to the nearest active cell it can be associated to. For example, users under cell 1 can associated to cell set, when cell 1 is closed, users under it will be associated to the active cell 7 from which they can receive the best average signal strength.

In a BS switching strategy, users under a closed sector are associated with neighboring cells. In a BS switching strategy, users under a closed cell are associated with neighboring cells. A cooperative relationship between cells is represented by a directed weighted graph. V is the set of sector nodes, and E is the set of edges of nodes. When 80% of users under a cell are under the coverage area of a cell, there are edges in the graph: the size of the edge is the average distance between the user and the sector under the cell. After the cell is closed, users under the sector can associate the set of cells.

3.2 Base Station Energy Comsumption Model

Each BS in the cellular network is consisted of multiple cells with different radiation azimuths, cells share the base station's infrastructure such as the refrigeration equipment. Energy consumption of a cell is consisted of static energy consumption and dynamic energy consumption. Static energy consumption concludes consumption of power amplifiers and antennas and etc. Dynamic energy consumption is needed for processing of the traffic loads, and is positively related to load ρ. Assuming that $\{\rho_1, \rho_2, \rho_3, ..., \rho_n\}$ represents the traffic load demands of cells, and $\{\rho_1^*, \rho_2^*, \rho_3^*, ..., \rho_n^*\}$ represents cells'current traffic loads with the energy-saving strategy. Power consumption of cells increases linearly with the traffic load:

$$P_{cell}(\rho) = k \cdot \rho + c \tag{1}$$

k is the coefficient, c is the static energy consumption of the cell. Consumption of a base station is:

$$P_{base} = \sum_{cell \in base} P_{cell}(\rho_{cell}) + C \qquad (2)$$

Among the function, C is the consumption of the base architecture of the BS.

3.3 User Experience Model

QoE was proposed by the ITU-T for measuring user's subjective acceptability to applications or services perceived. For the mapping from objective measurements (in terms of QoS) into subjective metrics (in terms of QoE perceived by the user), we adopt the utility function toward multi-services which is defined as the gain users obtained from a service according to the resource requirements. Mobile cellular network services are mainly classified into four types: VoIP services, streaming services, interactive services, and background services. Each type of services has specific characteristic and different transmission resource requirement. Therefore, different forms of utility function are required for modeling multi-service user experience.

VOIP: such as audio calls and video calls, is a hard real-time service that requires strict end-to-end guarantee and is particularly delay sensitive. Its utility function is a unit step function of the allocated resource r. When the allocated resource r is smaller than the minimum transmission resource requirement r_{min}, the utility value is 0, and when the allocated resource equals to r_{min}, the utility value steps to its max value 1 and will not increase anymore, the utility function is as follows

$$U_{VOIP}(r) = \begin{cases} 0, r < r_{\min} \\ 1, r \geq r_{\min} \end{cases} \qquad (3)$$

Streaming (STM): audio and video streaming services that can use data buffering technology, having a certain degree of tolerance for media distortions, and can be accepted when packets exceed the latency limitation slightly or even get some loss. The utility function is in exponential form. When the resource r is smaller than a certain smaller value r_{min}, the utility value increases from zero to r, and its growth rate increases. When r gets greater than r_{min}, the growth rate of utility function decreases. Due to the limited system transmission resource r_{max}, the value of the utility function reaches its maximum value when the resource reaches r_{max} and will no longer increase, the utility function is as follows

$$U_{STM}(r) = 1 - e^{-\frac{k_1 r^2}{k_2 + r}}, r \leq r_{\max} \qquad (4)$$

Interactive Services (WEB): Mainly are web browsing, chatting, games and other services that have a certain tolerance for delay. The utility function is an exponential function with the allocated resources r. When r is lower than the minimum resource requirement r_{min}, the utility value is 0; when r_{min} gets greater than r_{min}, the utility value steps to a larger value and begins to increase monotonously with r, and the growth rate keeps decreasing. The utility value reaches its maximum when r reaches the limited system transmission resource r_{max}, the utility function is as follows

$$U_{WEB} = \begin{cases} 0, r < r_{\min} \\ 1 - e^{-\frac{k_3 r}{r_{max}}}, r_{\min} \leq r \leq r_{max} \end{cases} \quad (5)$$

Background BK: Services such as file transferring and email, which has high tolerance of delay. The utility function is an exponential function of resource r and increases with the resource r with growth rate decreasing. When the allocated resource r reaches the system's maximum resource limit r_{max}, the utility function will reach its maximum value

$$U_{BK}(r) = 1 - e^{-\frac{k_4 r}{r_{max}}}, r \leq r_{max} \quad (6)$$

Among them, k_1, k_2, k_3, k_4 are positive model parameters used to adjust the growth rate of utility function. The range of value for utility function is $[0, 1]$.

The average transmission rate received by users under cell i is: $r_i = Wlog(1+ SINR)$, where W is the channel bandwidth, and $SINR = \frac{p_i + g_i}{\sum_{m \in N_i, m \neq j} g_m + \sigma_0}$ is the Signal to Interference plus Noise Ratio, in which p_i is the transmission power of antenna, σ_0 is white noise from the environment, $\sum_{m \in N_i, m \neq j} g_m$ is the inter-cell interference from the neighbor cells which can also be considered as Gaussian white noise, $g_i = L(d_i) = (1 + (\frac{d_i}{40})^{3.5})^{-1}$ is the channel gain caused by channel fading and Rayleigh fading, d_i is the average distance from users under cell i to the cell.

4   Strategy Formulation

In the last section we have introduced the system model in detail, include the base station energy model and multi-service user experience model. The base station switching strategy is closing some cells and offloading users under them to their neighbor cells according to cells cooperation relationship, and ensuring that the user experience be guaranteed. Our goal is to save as much energy as possible at the expense of a smaller loss of user experience, that is, base station energy saving is a multi-objective optimization problem of base station energy and multi-service user experience.

4.1   Optimization Model of DMUES

Assume that the status vector of cells is $\{x_1, x_2, x_3, ..., x_n\}$, $x_i = \{0, 1\}$, let $\{\rho_1, \rho_2, \rho_3..., \rho_n\}$ be the cell load demand vector, $\{\rho_1{}^*, \rho_2{}^*, \rho_3{}^*..., \rho_n{}^*\}$ be the current cell load vector. $\rho_i{}^*$ is related with the status of cell i and status of its neighbors.

From the user-cell affinity graph we can get the cell set N_i that users under cell i can associated to, and the cell set C_i whose serving users can associated to cell i. When cell j in C_i is closed, and neighbor cells closer to cell j than cell i are all closed, cell i will be the nearest active cell of cell j, then the load of cell j will be offloaded to cell i, that is, $\rho_i{}^*$ is related to state of N_i and state of neighbor cells of cells in N_i, $\rho_i{}^*$ can be expressed as follows

$$\rho_i^* = x_i \cdot \rho_i + (1 - x_j) \cdot \sum_{j \in C_i} \rho_j \cdot \prod_{m \in N_j, d_{jm} < d_{ji}} (1 - x_m) \tag{7}$$

As cell consumption is related with load, cell consumption will be

$$E_i = P_{cell}(\rho_i^*) \tag{8}$$

And BS infrastructure consumption is related with status of all cells under it

$$E_b = C \cdot (1 - \prod_{i \in b}(1 - x_i)) \tag{9}$$

We adopt the average distance from users' random location in the cell's coverage area to the cell as the distance from user to its accessing cell. Distance from user u under cell i to its accessing cell d_u is related to the state of cell i and N_i

$$d_u = x_i \cdot d_{ii} + (1 - x_i) \cdot \sum_{j \in N_i} x_j \cdot \prod_{m \in N_i, d_{im} < d_{ij}} (1 - x_m) \tag{10}$$

In formula (10), d_{ii} is the distance from user u to cell i, d_{ij} is the distance from user u to its neighbor cell j.

And QoE of user u under cell i whose accessing content type is *cont* is

$$q_u = U_{cont}(r(d_u)) \tag{11}$$

As value of QoE utility function (3–6) is normalized with a maximum of 1, we define the QoE loss as

$$c_u = 1 - U_{cont}(r(d_u)) \tag{12}$$

User set with different accessing content type under cell i is U_i, sum of QoE loss under cell i is

$$Q_i = \sum_{u \in U_i} c_u \tag{13}$$

The purpose of this paper is to achieve energy savings of BSs with less loss of user experience, so the goal can be transferred into getting the minimum value of the optimization function $min(f)$ which combines the energy consumptions and QoE losses.

$$\min(f) = (\sum_{i \in B} E_i + \sum_{b \in B} E_b)/P_i + \eta \cdot \sum_{i \in B} Q_i \tag{14}$$

$$s.t.\rho_i^* < \rho_{\max}, \forall i \in \{1, 2, ..., n\} \tag{15}$$

$$s.t.x_i + \sum_{m \in N_i} x_m >= 1, \forall i \in \{1, 2, ..., n\} \tag{16}$$

Among them, η is a parameter for adjustment, by adjusting the value of η we can change the proportion of energy consumption and user experience in the optimization. Increasing the value of η means increasing the importance of user experience. Decreasing the value of a corresponds to increase in importance of energy consumption. For example, if η equals to value 1, it indicates that user's optimal experience is equivalent to a cell's energy consumption. Formula (15) gives the burden limit of cells, and means that traffic load of each cell should not overpass its service capability ρ_{max}. Formula (16) gives the user association protection to ensure that each user should be able to connect to at least one cell.

The multi-objective programming problems of energy consumption and user experience are converted into a joint optimization goal min(f) in this paper. The energy-saving scheme is modeled as a 0-1 integer nonlinear programming problem of the cell status vector $\{x_1, x_2, x_3, ..., x_n\}$, $x_i = \{0, 1\}$. And the goal is to get a set $\{x_1, x_2, x_3, ..., x_n\}$ to achieve the joint optimization of energy consumption and user experience. And the tradeoff between the energy consumption and the user experience will be achieved.

This paper uses the classical branch-and-bound algorithm to solve the 0-1 integer nonlinear programming problem. The thought of branch-and-bound algorithm [14] is to relax discrete 0-1 variables into continuous variables range from 0 to 1, and decompose the original problem into disjoint relaxation sub-problems. Target value corresponding to the relaxation solution is taken as the upper bound of the original problem, after iterations, we can get the optimal solution of the original problem. In the end, we use the optimization software Lingo to solve the above 0-1 integer nonlinear programming problem.

4.2   Problem Solving

The optimization problem in this paper is a 0-1 polynomial programming problem. Branch-and-bound method solves the deterministic solution of nonlinear integer programming and is more efficient in solving hybrid nonlinear integer programming.The basic idea is to generate a branch and delimitation tree and a sequence of upper and lower bounds. By decomposing the original problem into a series of disjoint relaxed sub-problems, the target value corresponding to the solution of the relaxed sub-problem is taken as the upper bound of the original problem, and the iterative solution to the original problem is obtained [14].

The integer programming problem in this paper is a convex nonlinear 0-1 integer programming problem, which is a pure integer programming problem. Pure Integer Nonlinear Programing (PINLP). We use an improved linear/nonlinear branch and bound method for 0-1 integer programming(LP/NLP based branch-and-bound, LP/NLP-BB).

Relaxation strategies include relaxation of the original problem to continuous space (NLP sub-problems) and linearization of nonlinear constraints (ILP sub-problems).

The optimization goal of Eq. (14) can be expressed as follows:

$$
\begin{aligned}
& Z_{INLP} = \min f(x), \\
& s.t. g(x) \leq 0, \\
& m(x) \leq 0, \\
& x \in \{0, 1\}^n
\end{aligned}
\tag{17}
$$

$g(x) = \{g_1(x), g_2(x), ..., g_n(x)\}$ is the nonlinear constraint of Formula (15), $m(x) = \{m_1(x), m_2(x), ...m_n(x)\}$ is the linear constraint of Formula (16), $x = \{x_1, x_2, ..., x_n\}$

ILP sub-problems: If the original target (14) is non-linear, its optimal solution may be the interior point in the convex hull. Such a problem should not be solved directly. Therefore, we introduce an auxiliary variable to convert a nonlinear target into a linear target, and the original objective function is treated as a constraint to obtain the equivalent INLP problem.

$$
\begin{aligned}
& Z_{INLP} = \min \eta, \\
& s.t. f(x) \leq \eta, \\
& g(x) \leq 0, \\
& m(x) \leq 0, \\
& x \in \{0, 1\}^n, \eta \in R
\end{aligned}
\tag{18}
$$

Due to the convexity of the objective function and nonlinear constraints, so at the current point $\hat{x}$, the inequalities $f(x) + \nabla f(\hat{x})^T (x - \hat{x}) \leq f(x)$ and $g(x) + \nabla g(\hat{x})^T (x - \hat{x}) \leq g(x)$ are established. So we can convert constraints to linear constraints, then the original goal is relaxed as follows:

$$
\begin{aligned}
& Z_{INLP} = \min \eta, \\
& s.t. f(x) + \nabla f(\hat{x})^T (x - \hat{x}) \leq 0 \\
& g(x) + \nabla g(\hat{x})^T (x - \hat{x}) \leq 0 \\
& m(x) \leq 0
\end{aligned}
\tag{19}
$$

NLP sub-problems: Another relaxation relaxes the integer variable of the original problem to continuous space. Assume that each component meets the limit $0 \leq l_I \leq x \leq u_I \leq 1$, The original problem will be transformed into a general nonlinear programming sub-problem.

$$
\begin{aligned}
& Z_{NLPR}(l_I, u_I) = \min f(x), \\
& s.t. g(x) \leq 0 \\
& m(x) \leq 0 \\
& 0 \leq l_I \leq x \leq u_I \leq 1
\end{aligned}
\tag{20}
$$

If (l_I, u_I) is the upper bound of the feasible domain (17), then the corresponding target value of (20) is to provide an effective lower bound for the original problem. The upper bound of (17) is provided by a feasible solution to the relaxed sub-problem. In combination with the linear relaxation of constraints and the continuation of integer variables, when the branch-and-bound method is solved, if an integer point is considered as a feasible solution to the original problem, the original problem becomes a series of LP sub-problems.

$$
\begin{aligned}
& Z_{LP/NLP} = \min \eta, \\
& s.t. f(x) + \nabla f^T(\hat{x})(x - \hat{x}) \leq 0, \\
& g(x) + \nabla g^T(\hat{x})(x - \hat{x}) \leq 0, \\
& m(x) \leq 0, \\
& x \in \{0,1\}^n, \eta \in R
\end{aligned}
\tag{21}
$$

Relaxation algorithm provides a basis for the delimitation of the branch and bound method. The specific LP/NLP-branch-demarcation algorithm steps are as follows:

First, we use a heuristic algorithm to find the initial feasible solution to the optimization objective function. namely the root node, and then relax the integer variable to $l_I \leq \hat{x} \leq u_I$.

Step 1: Select node. Starting from the root node, we select a node in the branch-and-bound tree to solve the loose sub-problem. If this problem is not feasible, we delete this node and search for the child nodes of the branch tree. Otherwise we assume the solution $\hat{x}$.

Step 2: Pruning. If the value of the objective function corresponding to the solution at this node is greater than the current upper bound, the feasible region of this portion does not contain the optimal solution, and the branch is cut off.

Step 3: Check integer constraints. If the point $\hat{x}$ does not satisfy the integer constraint, we select a variable that does not satisfy the integer constraint and add the left and right branch constraints $\hat{x}_i = 0$ and $\hat{x}_i = 1$. Otherwise, if $\hat{x}$ satisfies the integer constraint condition and the objective function value is less than the current optimal value, the upper bound is updated, and the branch whose objective function value is greater than the current upper bound is trimmed.

Step 4: Check if the branch delimiter tree is empty. If the branch and delimitation tree is not empty, then it returns to step 1. Otherwise, the algorithm will be terminated and the current optimal solution will be output.

4.3   Implementation of DMUES

The branch-and-bound method finds the integer optimal solution in the feasible domain of linear relaxation model of integer programming according to certain search rules. The time complexity of its solution will still increase exponentially with the number of base stations. To implement base station energy-saving strategy in large-scale cellular network clusters, the time complexity is very high. We consider the community division of BS clusters based on the cooperative relationship between cells. BS energy saving strategy is implemented separately in each community BS to achieve distributed computing to reduce time complexity.

The BSs in the city are deployed according to the functional areas of the city and the users' demands, which are distributed unevenly. We use space cooperation network to describe the cooperation between BS cells in urban space.

We use space cooperation network G to describe the cooperation between cells in urban space. The graph is usually expressed as $G = (V, E)$. It consists of nodes and edges. V represents a set of nodes and E represents a set of edges. The network consists of the cell node $<V_i, V_j>$ and the associated edges W_{ij} between the sectors. When there is a cooperative relationship between sectors, increase the edge in .The edge weight is a measure of the tightness between cells and is inversely proportional to the distance $W_{ij} = e^{-d_{ij}^2/(2 \cdot delta^2)}$.

When there is a cooperative relationship between sectors, the smaller the distance between the sectors, the greater the connection tightness between them; the greater the distance between base stations, the smaller the connection tightness.

In the connection relationship between base station sectors in the main urban area of Jinhua City, the distribution of base stations in cities is uneven. And the closer we get to the city center, the more dense the base station is. The distance between the BS is close. The connection is more and the network structure, has certain community structure. In the suburban areas, the deployment of BSs is sparse and the connection between base stations is sparse, presenting a distinctly small community structure.

The Louvain algorithm is used to divide the network into communities, and the base station energy-saving strategy is implemented separately in each community, which can effectively reduce the time complexity and can be used to save energy in large-scale cellular networks.

5   Experiment Results

In this section, we numerically evaluate the proposed MUES by comparing its performance to several reference algorithms based on the real China Mobile UDR dataset in Jinhua District of Zhejiang province. We use the method of community division to divide the BS clusters in the city. And then we implement energy-saving strategies in each community to reduce the time complexity.

5.1   Description of Dataset

We analyze the cellular network of the urban areas in a city of Zhejiang province, China. 59 dense cells of a square area is selected for experiment, the coverage areas of cells is shown in Fig. 1. The UDRs used in this paper is based on users' Internet access behavior which conclude fields of session time, cell location information, URL and traffic load, etc. Table 1 shows the main fields and record example of UDRs.

5.2   Experiment Results and Analysis

Time Complexity. The optimization problem that needs to be solved in the BS energy-saving strategy in this paper is the 0-1 combination planning problem. The time complexity of the solution is exponentially increasing with the number

Table 1. Field of the usage detail records

userID	Session time	Location	URL	Traffic load/B
69201446765	2014-11-21 20:18:24	6893_379A	news.baidu.com	107031

of targets. Firstly, The community energy-saving strategy optimization model with different sectors is modeled. Then branch and bound method is used to solve the optimization problem. The logarithmic curve of the solution time and the number of cells is shown in Fig. 2.

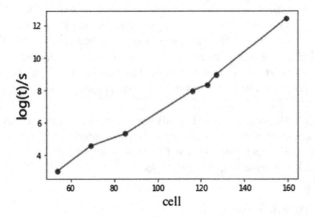

Fig. 2. Time logarithmic curve

The time complexity of the energy saving strategy optimization problem is an exponential function of the number of cells: $T(n) = k \cdot 2^n$. The branch-and-bound solver used in this paper runs on ordinary computer windows systems. When the number of cells is 127, the average optimization solution time reaches 20 min, which is more than 1/3 of the implementation period (1 h) of the energy saving strategy, and the implementation efficiency is low. When the number of cells is 160, the complete iterative search process time for the entire optimization problem reaches 1.5 h, which is much larger than the implementation period of the energy-saving strategy, and there is no possibility of implementation. Therefore, We consider the community division of BS clusters based on the cooperative relationship between cells. Community division can reduce the complexity of the network, so the efficiency of energy-saving strategies after community division is higher than that of energy-saving strategies based on global networks. For example, if we divide the BS into m communities and implement the energy saving strategy in each BS, then the time complexity of the energy saving strategy is $D(n) = k \cdot m \cdot 2^{\frac{n}{m}}$. And before the community is divided, the time complexity of the energy saving strategy is $T(n) = k \cdot 2^n$. Obviously, T(n) is greater than D(n), so community division can reduce the time complexity of energy saving strategy.

Community Division Results. In order to solve the problem of large-scale cellular networks and energy efficiency of energy-saving strategies, this paper adopts the method of community division of BS clusters to realize the distributed implementation of energy-saving strategies. The construction of the base station network and the edges status are described in Sect. 3.1. The Louvain algorithm was used to divide the BS network into communities. The results of the community division are shown as follows: The number of nodes is 1444. The number of edges is 3821. The number of communities is 39. The maximum number of BSs included in the community is 107. The minimal number of BS included in the community is 2. The average number of BSs included in the community is 37. The modularity 0.8745.

The total number of nodes of the BS in the network is 1,444, and the total number of edges of the network is 3,821, which is divided into 39 independent communities. The modularity range is $[-0.5, 1)$, The greater the degree of modularity is, the stronger the community characteristics of the network and the greater the independence of the divided communities are. That is, the better the result of community division is. Studies have shown that when the value of modularity is greater than 0.5, the results of community division are better. The modularity of the BS network is as high as 0.8745. It shows that the BS clusters in cities have strong community characteristics and strong independence between communities. At the same time, in the divided communities, there is no situation where the number of BSs in the community is particularly large, and the community is divided more evenly, which facilitates the implementation of distributed computing.

With arcgis you can project points in space into real geographic space. Figure 3 projects the nodes of 1444 BSs in Lucheng District of Jinhua City onto the streets of Jinhua City. Different colors are used to mark different communities so that the distribution of sector nodes in the network and the community structure of the network can be seen. It can be seen that the nodes of different communities are separated in geographical space. The BS in the same community are very close. The characteristics of the community structure are obvious, and the number of nodes in a single community is relatively uniform, which is conducive to the distributed implementation of the energy-saving strategy.

Performance Analysis. In order to verify the performance difference between implementing the BS energy-saving strategy for the BS cluster of the entire cellular network and implementing the energy-saving strategy for each community after dividing the community, this paper chooses to implement DMUES as a distributed implementation solution for two geographically adjacent communities respectively. We combine two communities as a community to implement DMUES as a centralized implementation plan and compare the results of the two scenarios. The number of cells selected for the community 1 is 54, and the number of cells selected for the community 2 is 59. The total number of cells after the merger is 113.

Fig. 3. Network community structure of base station

From Fig. 2, we can see that the complexity of solving the optimization problem has an exponential growth relationship with the number of variables. The experimental results show that the number of sectors in community 1 is 54. And the average calculation time is 8.14 s. The number of sectors in community 2 is 59. And the average calculation time is 23.7 s. But when merging the adjacent communities in these two spaces into a community with 113 sectors, the optimization solution time increases to 327 s, which is more than ten times.

We partition a day into 24 hourly intervals, the experiment is conducted on the off-peak hours from 0 o'clock to 6 o'clock. We first statistic the user numbers, access service types and traffic loads of cells. Then we construct the energy consumption model and user experience model according to the user-cell affinity graph. The object optimization problem is formulated and we solve this problem using branch-and-bound algorithm. Our strategy is compared with the energy saving strategy proposed in [11] that only considered the flow-level performance (ES-FLD) and the classical energy-saving strategy that used the blocking rate as the user experience (ES-BR) in literature [12]. The energy saving strategy is compared with the aspects of the number of active cells, energy saving ratio and user QoE loss. And the result is shown in Fig. 4. From the experimental results, it can be seen that the energy-saving strategy ES-FLD achieves a maximum of 86% energy saving. It only considers the flow-level performance. The QoE loss increases several times, which seriously affects the user experience. The energy-saving

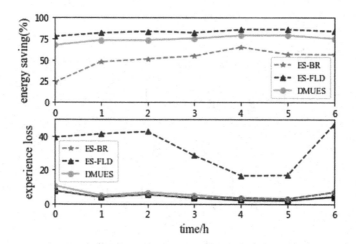

Fig. 4. Method performance at non-peak times

strategy in [12] achieves 50% energy saving. The growth rate of the QoE loss in [12] is approximately the same as DMUES proposed in this paper. DMUES proposed in this paper achieves a maximum of 79% energy saving, with very little increase in user experience loss with better performance.

Therefore, compared with ES-FLD, which considers only the flow-level performance cost, the DMUES achieves a higher energy saving rate with only a little increase in the user experience cost. Compared with the energy-saving strategy in [12], under the premise of guaranteeing the cost of user experience, more than 20% of energy is saved. In general, compared with traditional base station energy-saving strategies, DMUES achieves a good energy-saving effect and guarantees the quality of user experience, and achieves the best combination of the two.

At the same time, this paper discusses the load utilization of active cells before and after implementing the DMUES at 0 o'clock, which is shown in Fig. 5. The results show that most of the cells in the city are under low utilization at 0 o'clock. And after the MUES is implemented, most of the cells with low utilization are turned off while cells whose utilizations are high are basically been retained. The strategy also ensures that load of a single cell is in the affordable range. In conclusion, the strategy not only improves the energy efficiency of cellular network base station, but also ensures the load balance of the active cell. Furthermore, the computational complexity and time complexity is greatly reduced. This proves that the DMUES proposed in this paper is very effective and feasible.

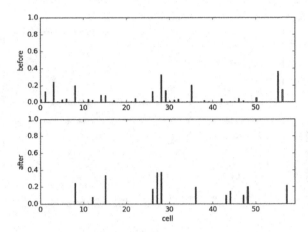

Fig. 5. Traffic loads of cells before and after implementing the DMUES

6   Conclusion

Current base station energy-saving strategy has not fully considered the impact of service characteristics on user experience and the problem of high time complexity of implementing the energy-saving strategy caused by the large scale of the 5G mobile network. In this paper, we introduce user experience quality as the measure of the subjective experience of users on the received service and propose a Distributed Multiple-service User-experience Energy Saving Algorithm for base station. And we use a complex network graph model to describe the cooperation relationships between BSs based on the proximity of BSs and the closeness of interaction in the city. Using the method of community division, the urban BS is divided into multiple communities, and the energy-saving strategy is implemented separately for each community. Part of the cellular network in a city of China is selected, and the experiment was conducted on the non-peak hours in this scenario based on real UDRs. Compared with the existing energy-saving strategies, the results show that the DMUES proposed in this paper can achieve good energy savings under the premise of less user experience loss. Furthermore, the time complexity of energy saving strategy is reduced due to community partition.

References

1. Budzisz, L., Ganji, F., Rizzo, G., Marsan, M.A.: Dynamic resource provisioning for energy efficiency in wireless access networks: a survey and an outlook. IEEE Commun. Surv. Tutor. **16**(4), 2259–2285 (2014)
2. Ding, M., Wang, P., López-Pérez, D., Mao, G., Lin, Z.: Performance impact of LoS and NLoS transmissions in dense cellular networks. IEEE Trans. Wirel. Commun. **15**(3), 2365–2380 (2016)

3. Feng, M., Mao, S., Jiang, T.: Base station ON-OFF switching in 5G wireless networks: approaches and challenges. IEEE Wirel. Commun. **24**(4), 46–54 (2017)
4. Fiedler, M., Hossfeld, T., Tran-Gia, P.: A generic quantitative relationship between quality of experience and quality of service. IEEE Press (2010)
5. Gómez, G., de Torres, E., Lorca, J., García, R., Pérez, Q., Arias, E.: Assessment of multimedia services QoS/QoE over LTE networks. In: Obaidat, M.S., Filipe, J. (eds.) ICETE 2012. CCIS, vol. 455, pp. 257–272. Springer, Heidelberg (2014). https://doi.org/10.1007/978-3-662-44791-8_16
6. Han, T., Ansari, N.: Enabling mobile traffic offloading via energy spectrum trading. IEEE Trans. Wirel. Commun. **13**(6), 3317–3328 (2014)
7. Hu, R.Q., Qian, Y.: Macro-Femto Heterogeneous Network Deployment and Management. Wiley, Hoboken (2013)
8. Jiang, H., et al.: Data-driven cell zooming for large-scale mobile networks. IEEE Trans. Netw. Serv. Manag. **15**(1), 156–168 (2018)
9. Khan, M.A., Toseef, U.: User utility function as quality of experience (QoE). In: Proceedings of the ICN, vol. 11, pp. 99–104. Citeseer (2011)
10. Li, W., Zheng, W., Xie, Y., Wen, X.: Clustering based power saving algorithm for self-organized sleep mode in femtocell networks. In: International Symposium on Wireless Personal Multimedia Communications, pp. 379–383 (2012)
11. Liu, B., Zhao, M., Zhou, W., Zhu, J.: Flow-level-delay constraint small cell sleeping with macro base station cooperation for energy saving in hetnet. In: Vehicular Technology Conference, pp. 1–5 (2015)
12. Niu, Z., Wu, Y., Gong, J., Yang, Z.: Cell zooming for cost-efficient green cellular networks. IEEE Commun. Mag. **48**(11), 74–79 (2010)
13. Oh, E., Son, K., Krishnamachari, B.: Dynamic base station switching-on/off strategies for green cellular networks. IEEE Trans. Wirel. Commun. **12**(5), 2126–2136 (2013)
14. Quesada, I., Grossmann, I.E.: An LP/NLP based branch and bound algorithm for convex MINLP optimization problems. Comput. Chem. Eng. **16**(10–11), 937–947 (1991)
15. Shaikh, J., Fiedler, M., Collange, D.: Quality of experience from user and network perspectives. Ann. Telecommun. - annales des télécommunications **65**(1–2), 47–57 (2010)
16. Son, K., Kim, H., Yi, Y., Krishnamachari, B.: Base station operation and user association mechanisms for energy-delay tradeoffs in green cellular networks. IEEE J. Sel. Areas Commun. **29**(8), 1525–1536 (2011)
17. Wu, J., Zhang, Y., Zukerman, M., Yung, K.N.: Energy-efficient base-stations sleep-mode techniques in green cellular networks: a survey. IEEE Commun. Surv. Tutor. **17**(2), 803–826 (2015)
18. Zhao, T., Liu, Q., Chen, C.W.: Qoe in video transmission: a user experience-driven strategy. IEEE Commun. Surv. Tutor. **19**(1), 285–302 (2017)
19. Zhu, Y., Kang, T., Zhang, T., Zeng, Z.: QoS-aware user association based on cell zooming for energy efficiency in cellular networks. In: IEEE International Symposium on Personal, Indoor and Mobile Radio Communications, pp. 6–10 (2014)

Alarm Sound Recommendation Based on Music Generating System

Wenhan Han[1,2](✉) and Xiping Hu[1,2]

[1] Shenzhen Institutes of Advanced Technology, Chinese Academy of Sciences,
Beijing, China
{wh.han,xp.hu}@siat.ac.cn
[2] The Chinese University of Hong Kong, Sha Tin, Hong Kong

Abstract. In this paper, we propose an alarm sound recommendation system based on music generation. The recommendation system will be integrated with an application named iSmile, which is a sleep analysis and depression detection application built by the authors in previous work. We use a music generating algorithm based on GAN (Generative Adversarial Nets) as the core of the recommendation system. To the best of our knowledge, it is the first application recommending real-time generated music rather than existing music. In the following part of the paper, we detail the algorithm, the experiment we conducted and the result analysis. The result shows that the recommendation system can effectively generate and recommend proper alarm sound according to the emotion prediction.

Keywords: Music generation · Alarm sound recommendation

1 Introduction

"5G" is a popular word nowadays. It is expected to have explosive bandwidth increment and much higher efficiency [1]. From an economic point of view, as the technology and devices upgraded, the cost of using wireless network can be much reduced. "5G" must change people's lives from a lot of aspects. For examples, people's demand for WIFI can be greatly reduced, the devices around people can keep online all the time and applications can provide more creative services. "5G" means not only the improvement of hardware technology but also the applications on mobile platforms. Benefited from the "5G" network, applications driven by big data will be more common in people's lives.

Previously, we have conducted a research about the impact of digital alarm sound to human emotions and constructed an application named iSmile. ISmile includes an Android application and an alarm sound recommendation system on the cloud. The Android application is used to collect users' sleep data, provide alarm service and request the feedback of users. The cloud accepts user data, building context profiles of users and pushing proper alarm sounds to users.

© ICST Institute for Computer Sciences, Social Informatics and Telecommunications Engineering 2019
Published by Springer Nature Switzerland AG 2019. All Rights Reserved
V. C. M. Leung et al. (Eds.): 5GWN 2019, LNICST 278, pp. 86–95, 2019.
https://doi.org/10.1007/978-3-030-17513-9_7

In the previous work, the alarm sound recommendation system in the back-end mainly consists of two parts, an alarm sound library, and a sleep data analysis model. The alarm sound library uses music genre classification [18] to classify existing music, then the sleep analysis model analyzes the uploaded data and selects proper alarm sounds to push. Many sounds or music recommendation systems are constructed in this way, for example, Hu et al. proposed a music recommendation system in [13], which aimed at helping drivers adjust their emotions and making a safe driving environment. However, recommending existing music to users is not flexible enough to satisfy the users due to the diverse preferences of individuals. Now, we think about doing something new. To make the sounds recommended more personalized, We alter the back-end of the application from recommending existing alarm sound to generating new music.

After GAN (Generative Adversarial Network) was proposed [10], many derivations of GAN have sprung up. GAN is applied to various fields and achieves a lot of amazing results, for examples, seqGAN [22], IRGAN [19] and AE-GAN [16]. It can be used for generating pictures, texts, etc. Recently, applying GAN to music generating becomes a popular topic. Dong et al. proposed MuseGAN [6–8], a GAN model which can generate 4-bar multi-track music phrases. Before that, there are many trials to make computers generate music automatically. Wolfram used his theory "a new kind of science" [21] to generate music, but it is more like a sequence of chaotic notes rather than music, although it has some potential regularity. Sturm et al. used RNNs to generate monophonic melodies [17]. Hadjeres et al. also used RNNs, and proposed a model to generate four-voice chorales [12]. RNN-RBM [4] was able to generate polyphonic single-track pianorolls. Using hierarchical RNNs to coordinate three tracks, Song from PI [5] can generate a lead sheet with an additional monophonic drums track. C-RNN-GAN [14] were able to generate music as a series of note events. Compared with MuseGAN, all those previous works can only generate single-track music or have limitations in performance. Our model built in the back-end of iSmile is inspired by MuseGAN actually.

The contributions are as follows:

- We use a GAN-based model to alter the previous alarm sound library, which can generate new alarm sounds according to the user context information.
- We conduct experiments to evaluate the results of the new recommendation system.

In Sect. 2, we introduce some related works. We detail the method of building the recommendation system in Sect. 3. Section 4 is mainly about the experiments we conduct. Finally, we conclude the work we do in Sect. 5.

2   Related Work

2.1   GAN

GAN [10] consists of a generator and a discriminator. The generator tries to generate fake data to fool the discriminator, while the discriminator tries to distinguish the fake data from the true data. The generator and the discriminator play a minimax game and compete with each other. Finally, the generator and the discriminator will both obtain better performances.

2.2 MuseGAN

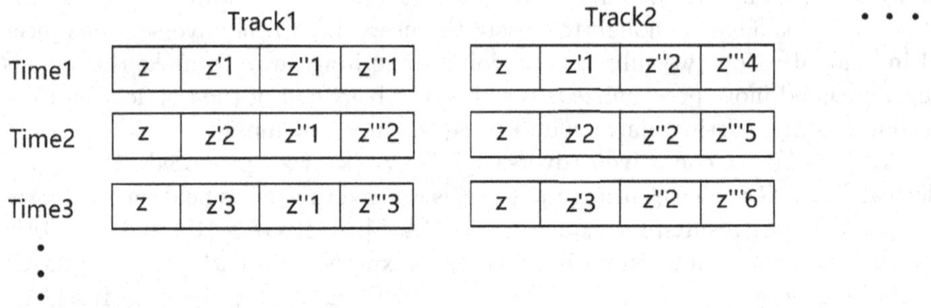

	Track1				Track2				• • •
Time1	z	z'1	z"1	z'''1	z	z'1	z"2	z'''4	
Time2	z	z'2	z"1	z'''2	z	z'2	z"2	z'''5	
Time3	z	z'3	z"1	z'''3	z	z'3	z"2	z'''6	

Fig. 1. The input format of the generator.

MuseGAN has a great performance in generating multi-track music. The model in [7] is designed to generate 5-track music with 4-bar length. Naturally, MuseGAN consists of two parts, a generator and a discriminator. In the generator, each track has a network to generate single-track music, which has the same network structure with each other. In order to simulate the regularity and randomness of music, the input of those 5 tracks is set to have 4 parts: the inter-track time-independent random vector, the intra-track time-independent random vector, the inter-track time-dependent random vector, and the intra-track time-dependent random vector. Figure 1 shows the format of the input, where the horizontal axis denotes the tracks, the vertical axis denotes the time steps, and the rectangles denote the input vectors.

2.3 iSmile

ISmile is the previous work of our team. It includes the front-end, an Android application, and the back-end, which is built on the cloud. Users can set the time when they will get up before they sleep using iSmile installed on their smartphones, then their smartphones will record and upload their sleep status data. Before the time when they are supposed to be woken up, the cloud will have analyzed their sleep data and push proper alarm sounds to their smartphones. The analyzer on the cloud is based on an approach named Emotion-Aware Smart Tips (EAST), which combines multivariate regression, random forest, and neural network to quantify the relations between sleep patterns and emotional states [11]. In the experiments we have conducted, the alarm sounds pushed by the cloud are selected from the existing music library.

3   Method

3.1   Model Design

Inspired by MuseGAN, we use an analogous network structure to generate alarm sounds. The alarm sounds generated by the network are 4-bar 8-track music. The input of each track in the generator is a 128-dimension random tensor, which is formatted as what mentioned in Sect. 3.2. With the time solution 24 (one beat), the output of each track in the generator is a $4 \times 96 \times 84$ tensor, where the 84 denotes 84 kinds of pitches. After merging whole 8 tracks' outputs as one tensor, it is input into the discriminator, whose output is a float between 0 and 1, indicating how it looks like the music created by human composers. Figure 2 shows the general structure of the whole model, where G denotes a single-track generator, and D is the discriminator. The model has 8 tracks, generating 8 music tracks of different instruments, which are drums, piano, guitar, bass, ensemble, reed, synth lead and synth pad. To save space, Fig. 2 just depicts 3 tracks. Figure 3 gives the detail about the single-track generator G. Similarly, to save space, the number of the layers is not the same as the figure. Actually, we use 7 layers of transposed CNN [9] to generate a single-track pianoroll.

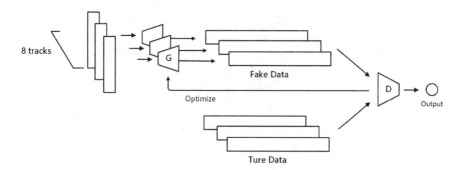

Fig. 2. The general structure of the GAN model.

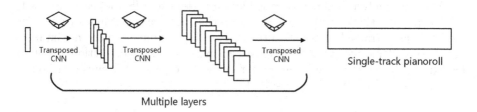

Fig. 3. The general structure of the single-track generator.

The whole generator acts as an interpreter. Before the generator, there is an encoding model, who encodes the result of emotion prediction made by the EAST system. The encoding model is formed with 3 layers of transposed CNN. It controls the inter-track time-independent random vector z in the input of the generator, which decides the base style of the whole music.

3.2 System Structure

In the previous work, iSmile has the structure as Fig. 4. All users have the same sound recommendation model. It limits the variety and personality of the sounds that are pushed to users' smartphones. Although the process of predicting emotions takes users' context information in consideration, the results of the sound recommendation system reacting to the same emotion predictions never change.

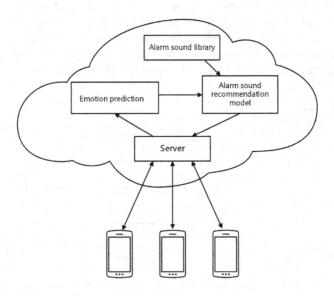

Fig. 4. Previous structure of iSmile.

After we apply the new recommendation system into iSmile, each user will have a private alarm sound generator. During users using iSmile, their own models will be trained to adapt to themselves. For example, a person who likes quietness will receive some light music when his emotion prediction result is looked happy, while another one may receive some passionate music although they have the same prediction result (Fig. 5).

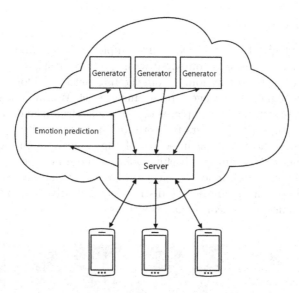

Fig. 5. New structure of iSmile.

4 Experiment

4.1 GAN Model Training

Original GAN is difficult to train. The reason is that when the support of the true set and the fake set generated by the generator is a low dimension manifold in high dimension, the possibility is almost 1 that the intersection measure of the true set and the fake set is 0 [2,3]. The performance of the generator and the discriminator must be in a relative balance. Excessively great performance of the discriminator will make the generator learn nothing. So we strictly control and dynamically adjust the optimization times of the generator and the discriminator in an iteration period when training the GAN model. The data set is Lakh Pianoroll Dataset built by Dong et al. [7,15].

4.2 Encoding Model Training

The purpose of the GAN model is to make the music generated be more like music created by human composers. The encoding model decides the style and emotion of the music. The result of the emotion prediction is a 2-D tensor, which includes arousal value and valence value (both are 0–10) as our previous work [11]. We set those two values to extremes respectively in order to evaluate the performance of the encoding model. We give feedback (arousal value and valence value) that how it fits the emotion we expect after the generator interprets the output of the encoding model. Policy gradient based REINFORCE learning [20] is utilized to train the encoding model. The encoding model adjusts the parameters according to the feedback we give, increasing the possibility of outputs that can make we give high scores.

4.3   Result Evaluation

Figures 6, 7 and 8 give the visualized result samples during training. To evaluate the authenticity of the results compared with the true music, we find 20 people to do a test. All test takers are found from the Internet by random, where 10 are male and 10 are female. Their ages are in range 18–24. We randomly selected 10 pieces of generated music and 10 pieces of true music from the dataset and mix them up, then ask our test takers to score for the authenticity of those pieces of music. Figure 9 shows the mean scores of those pieces of music, where the black points denote true ones and white points denote fake ones. The vertical positions of the points are randomly selected to avoid overlapping. Generally, the fake music and true music are not be distinguished clearly, but some generated pieces still get much lower scores than the trues.

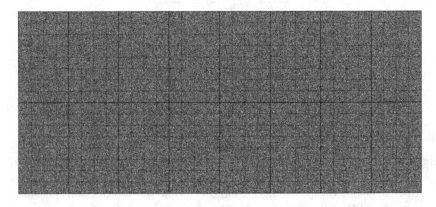

Fig. 6. The sample of results at the beginning

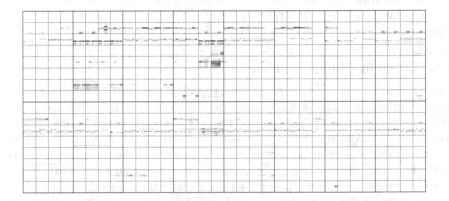

Fig. 7. The sample of results at the 3000th iteration

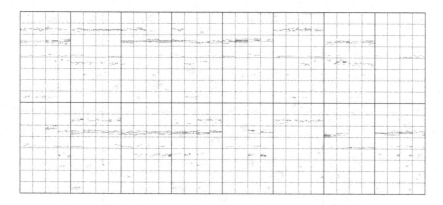

Fig. 8. The sample of results at the 20000th iteration

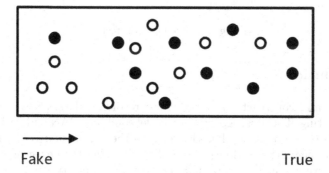

Fake   True

Fig. 9. The authenticity test

We also make a test about the emotion of the generated music. Arousal value and valence value are used to evaluate the emotion. We set both the arousal and valence values to 10 for the generator to produce music, and ask test takers to score for their moods and feelings after hearing these pieces of music. Figure 10 shows the mean scores, where black points are positive ones and white points are negative ones. To avoid overlapping, all positions of the points are handled by randomly jittering in range −0.5 to 0.5.

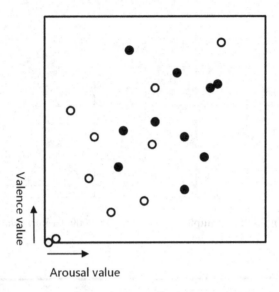

Fig. 10. The emotion test

5 Conclusion

We propose and construct an alarm sound recommendation system based on music generating. The music generating model combines GAN and REINFORCE learning. To the best of our knowledge, it is the first sound recommendation system recommending real-time generated music rather than existing music. The experiments we conducted show that the system has pretty good performance. However, the generated music still has a little distance to the true pieces, and the model is not very stable. Due to the limitation of time, the experiments are not very comprehensive. We need more user data to optimize and evaluate the recommendation system. More details will be shown in our full paper version soon.

References

1. Andrews, J.G., et al.: What will 5G be? IEEE J. Sel. Areas Commun. **32**(6), 1065–1082 (2014)
2. Arjovsky, M., Bottou, L.: Towards principled methods for training generative adversarial networks. arXiv preprint arXiv:1701.04862 (2017)
3. Arjovsky, M., Chintala, S., Bottou, L.: Wasserstein generative adversarial networks. In: International Conference on Machine Learning, pp. 214–223 (2017)
4. Boulanger-Lewandowski, N., Bengio, Y., Vincent, P.: Modeling temporal dependencies in high-dimensional sequences: application to polyphonic music generation and transcription. arXiv preprint arXiv:1206.6392 (2012)
5. Chu, H., Urtasun, R., Fidler, S.: Song from pi: a musically plausible network for pop music generation. arXiv preprint arXiv:1611.03477 (2016)

6. Dong, H.W., Hsiao, W.Y., Yang, L.C., Yang, Y.H.: MuseGAN: demonstration of a convolutional gan based model for generating multi-track piano-rolls. In: Proceedings of International Society of Music Information Retrieval Conference (2017)
7. Dong, H.W., Hsiao, W.Y., Yang, L.C., Yang, Y.H.: MuseGAN: multi-track sequential generative adversarial networks for symbolic music generation and accompaniment. In: Proceedings of AAAI Conference on Artificial Intelligence (2018)
8. Dong, H.W., Yang, Y.H.: Convolutional generative adversarial networks with binary neurons for polyphonic music generation. arXiv preprint arXiv:1804.09399 (2018)
9. Dumoulin, V., Visin, F.: A guide to convolution arithmetic for deep learning. arXiv preprint arXiv:1603.07285 (2016)
10. Goodfellow, I., et al.: Generative adversarial nets. In: Advances in Neural Information Processing Systems, pp. 2672–2680 (2014)
11. Guo, Y., et al.: Poster: emotion-aware smart tips for healthy and happy sleep. In: Proceedings of the 23rd Annual International Conference on Mobile Computing and Networking, pp. 549–551. ACM (2017)
12. Hadjeres, G., Pachet, F., Nielsen, F.: DeepBach: a steerable model for bach chorales generation. arXiv preprint arXiv:1612.01010 (2016)
13. Hu, X., et al.: SAFeDJ: a crowd-cloud codesign approach to situation-aware music delivery for drivers. ACM Trans. Multimed. Comput. Commun. Appl. (TOMM) **12**(1s), 21 (2015)
14. Mogren, O.: C-RNN-GAN: continuous recurrent neural networks with adversarial training. arXiv preprint arXiv:1611.09904 (2016)
15. Raffel, C.: Learning-based methods for comparing sequences, with applications to audio-to-midi alignment and matching. Columbia University (2016)
16. Shen, S., Jin, G., Gao, K., Zhang, Y.: AE-GAN: adversarial eliminating with GAN. arXiv preprint arXiv:1707.05474 (2017)
17. Sturm, B.L., Santos, J.F., Ben-Tal, O., Korshunova, I.: Music transcription modelling and composition using deep learning. arXiv preprint arXiv:1604.08723 (2016)
18. Tzanetakis, G., Cook, P.: Musical genre classification of audio signals. IEEE Trans. Speech Audio Process. **10**(5), 293–302 (2002)
19. Wang, J., et al.: Irgan: a minimax game for unifying generative and discriminative information retrieval models. In: Proceedings of the 40th International ACM SIGIR conference on Research and Development in Information Retrieval, pp. 515–524. ACM (2017)
20. Williams, R.J.: Simple statistical gradient-following algorithms for connectionist reinforcement learning. Mach. Learn. **8**(3–4), 229–256 (1992)
21. Wolfram, S.: A New Kind of Science, vol. 5. Wolfram Media, Champaign (2002)
22. Yu, L., Zhang, W., Wang, J., Yu, Y.: SeqGAN: sequence generative adversarial nets with policy gradient. In: AAAI, pp. 2852–2858 (2017)

Resource Allocation and Management

Cooperative Caching and Delivery Algorithm Based on Content Access Patterns at Network Edge

Lintao Yang[1], Yanqiu Chen[2], Luqi Li[2], and Hao Jiang[2(✉)]

[1] College of Physical Science and Technology, Central China Normal University, Wuhan 430079, China
[2] School of Electronic Information, Wuhan University, Wuhan 430072, China
jh@whu.edu.cn

Abstract. Mobile network performance and user Quality of Experience (QoE) will be negatively affected by the explosion of mobile data traffic. Recent research has focused on local caching at the wireless edge, as motivated by the 80/20 rule regarding content popularity. By caching popular contents at base stations (BSs), backhaul congestion and content access latency can be dramatically reduced. To address the limited storage size of BSs, an algorithm optimizing cooperative caching has been highlighted. Contents requested by mobile users that cannot be obtained locally could be transferred by cooperative BSs. In this paper, we propose a cooperative caching algorithm based on BS content access patterns. We use tensor decompositions with distance constraint to analyze interaction between users, contents and base stations. Thus, BSs with small geographical distances and similar content access patterns constitute a cooperative caching domain. Simulation results based on a real dataset of usage detail records (UDRs) demonstrate the superior performance and promising practical gains in caching of the proposed caching method compared to user clustering and BS clustering.

Keywords: Cooperative caching · Mobile Internet ·
Multi-aspect data and analysis · Network edge · Tensor decomposition

1 Introduction

In recent years, rapid ubiquity of advanced mobile applications with huge bandwidth requirements has dramatically increased mobile and Wi-Fi traffic. The Cisco Visual Networking Index (VNI) predicts that mobile data traffic will increase at a compound annual growth rate of 47% resulting in an increase to 49 exabytes monthly by 2021, which is a 7-fold increase over mobile data traffic in 2016. Globally, the proportion of smart devices and connections will increase to 75% in 2021, compared to 46% in 2016. As the explosive growth of network traffic, traditional core network architecture cannot accommodate rapidly increasing

© ICST Institute for Computer Sciences, Social Informatics and Telecommunications Engineering 2019
Published by Springer Nature Switzerland AG 2019. All Rights Reserved
V. C. M. Leung et al. (Eds.): 5GWN 2019, LNICST 278, pp. 99–123, 2019.
https://doi.org/10.1007/978-3-030-17513-9_8

user demand generated by the explosive growth of network traffic, due to long latency and the heavy burden on backhaul links.

Mobile edge caching [1,2] has been identified as one of the most disruptive enablers for 5G networks by the 5G Infrastructure Public Private Partnership, both to reduce content access latency and to alleviate backhaul congestion by relocating computing and storage units closer to the edge of the network [3]. This approach better accommodates proximal user demand while eliminating redundant transmissions from the remote sources [4].

To meet the ever-increasing demand for resource utilization and Quality of Experience (QoE), efficient cooperative content caching and delivery algorithm is suggested for cooperative caching between users and BSs. In most previous research on cooperative caching, cooperative base stations (BSs) are grouped based on placement, without considering content access behavior at the network edge or the interest distribution of mobile users. Thus, the cache hit ratio is not maximized.

With the popularity of the mobile Internet, the diversity of user content access behavior reflects to the heterogeneity of users [5]. With certain numbers of BSs, the distribution of mobile user interest and the effect of spatial-temporal information are predictable [6]. Therefore, we can apply cooperative caching based on user access patterns at the network edge to facilitate familiar content access behavior in clusters of BSs and achieve more efficient utilization of network resources. In next-generation cellular networks, the distance between small cells decreases and while physical layer technology is already at the boundary of Shannon capacity [7,8]. The proposed method would decrease the cost of collaboration, making cooperation caching based on user access patterns reasonable and feasible.

This paper proposes a cooperative caching algorithm based on user access patterns at the network edge. Local caching by cooperative base stations at the network edge constitutes a cooperative domain, in which base stations share contents. The cooperative domain is determined by clustering based on multiple aspects of mobile user content requests at the network edge. We have designed an efficient content placement and delivery algorithm that maximizes the cache hit ratios. Based on a dataset of real usage detail records (UDRs), results demonstrate that the proposed algorithm achieves a higher hit ratio while controlling the cooperative cost and improving QoE.

2   Related Work

Cooperative caching eases the traffic in the core network and reduces the overall download time, hence enhancing user perceptions of QoE [9]. Some studies have focused on cooperation between caching nodes, grouping them to improve the efficiency of network resource utilization and QoE.

Chen et al. [10,11] proposed a cluster-centric small cell network with a combined cooperative caching and delivery algorithm. Small base stations (SBSs) were grouped into disjoint clusters based on geographic position information, in which in-cluster cache space was utilized as an entity. Wang et al. [12] proposed a beamforming scheme that coordinates multiple remote radio heads (RRHs) in C-RAN to improve the quality of experience (QoE) of users by maximizing their aggregate weighted quality of service (QoS). Hu et al. [13] presented a general framework to model the video diffusion among mobile users and user QoS of the MSVS service over the wireless infrastructure. Li et al. [14] focused on the cooperative cell caching for future mobile networks, where each cell (e.g., base station) can cache popular contents for improving QoS. Fan et al. [15] proposed a clustering-based downlink resource allocation algorithm to allocate downlink spectrum resources in small cell networks. Yan et al. [16] proposed a hierarchical clustering-based caching strategy that improved caching efficiency by using cooperative caching for BS communication.

Another well-known strategy is cooperative caching based on user clustering. In [17,18], the users within the network were clustered according to their content popularity distribution and caching was executed accordingly to maximize the hit ratios. Unlike clustering algorithms based on user interest distribution, in [19], users were grouped based on their locations. To maximize the cache hit ratios, BSs used joint caching and delivery policies for users within communication range.

Cooperative content placement and delivery algorithms for known cooperative BSs is a popular research topic in cooperative caching. These studies generally assume or emulate the cooperation relationships of BSs directly, using this as basis of efficient algorithms designed to improve QoE. In [20], Scalable Video Coding (SVC) with cooperative caching was used to enable caching and serve sliced video layers that can serve different bitrates to improve utilization of caching resources. In [21,22], the authors developed light-weight cooperative cache management algorithms based on a heterogeneous cellular network (HetNet). These algorithms are considered promising architectural techniques for 5G as they maximize the traffic volume served by caching while minimizing the bandwidth cost.

The prior studies explore cooperation caching design content replacement and delivery algorithms for cooperative BSs to maximize QoE. Though diverse results have been acquired, the determination of cooperative relationship must be revised. When the cooperative relationship of base stations is directly assumed, cooperative BSs are not grouped and only a few base stations are considered in the simulation. Conversely, in cooperation caching, in which BSs are grouped based on geographical positions, user mobile access behavior is ignored. Cooperation caching, that is, grouping users based on interest distribution or placement, should inform the cooperative relationship with BSs. However, this approach generates suboptimal results in terms of precision.

Inspired by the preceding studies, we assert that grouping BSs into clusters is more direct because the cooperation caching occurs on the caching unit. Cooperative BSs with close geographical distances access similar content, thus efficiently utilizing caching resources. The method proposed in this paper can cluster BSs based on mobile user content access behavior at the network edge by considering multiple aspects to determine a suitable set of cooperative BSs.

3   User Behaviour Analysis

Before introducing the cooperative caching algorithm, we will analyze user access patterns and show the feasibility of our method.

We considered a real dataset of UDRs obtained from a mobile network operator in Jinhua, China. The dataset contained the data access records of 1.6 million mobile phone users over 23 days, covering 8,845 base stations, and involving up to 172,324 contents.

The dataset, which was stored in MySQL, contained information about the content access behavior of mobile users and as described by the fields listed in Table 1. Note that user information privacy was preserved by encrypting sensitive data.

Table 1. Data of the usage detail records.

Fields	Description
UID	An encrypted telephone number indicating a mobile user
Time_start	The time that a user begins the content request
Time_end	The time that a user ends the content request
LAC & CID	The base station providing content resources
URL	The identity of the content access

The UDR dataset also contained the geographical position information provided by the corresponding relationship of local area code (LAC) and cell ID (CID) and position as depicted in Table 2.

Table 2. Description of BSs geographical position information.

Fields	Description
LAC & CID	The base station providing content resources
Longitude	Longitude of BSs
Latitude	Latitude of BSs

First, we consider content popularity. Various types of content are available to mobile users. But, owing to the individuality reflected by user preferences and the demonstration effect, the popularity of diverse content differs among users.

Figure 1 shows the diversity content popularity distribution. Content popularity reflects average interests of multiple users.

From Fig. 1(b), we observe that within 23 days, the content with a total visit frequency greater than 100 accounted for only 4.659% of traffic, and the content with a total visit frequency greater than 1000 accounted for only 1.166% of traffic. This demonstrates that content popularity follows the power-law distribution. Fewer popular contents are accessed by larger numbers of users. This imbalance in content popularity follows the Pareto principle, that is, roughly 80% of traffic is attributed to 20% of the content. Thus, it is sensible to cache content with high popularity at base stations, as this practice would consume little cache space relative to the vast majority of user interests covered, thereby greatly improving the utilization of cache resources and enhancing QoE.

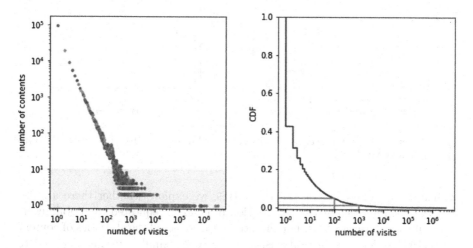

Fig. 1. Content popularity: (a) statistical distribution and (b) cumulative distribution function (CDF).

From Fig. 1 also note that the content popularity distributions exhibited a long-tail effect, and the second gradient of access, in which access frequency was less than 100, contained many types of content. Although the number of visits did not reach the maximum, the total number of visits and the coverage of the mobile user group cannot be ignored [23]. The long tail effect is fully utilized in recommender systems [24]. Based on this observation, we suggest that when considering edge caching, we should increase content diversity as much as possible while still guaranteeing the popularity of cached content. Thus, we maximize the limited cache size to satisfy more users' requests locally. The second consideration concerns user behavior. Mobile networks offer a broad range of content, available anywhere at any time, without any cost difference. But, whether every user will access the majority of network content is questionable. We use the UDR dataset to answer this question. Per Fig. 2, a total of 84.835% of mobile users had fewer than 10 visits during the 23-day observation period. This indicates that most mobile users were interested in a low variety of content. From Fig. 2, we learn that every user prefers certain content, but that less popular content is accessed by most mobile users. Hence, there must be an overlap of the individual user preferences, making the sharing of cached content feasible.

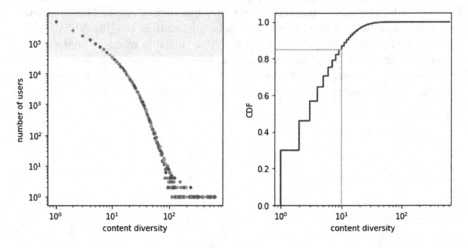

Fig. 2. Mobile user preference: (a) statistical distribution and (b) cumulative distribution function (CDF).

Regarding the content to be cached at BSs, we explore whether there are differences or similarities in the distribution of content requested by mobile users under different base stations. For this study, we collected the statistics of content accessed via different base stations, and the cosine similarity [25] was used to measure the similarity of content popularity distributions at BSs. Cosine similarity characterizes similarity by measuring the cosine of the angle between the vectors characterizing individual characteristics. The value range was $[-1, 1]$, where greater values reflect stronger similarity in the individual. The heat map shown in Fig. 3 visually demonstrates the similarity of content popularity at different base stations. Overall, there is a certain degree of similarity in the user preference at different base stations. Each base station has a certain coverage area where mobile users access different contents. Although each user has a personalized preference [11], the role of the group reduces this difference. Hence, the requested contents at different BSs share similarities. At the same time, it can be observed that there is a non-negligible difference in the content popularity at base stations. Different base stations serve different users. As observed in Fig. 2, most users have a low diversity of interests, which produces differences in content popularity among base stations with small intersections of user groups. Furthermore, similarities and differences also exist in the interest distribution of Internet content served by base stations. Hence, base stations with similar distributions of content interests can be clustered together to respond to more requests for user content by employing content-sharing. Thus, the core network traffic can be uploaded and user QoE is improved.

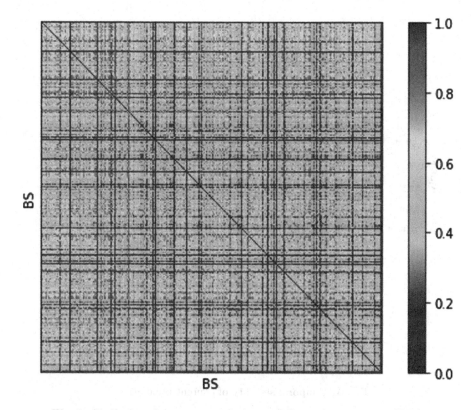

Fig. 3. Similarity of content popularity at different base stations (BSs).

Based on the above, we cache content with high popularity at BSs. Given that the content accessed is dynamic and changes over time, then how does content popularity changes with time? To answer this question, we measured the similarity of the content popularity of any two days within the 23-day observation period for the entire dataset using Jensen-Shannon (JS) divergence. The result is as depicted in Fig. 4.

The JS divergence, with range $[0, 1]$, measures the difference between the two probability distributions using the arithmetic mean of the correlation entropy of each probability distribution and the mean of the two probability distributions. When the two probability distributions are the same, the JS divergence is 0, otherwise it is 1. In this paper, 1-JS divergence is used as a measure of the degree of similarity between two probability distributions of content popularity. As observed in Fig. 4, the similarity is exhibited scores of 0.93 and higher. Note that the closer the two dates, the higher the similarity. Hence, the distribution of content popularity is stable over time, which probably results from the low diversity of user preference and the strong stickiness of Internet content. Based on this observation, we suggest that it is feasible to use online records from the previous day to guide follow-up cooperative caching.

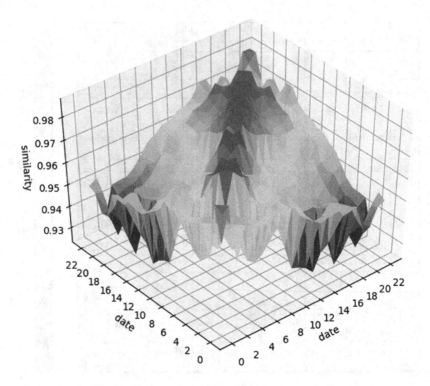

Fig. 4. Temporal stability of content popularity.

To summarize, we observe that the preferences of different users overlap and that similarities and differences exist in the interest distribution of Internet content served by base stations. As much high popularity content as possible can be cached at BSs within constraints of storage size if BSs with similar content popularity distribution can share the cached content to reduce the storage size. The stability of the content popularity distribution guarantees the feasibility of caching content with high popularity at BSs using the proposed cooperative caching and delivery algorithm.

4   System Model and Problem Analysis

4.1   System Model

The cooperative edge caching architecture focused on cooperation among BSs is illustrated in Fig. 5. Outside the mobile network operator (MNO) network, some service providers (SPs), such as YouTube and Facebook, offer content files over the Internet. Inside the MNO network, numerous BSs cover the service area. Mobile user content requests are received and served by their associated BSs, while SPs cache content onto the core network supported by the MNO. These contents are transmitted to BSs via backhaul link to satisfy the content requests of mobile users served by the BSs. Because the content requests made by different users or from different locations are inevitably intersected [5], the transmission of contents increases backhaul traffic and is frequently duplicated.

To alleviate backhaul congestion and enhance QoE, cache-enabled Cloudlets can be combined with traditional base stations distributed at the edge of the network. Each Cloudlet provides content services for mobile users in their respective regions. Data Centers (DCs) and Distributed Cloudlets use backhaul links to control information transmission and distribute content to various local caches. Each Cloudlet communicates with each other Cloudlet to transfer information and share content, reducing data traffic to and from remote DCs and improving caching capability.

Cloudlets and their neighboring BSs constitute cooperative caching domains. As shown in Fig. 5, several cooperative caching domains exist at the network edge. The caching-enabled BSs are connected and communicate with each other via X2 link [26]. To satisfy as many content requests from mobile users in the network edge as possible, the associated local BS either returns the content if it is locally available or retrieves the content from other BSs. In this way, some of the congested and costly backhaul link traffic becomes lower cost, internal traffic between BSs, reducing content access latency and increase quality of service (QoS).

Under this architecture, data content services are implemented. This paper focuses on two problems:

1. The definition of cooperative caching domains and storage of valuable contents.
2. Intercommunication between neighboring BSs in limited-capacity local caching within a cooperative domain.

In response to above issues, this paper tends to make an analysis and discussion in the following sections.

4.2 Problem Statement

Through the tensor decomposition of multi-source relational data, base station clustering with relatively consistent content access patterns and close spatial distances was achieved and base station clustering was correlated with content clustering. If the content accessed via the base station was relatively similar, and the set of users served by the base station also exhibited similarity, then these base stations were considered to have a large overlap in the content that can be cached because of the low diversity of user interests and the reduced variation in services requested by similar user sets. As content access increases in similarity, increasing portions of base station collections of user interests may be cached by each base station, without having to cache the same or similar content on each base station. Thus the base stations use surrounding base stations collaboratively. The cached content can substantially increase the heterogeneity of the content of the edge base station cache and greatly increase the utilization of cache resources, which is equivalent to expanding the cache size.

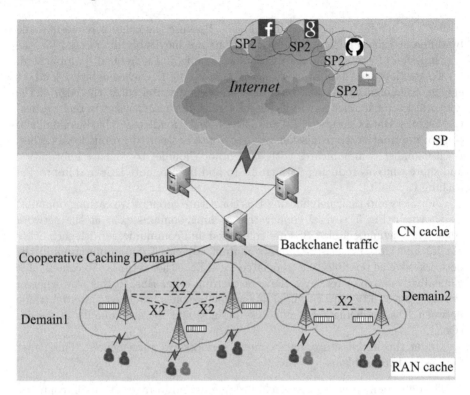

Fig. 5. Illustration of the cooperative edge caching architecture focused on collaborations among back stations (BSs).

It is worth noting that to mitigate the negative influence of content sharing between the base stations on request delay and user experience, the base stations with content sharing relationships should have shorter duration transmission time. This indicator is measured by attributes such as transmission bandwidth, transmit power, data rate, path loss index, transmission power, signal-to-interference-plus-noise ratio (SINR), channel fluctuation, and geographical distance [27]. This study defines the cost of collaboration as the effect of network content sharing among base stations on user experience. When hitting the user experience quality index and optimizing it, the negative impact of collaboration costs cannot be ignored. In this paper, the cost of content transmission between the base stations is measured by the geographical distance between base stations, as shown in (1).

$$cost_{ij} = cost(BS_i, BS_j) = f(d_{ij}) \tag{1}$$

Intuitively, to minimize the impact of content delivery on the average request latency of mobile users, the geographical distance between the base stations attempting to cooperate should also be minimized. In the case of transmission bandwidth, data rate and other parameters, the cost of cooperation can be more complex and refined. Therefore, the collaboration cost defined in this paper is universal, and can be used in applications that consider additional factors by introducing new parameters to further describe collaboration cost.

To simplify the problem complexity and highlight the content placement and transmission strategies that this study attempted to optimize, we assumed that each content file was of equal length and normalized this length to one byte. As do many papers on cooperative caching [19, 28–30], we assume that it is reasonable to set the value of all file lengths to one byte because files of different lengths may be segmented into equal-length fragments that implement code-based cooperative caching [30]. Hence, the maximum amount of content that can be stored on each base station is the number of cache units.

Base station clustering is applied to form cooperative cache domains by identifying clusters of base stations with cooperative relationships. After determining the cooperation cache domain and selecting the content collections to be cached in this domain, it was necessary to determine which contents should be cached given the limited cache capacity and how the base stations should execute routing to maximize the hit rate while controlling the cooperation cost. Hence, the importance of determining the types and contents to be cached.

5   Cooperative Content Caching and Delivery Algorithm

5.1   Framework

The framework of algorithm proposed in this paper is diagrammed in Fig. 6. The framework of the method can be divided into three stages. In the first stage, the content access behavior will be extracted from the original UDRs through a 3-order tensor while simultaneously obtaining the geographical distribution of BSs. In the second stage, we use tensor decomposition to mine content access patterns. The tensor can extract and model interaction relationships between base stations, users, and content. Hence, BS clustering based on similar content access patterns that considers geographical distances informs the construction of various cooperative caching domains. In the final stage, after comprehensive consideration of the cache ratio and the content transmission cost, a distributed optimization cooperative caching and delivery algorithm is proposed.

5.2   Cooperative Caching Domain

Cooperative caching domain consists of several cooperative BSs. Base station cooperation occurs when the BSs share content by caching content at one BS and using it to satisfy content requests from mobile users served by other BSs in the same cooperative caching domain. This efficiency is based on the expected similarity of the content served by different BSs in the same caching domain.

Our previous research demonstrated that mobile user content preferences exhibit individual characteristics and stability [5]. Correspondingly, content access at BSs serving similar mobile users is expected to be similar. Therefore,

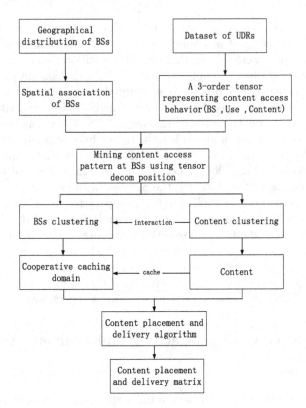

Fig. 6. Algorithm framework.

we assert that BSs with similar requested content and users share similar user access patterns. Thus, cooperative caching domains can be determined based on the aspects of content access and mobile users.

Like [27], we assume that caching-enabled BSs in the same cooperative domain are connected via X2 link. To reduce the transmission cost, cooperative BSs operating in the same cooperative caching domain should be close in geographical distance.

In conclusion, BSs in a single cooperative caching domain should satisfy requests for similar user access patterns within a smaller geographical distribution.

As mentioned previously, content access behavior of the base station from the service user and content must be mined and analyzed. All three dimensions, base station, user, and content, must be considered. The traditional matrix can only capture two dimensions of information [31]. In the application scenario of this paper, it is necessary to perform two-dimensional data analysis and then integrate it. In the analysis of two-dimensional data, other dimensions of information were not involved, thus introducing errors. Hence, this paper attempts to capture and analyze multiple dimensions of information simultaneously, to better examine interactions between different dimensions of information.

To discover neighbor BSs accessing similar content requested by similar users, this paper used tensor decompositions [32] to achieve pattern mining. It extended data analysis to multiple dimensions and captured multiple facets of access patterns, thus outweighing the two-dimensional representation of data [31]. Tensors captured users content access behavior at BSs while Tucker decompositions realized multi-faceted analysis for content access behavioral pattern discovery.

Using the mobile user UDR dataset, we focused on identifying patterns of content access behavior at the network edge. Let the dataset be a list of tuples (u, b, c) denoting that a mobile user via BS visits content c. We model the data as a 3-order tensor $X \in \mathbb{R}^{n(a) \times n(b) \times n(c)}$, where $n(u)$ is the number of mobile users, $n(b)$ is the number of BSs, and $n(c)$ is the number of contents. Tensor $X(u, b, c)$ has a value of the number of existing tuples (u, b, c). Our goal is to factorize the tensor

$$X \approx G \times_{(u)} U \times_{(b)} B \times_{(c)} C \tag{2}$$

where $G \in \mathbb{R}^{R_{(a)} \times R_{(b)} \times R_{(c)}}$ is the core tensor, which encodes the behavioral patterns, i.e., the relationships among users, BSs, and content groups. The probability represented by $G(r(u), r(b), r(c))$ indicates the behavior of the r(u)-th user group via the r(b)-th BS group visits the r(c)-th content group, which can be expressed by simple mathematical formulae as (3)

$$G(r^{(u)}, r^{(b)}, r^{(c)}) \approx$$
$$p(user \in r^{(u)}, BS \in r^{(b)}, content \in r^{(c)} \mid (user, BS, content) happens) \tag{3}$$

The user projection matrix is given as $U \in Rn(u) \times R(u)$. where $U(i(u), r(u))$ represents the probability that the i(u)-th user belongs to the r(u)-th group, which can be formulated as (4)

$$U(i^{(u)}, r^{(u)}) = p(user_{i^{(u)}} \mid r^{(u)}) = p(user_{i^{(u)}} \in r^{(u)}) \tag{4}$$

where $B \in Rn(b) \times R(b)$ is the BSs' projection matrix and B(i(b), r(b)) represents the probability that the i(b)-th BS belongs to the r(b)-th group, which can be formulated as (5)

$$B(i^{(b)}, r^{(b)}) = p(BS_{i_{(b)}} \mid r^{(b)}) = p(BS_{i_{(b)}} \in r^{(b)}) \tag{5}$$

where $C \in Rn(c) \times R(c)$ is the contents' projection matrix and Ct(i(c), r(c)) represents the probability that the i(c)-th content belongs to the r(c)-th group, which can be formulated as (6)

$$C(i^{(c)}, r^{(c)}) = p(content_{i_{(c)}} \mid r^{(c)}) = p(content_{i_{(c)}} \in r^{(c)}) \tag{6}$$

Note that in many applications including UDRs, the tensor is highly sparse, that is, many of the values are zero, because of the very nature of the application [32]. Commonly, elements in the tensor may be constrained by practical factors, such as distance constraint in this paper, which considers distance factors in the proposed cooperative content caching and delivery algorithm.

To solve the sparsity problem and introduce realistic constraints in tensor decompositions, as well as to guide the decomposition to identify the correct structure coinciding with features of cooperative caching domain, we introduce the BSs' geographical distance as side information and impose regularization to tackle sparsity and constraints. The regularizers can be encoded as Laplacian matrices L(b), where the (i, j)-th element represents the similarity between the i-th and j-th entities, i.e., BSs. The similarity should be inversely proportional to how far apart the BSs are located.

Referencing multi-faceted analysis method for behavioral pattern discovery proposed in [33], we incorporate the multi-faceted information and constraints into the tensor decomposition. We denote by μ(b) the weight of the BS-pattern Laplacian matrix L(b). The covariance matrix of the m-th pattern is

$$C^{(m)} = X^{(m)} X^{(m)T} + \mu^{(m)} L^{(m)} \tag{7}$$

where $X^{(m)}$ is the pattern-m matricizing of the tensor X. The projection matrices can be computed by diagonalization: they are the top r(m) eigenvectors of the covariance matrix C(m).

At the same time, benefiting from the tensor's extreme sparsity, the computational complexity of the algorithm in [33] appears as a linear relationship with the sum of the number of elements in each dimension. Additional details about multi-faceted tensor decomposition are available in [33].

To summarize, after incorporating the multi-faceted information and constraints into the tensor decomposition, clustering is executed based on BSs, content, and their interactions. The in-cluster BSs serve similar content to similar mobile users [34]. In addition, the distance constraint minimizes the in-cluster geographical distribution of BSs. As a result, BS clusters can be used to determine cooperative caching domain, while simultaneously clustering users with strong interactions with clustered BSs establishes the caching content set in a given cooperative domain.

5.3 Cooperative Content Caching and Delivery Method

After determining the cooperative caching domain and its content set, we should consider efficient content placement and delivery algorithm with limited caching capacity to maximize cache hit ratios and reduce cooperative cost. It is crucial to decide which files should be cached and where to cache them.

Given N BSs composing R collaboration caching domains, where the r-th collaboration caching domain contains N_r BSs. The frequency of an interaction involving BS_j in one cooperative caching domain is ω_j, considered to be the probability of BS_j belonging to this cooperative caching domain. The content set associated strongly with the r-th cooperative caching domain is $\{f_1, f_2, ...F_n, ...f_{F_r}\}$,where $F_r = N_r * cachesize$, $cachesize$ denotes the size of the space available for BS caching. The number of files involved is F, the popularity of f_n at BS_j is $(p_j)^n$.

For convenience, we assumed that each file has the same file length and normalized to 1 byte. This is reasonable because files of different length can be divided into groups of the same length. Thus, the maximum number of files each BS can store is also the cache size. Constraint to the feature of dataset, we measure transmission cost in terms of geographical distance, namely, $cost_{ij} = cost(BS_i, BS_j) = f(d_{ij})$. In real-world experience, the cooperative cost is related to many factors such as transmission bandwidth, data rate, path loss index, signal-to-interference-plus-noise (SINR) ratio, and geographical distance. With these factors obtained, the cooperative cost realizes greater complexity and sophistication. The cost we defined here has universality. In applications considering more factors, we can incorporate the additional factors in the definition of cooperative cost.

To achieve a distributed caching mechanism aimed at maximizing the cache hit ratio and reducing the cooperative cost, we must determine which files are to be cached and where to cache them in every cooperative caching domain. Meanwhile, we must also determine which BSs can satisfy the content requests that cannot be served locally. That is, we must solve the problems of what to cache, where to cache, and how to cooperate, which is realized by the proposed caching placement and delivery algorithm.

Content placement matrix $(x_j^f)_{N \times F}$, where $x_j^f \in 0, 1$ denotes whether or not f is cached at BS_j.

Content delivery matrix $\delta = \delta_{jk N \times N \times F}^f$, where $\delta_{jk}^f \in \{0,1\}$ denotes that whether BS_j will ask BS_k to transfer the file f which is stored not in BS_j but in BS_k and is requested by users serviced by BS_j.

$$\max_{x_j^f, \delta_{jk}^f} \sum_{r=1}^{R} (\sum_{j=1}^{Nr} \omega_j \sum_{f=1}^{Tr} p_j^f (x_j^f + \sum_{k=1}^{Nr} \delta_{jk}^f)) \tag{8a}$$

$$\min_{\delta_{jk}^f} \sum_{r=1}^{R} (\sum_{j=1}^{Nr} \sum_{k=1}^{Nr} \sum_{f=1}^{Tr} \delta_{jk}^f \cdot p_j^f \cdot e^{d_{jk}}) \tag{8b}$$

$$s.t. \quad x_j^f + \sum_{k=1}^{Ni} \delta_{jk}^f \leq 1 \quad \forall i, \forall f \tag{8c}$$

$$delta_{jk}^f \leq X_k^f \quad \forall i, \forall k, \forall f \tag{8d}$$

$$\sum_{f=1}^{F} x_j^f \leq cachesize \quad \forall j \tag{8e}$$

$$\delta_{jj}^f = 0 \quad \forall j, \forall f \tag{8f}$$

$$x_j^f \in 0, 1, \delta_{jk}^f \in 0, 1 \quad \forall i, \forall k, \forall f \tag{8g}$$

- Our objective is measured in terms of both the hit ratio and cost of the information exchange between BSs incurred by the users of each cooperative caching domain. The objective is to maximize the hit ratio for serving users, while minimizing the cooperation cost, as shown in (8a) and (8b).

- The constraints in (8c) denote the cooperation among BSs and guarantee that any content request will not be routed to other BSs if the content is locally available.
- Constraint (8d) states that a content can be fetched from the BS only if the BS caches that content.
- The constraints in (8e) enforce resource limits at each BS, stating that all the items cached at a BS cannot exceed its cache capacity.
- Constraint (8f) guarantees the nonexistence of the content request transferring to local BS.
- Constraint (8g) defines this problem as 0–1 integer programming.

The problems expressed in (8a) and (8b) constitute a multi-objective optimization problem. The value range and dimension of the hit ratio and cooperative cost are not uniform. Therefore, we first set the min-max standardization of the collaboration cost to be in the range of $[0, 1]$. Then we used the linear weighted method to integrate the two optimization goals into a single optimization formula, given as (9).

$$min_{x_j^f, \delta_{jk}^f} \sum_{r=1}^{R} (S(\sum_{j=1}^{Nr} \sum_{k=1}^{Nr} \sum_{f=1}^{Tr} \delta_{jk}^f \cdot p_j^f \cdot e^{d_{jk}})) \qquad (9)$$

The standardization of the collaboration cost is shown in (10).

$$S(x) = \frac{x - \min(x)}{\max(x) - \min(x)} \qquad (10)$$

In the application scenario of this article, as expressed in (10), $\min(x) = 0$, $\max_{\substack{j,k \in Br \\ f \in Cr}} \sum_{j=1}^{Nr} \sum_{k=1}^{Nr} \sum_{f=1}^{Tr} p_j^f \cdot e^{d_{jk}}$.

When the linear weighting method is used to solve multi-objective optimization problems, the weighting coefficients must be carefully selected according to the problem scenario. However, in this paper, the coordination cost is normalized so that it is within the range of fluctuations that are equivalent to the hit rate, effectively avoiding problem-dependent weight coefficient selections that could introduce excessive subjectivity.

To obtain the optimal solution under the constraint conditions described by (8c) through (8f) for the optimization goals declared in (8a) and (8b), this paper uses Lagrangian duality to convert the original problem into a dual problem and then apply the solution to the dual problem to obtain the solution to the original problem. By introducing the Lagrangian multiplier, the optimization problem with d variables and k constraints can be transformed into an unconstrained optimization problem with $d + k$ variables.

First, we investigate the feasibility of solving the dual problem instead of solving the original problem. If the decision variable is a continuous value in the range $[0, 1]$, then the optimization objectives of (8a) and (8b) and the inequality constraints given in (8c) through (8e) are all linear functions related to the decision variable, belonging to the convex function. One function, the equality constraint (8f), belongs to the affine function, and the presence of a certain value of the decision variable makes the inequality constraint strictly feasible, so there is a precondition for solving the original problem by solving the dual problem [32]. To take advantage of the computational simplicity of the dual problem, we relaxed the original problem into a generalized linear program (LP)-type problem that does not contain integer constraints. Then, we used the Lagrangian duality to convert it into a dual problem, as delineated in (11).

$$
\begin{aligned}
L(x, \delta, \alpha, \beta, \gamma, \omega, \mu, \eta, \nu, \sigma) = \sum_{r=1}^{R} (S(\sum_{j=1}^{Nr} \sum_{k=1}^{Nr} \sum_{f=1}^{Tr} \delta_{jk}^{f} \cdot p_{j}^{f} \cdot e^{d_{jk}}) \\
- \sum_{j=1}^{Nr} \omega_{j} \sum_{f=1}^{T} p_{j}^{f} (x_{j}^{f} + \sum_{k=1}^{Nr} \delta_{jk}^{f} \\
+ \alpha_{j}^{k} (x_{j}^{k} + \sum_{k=1}^{Nr} \delta_{jf}^{f} - 1) + \beta_{jk}^{f} (\delta_{jk}^{f} - x_{k}^{f}) \\
+ \gamma_{j} (\sum_{f=1}^{Tr} s_{j}^{f} - cachesize) - \omega_{j}^{f} x_{j}^{f} - \mu_{jk}^{f} \delta_{jk}^{f} \\
+ \eta_{j}^{f} (x_{j}^{f} - 1) + \nu_{jk}^{f} (1 - \delta_{jk}^{f} + \sigma_{j}^{f} \delta_{jj}^{f})) \quad (11)
\end{aligned}
$$

where are Lagrange multipliers and non-negative. Then, in (12), we solve the dual problem.

$$
\max_{\substack{\alpha, \beta, \gamma, \omega, \mu, \eta, \nu, \sigma \\ \alpha, \beta, \gamma, \omega, \mu, \eta, \nu \geq 0}} \min_{x, \delta} L(x, \delta, \alpha, \beta, \gamma, \omega, \mu, \eta, \nu, \sigma) \quad (12)
$$

Solving the dual problem can obtain an analytical solution without having to iterate to obtain the numerical solution, which can greatly reduce the solution complexity. Finally, the connection between the solution to the original problem x^{*}, δ^{*} and the optimal solution to the dual problem $\alpha^{*}, \beta^{*}, \gamma^{*}, \omega^{*}, \mu^{*}, \eta^{*}, \nu^{*}, \sigma^{*}$ is established through the Karush-Kuhn-Tucker (KKT) condition [35].

Because of the relaxation of the original problem, in using the sequential minimal optimization (SMO) algorithm to solve, we must integerize the non-integer solution. Assume that the non-integer values between $[0, a]$ and $[a, 1]$ $(0 \leq a \leq 1)$ are integerized to 0 and 1 respectively, and then driven by the optimization goal expressed in (11). A grid search is used to determine the rounding decision boundaries of content placement decision variables and content delivery decision variables. Based on this, the content placement matrix and routing matrix can be obtained. While controlling the collaboration cost, the hit rate of the cache resources is high, thus satisfying more user content requests at the edge of the network.

6 Performance Evaluation

6.1 Simulation Setup

We used the UDR dataset introduced in Sect. 3 to evaluate the proposed algorithm. Because of limited cache space and the power-law distributions of access popularity, most contents are rarely accessed. Hence, we preprocessed the data to remove contents with small popularity values. To reduce the complexity of tensor decomposition and the distributed caching mechanism, contents with large popularity values were selected for caching. In this paper, the first three days of UDRs were used as a training set and the test set comprised the remaining twenty days of data. The tensor was obtained based on the training set. The proportion of non-zero elements in the tensor was as low as 5.194e−09. After preprocessing the dataset, the proportion of non-zero elements in the tensor was as low as 2.17943605808e−05. This demonstrates that the tensor representing the interactions among users, BSs, and contents derived from UDRs is extremely sparse and well-suited to storage and decomposition.

In this experience, we obtained a BS distance matrix based on the geographical position information of BSs. The user access patterns at the network edge were calculated using the Tucker decomposition subject to distance constraints. Per the objective of (7), we have designed a content placement and delivery algorithm. We evaluated the performance of the proposed algorithm using the test set.

6.2 Performance Results

We considered the following four content caching schemes:

1. User_Cluster: Users are clustered and BSs providing contents are allocated to maximize the hit ratio [17].
2. BS_Cluster_Geo: Base stations are clustered based on geographical position [11].
3. BS_Cluster_ContentModePattern: Based on user access patterns at the network edge, the purpose is to identify cooperative caching domains and the content contained in each domain without considering a distance constraint.
4. BS_Cluster_ContentModePattern_Geo: Based on user access patterns at the network edge and a distance constraint, the proposed algorithm attempts to identify cooperative caching domains and their respective contents.

We compare the efficiency of the four content caching schemes using the UDR dataset. After determining the cooperative domain, all four schemes designed content placement and delivery algorithms that were evaluated based on their performance on the test set as defined by the content distribution mechanism in (7). Specifically, we compared performance using three metrics, the hit ratio, cooperative cost, and the content utilization ratio, and then considered stability over time.

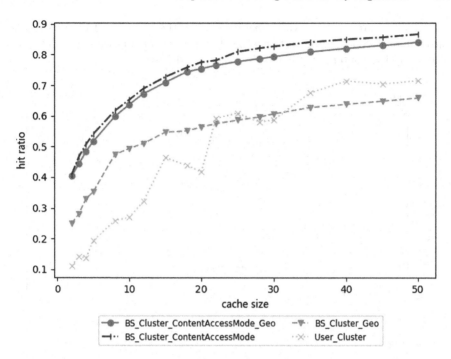

Fig. 7. Cache hit ratio versus cache size.

Hit Ratio. First, we investigated the hit ratio. Figure 7 depicts the total cache hit ratio of UDRs collected during the 20-day period covered by the test set, for different cache sizes C, we considered BS cache sizes of two to fifty contents. The simulations suggest that the cache ratio of all the cooperative caching mechanisms is positively related to the cache size. With the increase of cache size, the impact on the hit ratio slows down. Overall, in terms of satisfying user content requests, cooperative caching that considers user access patterns achieves a hit ratio increase of approximately 25% compared to cooperative caching based on BS or user clustering. However, enforcing distance constraints resulted in a slight decrease in the hit ratio. This demonstrates the superiority of the proposed method in satisfying user content requests.

Furthermore, we note that even when the cache storage size was small, many user content requests were satisfied. For example, when cache size was 10,0 63% of user content requests were satisfied. This demonstrates that less popular content can cover most user interests, which is consistent with the power-law characteristic of content access behavior [4].

Cooperative Cost. The definition of cooperative cost is in part D of Method. The cooperative cost which is for all UDRs in the test set in Fig. 8 show a trend of increasing first and decreasing then with the increase of cache size. When the cooperative size is small, the most popular contents are cached and BSs can achieve more cooperative probability. With the increase of cache size and constraints of cooperative cost, the most popular contents are cached at BSs locally and the content transfer is decreased gradually.

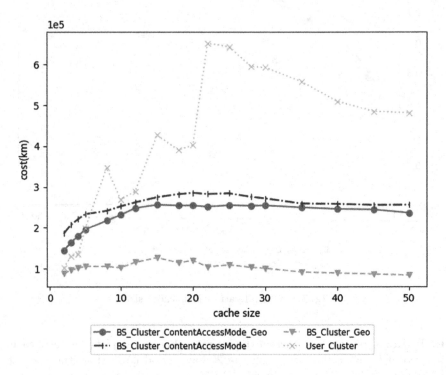

Fig. 8. Cooperative cost versus cache size.

The transmission cost of cooperative caching that considers user access patterns is higher than that based on BS clustering and lower than that based on user clustering. When setting the file size to 1 byte, cooperative caching based on the geographical positions of BSs has a lower transmission cost, but this is paired with a lower hit ratio, as observed in Fig. 7. Cooperative cost increases for cooperative caching based on user clustering, as this approach does not consider the geographical distribution of users, and thus clusters users with varied geographical distances and similar interests. Although the proposed method includes a distance constraint that slightly reduces the hit ratio, the constraint also reduces the cooperative cost.

Content Utilization Ratio. The hit ratio indicates the probability of responses to user content requests, while how many the cached files users can access is referred to as the content utilization ratio. Figure 9 depicts the content utilization ratio achieved by each algorithm with various cache sizes. As cache size increases, the utilization ratio of cached content correspondingly decreases.

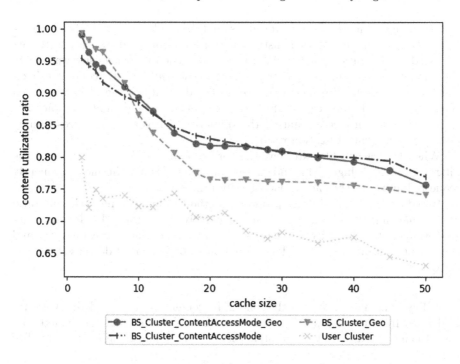

Fig. 9. Caching utilization ratio versus cache size.

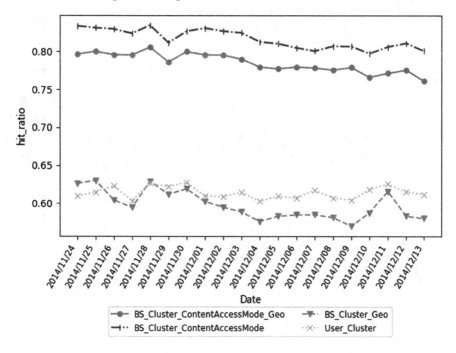

Fig. 10. Stability of hit ratio over time.

Cooperative caching based on user access patterns achieves the highest utilization ratio. As previously demonstrated, consideration of distance constraints balanced the hit ratio against cooperative cost. When the cache size was small, the distance constraint lowered transmission cost while raising content utilization ratio. As cache size increased, so did the diversity of the contents, which then decreased the possibility of sharing contents. We highlight the inference effect of the distance constraint on the similarity of BSs and the corresponding decrease in content utilization ratio.

When the cached files are few, the corresponding utilization ratio and the hit ratio are both high. This indicates that these files are the most frequently requested and that the cache space is fully utilized [4].

Based on our analysis, the proposed method improved the cache hit ratio while balancing the hit ratio and the cooperative cost using the distance constraint. Although the distance constraint slightly decreased the hit ratio and content utilization ratio, these losses were offset by benefit of decreased cooperative cost.

Stability over Time. We use the content placement matrix and delivery matrix in derived from the test set to evaluate the stability over time, as depicted by Figs. 10 and 11. Note that cooperative caching based on user access patterns has

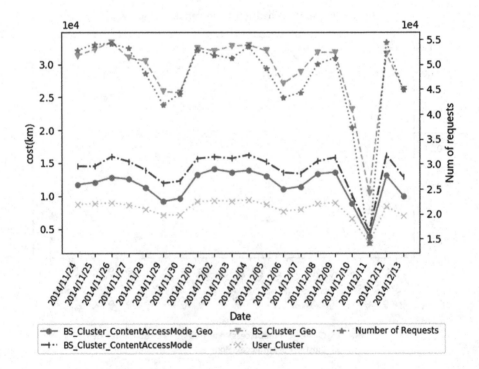

Fig. 11. Stability of cooperation cost over time.

a higher hit ratio, which is consistent with observation regarding Fig. 7. In terms of stability over time, cooperative caching based on user access patterns was superior to that based on user clustering, while slight fluctuations were observed in cooperative caching based on BS clustering.

From the results, we establish that the proposed method improves user QoE and is stable over time. The content placement caching algorithm also guarantees the long-term popularity of cached contents. Meanwhile, the long-term stabilization effect can also be observed using the three days of training data, underscoring the stability of the proposed caching algorithm even when applied to small datasets. This attribute indicates that the proposed method could be applied to mobile big data scenarios.

7   Conclusion

This paper proposed cooperative caching based on user access patterns at the network edge. Tensor decompositions of multi-aspect data were applied. We find that BSs with close geographical distances accessed similar content at the request of similar users. There was a greater demand for content sharing among these BSs and the costs were not high, thus hey constituted cooperative caching domains. Furthermore, we designed a content placement algorithm that simultaneously considered the hit ratio and the cooperative cost. In every cooperative caching domain, the contents that frequently interacted with the BSs in the domain were placed and shared accordingly.

We evaluate the performance using a real UDR dataset. The results show that the method proposed in this paper can improve the caching hit ratio and the content cache utilization ratio while moderating cooperative cost and maintaining stability overlong time. The overall performance was superior, and thus able to meet user content access demand and be applied to mobile data.

Acknowledgment. This work was supported in part by the National Natural Science Foundation of China (NSFC), Grant No. 61371126. This work was financially supported by self-determined research funds of CCNU from the colleges basic research and operation of MOE (CCNU17QN0011) and specific funding for education science research by self-determined research funds of CCNU from the colleges basic research and operation of MOE (ccnu16JYKX019).

References

1. Ahmed, A., Ahmed, E.: A survey on mobile edge computing. In: International Conference on Intelligent Systems and Control (2016)
2. Wang, S., Zhang, X., Zhang, Y., Wang, L., Yang, J., Wang, W.: A survey on mobile edge networks: convergence of computing, caching and communications. IEEE Access **5**(99), 6757–6779 (2017)
3. Li, X., Wang, X., Li, K., Leung, V.: CaaS: caching as a service for 5G networks. IEEE Access **5**, 5982–5993 (2017)

4. Wang, C.X., et al.: Cellular architecture and key technologies for 5G wireless communication networks. J. Chongqing Univ. Posts Telecommun. **52**(2), 122–130 (2014)
5. Zhou, C., Jiang, H., Chen, Y., Wu, L., Yi, S.: User interest acquisition by adding home and work related contexts on mobile big data analysis. In: Computer Communications Workshops (2016)
6. Zhou, C., Jiang, H., Chen, Y., Wu, J., Zhou, J., Wu, Y.: TCB: a feature transformation method based central behavior for user interest prediction on mobile big data. Int. J. Distrib. Sens. Netw. **12**(9) (2016)
7. Agiwal, M., Roy, A., Saxena, N.: Next generation 5G wireless networks: a comprehensive survey. IEEE Commun. Surv. Tutor. **18**(3), 1617–1655 (2017)
8. Bastug, E., Bennis, M., Debbah, M.: Living on the edge: the role of proactive caching in 5G wireless networks. IEEE Commun. Mag. **52**(8), 82–89 (2014)
9. Ramanan, B.A., Drabeck, L.M., Haner, M., Nithi, N.: Cacheability analysis of http traffic in an operational LTE network, pp. 1–8 (2013)
10. Chen, Z., Lee, J., Quek, T.Q.S., Kountouris, M.: Cluster-centric cache utilization design in cooperative small cell networks. In: IEEE International Conference on Communications (2016)
11. Chen, Z., Lee, J., Quek, T.Q.S., Kountouris, M.: Cooperative caching and transmission design in cluster-centric small cell networks. IEEE Trans. Wirel. Commun. **16**(5), 3401–3415 (2017)
12. Wang, Z., Ng, D.W.K., Wong, V.W.S., Schober, R.: Transmit beamforming for QoE improvement in C-RAN with mobile virtual network operators. In: IEEE International Conference on Communications, pp. 1–6 (2016)
13. Hu, H., Wen, Y., Niyato, D.: Spectrum allocation and bitrate adjustment for mobile social video sharing: a potential game with online QoS learning approach. IEEE J. Sel. Areas Commun. **35**(4), 935–948 (2017)
14. Li, X., Wang, X., Xiao, S., Leung, V.C.M.: Delay performance analysis of cooperative cell caching in future mobile networks. In: IEEE International Conference on Communications, pp. 5652–5657 (2015)
15. Fan, S., Zheng, J., Xiao, J.: A clustering-based downlink resource allocation algorithm for small cell networks. In: International Conference on Wireless Communications & Signal Processing, pp. 1–5 (2015)
16. Yan, H., Gao, D., Su, W., Foh, C.H., Zhang, H., Vasilakos, A.V.: Caching strategy based on hierarchical cluster for named data networking. IEEE Access **5**, 8433–8443 (2017)
17. Elbamby, M.S., Bennis, M., Saad, W., Latva-Aho, M.: Content-aware user clustering and caching in wireless small cell networks. In: International Symposium on Wireless Communications Systems, pp. 945–949 (2014)
18. Hajri, S.E., Assaad, M.: Caching improvement using adaptive user clustering. In: IEEE International Workshop on Signal Processing Advances in Wireless Communications, pp. 1–5 (2016)
19. Poularakis, K., Iosifidis, G., Tassiulas, L.: Approximation caching and routing algorithms for massive mobile data delivery. In: Global Communications Conference, pp. 3534–3539 (2014)
20. Yu, R., et al.: Enhancing software-defined ran with collaborative caching and scalable video coding. In: ICC 2016–2016 IEEE International Conference on Communications, pp. 1–6 (2016)
21. Jiang, W., Feng, G., Qin, S.: Optimal cooperative content caching and delivery policy for heterogeneous cellular networks. IEEE Trans. Mob. Comput. **16**(5), 1382–1393 (2017)

22. Borst, S., Gupta, V., Walid, A.: Distributed caching algorithms for content distribution networks. In: Conference on Information Communications, pp. 1478–1486 (2010)
23. Bao, J., Zheng, Y., Wilkie, D., Mokbel, M.: Recommendations in location-based social networks: a survey. Geoinformatica **19**(3), 525–565 (2015)
24. Ren, X.Y., Song, M.N., De Song, J.: Context-aware point-of-interest recommendation in location-based social networks. Chin. J. Comput. (2017)
25. Sidorov, G., Gelbukh, A., Gómezadorno, H., Pinto, D.: Soft similarity and soft cosine measure: similarity of features in vector space model. Computación Y Sistemas **18**(3), 491–504 (2014)
26. Ranaweera, C., Wong, E., Lim, C., Nirmalathas, A.: Next generation optical-wireless converged network architectures. IEEE Netw. **26**(2), 22–27 (2012)
27. Wang, S., Zhang, X., Yang, K., Wang, L., Wang, W.: Distributed edge caching scheme considering the tradeoff between the diversity and redundancy of cached content. In: IEEE/CIC International Conference on Communications in China, pp. 1–5 (2016)
28. Sermpezis, P., Spyropoulos, T., Vigneri, L., Giannakas, T.: Femto-caching with soft cache hits: improving performance with related content recommendation. In: GLOBECOM 2017–2017 IEEE Global Communications Conference, pp. 1–7 (2018)
29. Golrezaei, N., Shanmugam, K., Dimakis, A.G., Molisch, A.F.: Femtocaching: wireless video content delivery through distributed caching helpers. In: IEEE INFOCOM, pp. 1107–1115 (2013)
30. Borst, S.C.: Distributed caching algorithms for content distribution networks, **54**(1), 1–9 (2015)
31. Acar, E., Çamtepe, S.A., Krishnamoorthy, M.S., Yener, B.: Modeling and multiway analysis of chatroom tensors. In: IEEE International Conference on Intelligence and Security Informatics, pp. 256–268 (2005)
32. Papalexakis, E.E., Faloutsos, C., Sidiropoulos, N.D.: Tensors for data mining and data fusion: models, applications, and scalable algorithms. ACM (2016)
33. Jiang, M., Cui, P., Wang, F., Xu, X., Zhu, W., Yang, S.: FEMA: flexible evolutionary multi-faceted analysis for dynamic behavioral pattern discovery, pp. 1186–1195 (2014)
34. Schein, A., Zhou, M., Blei, D.M., Wallach, H.: Bayesian Poisson tucker decomposition for learning the structure of international relations (2016)
35. Joachims, T.: Training linear SVMs in linear time. In: ACM SIGKDD International Conference on Knowledge Discovery and Data Mining, pp. 217–226 (2006)

An Energy Efficient Uplink Scheduling and Resource Allocation for M2M Communications in SC-FDMA Based LTE-A Networks

Qiyue Li[1](✉), Yuling Ge[1], Yangzhao Yang[2], Yadong Zhu[1], Wei Sun[1], and Jie Li[3]

[1] School of Electrical Engineering and Automation, Hefei University of Technology, Hefei, Anhui, China
liqiyue@mail.ustc.edu.cn, 2018110326@mail.hfut.edu.cn, 2018170323@mail.hfut.edu.cn, wsun@hfut.edu.cn
[2] China Academy of Electronics and Information Technology, Beijing, China
forester@mail.ustc.edu.cn
[3] School of Computer and Information, Hefei University of Technology, Hefei, Anhui, China
lijie@hfut.edu.cn

Abstract. In future wireless communications, there will be a large number of devices equipped with several different types of sensors need to access networks with diverse quality of service requirements. In cellular network evolution, the long term evolution advanced (LTE-A) networks has standardized Machine-to-Machine (M2M) features. Such M2M technology can provide a promising infrastructure for Internet of things (IoT) sensing applications, which usually require real-time data reporting. However, LTE-A is not designed for directly supporting such low-data-rate devices with optimized energy efficiency since it depends on core technologies of LTE that are originally designed for high-data-rate services. This paper investigate the maximum energy efficient data packets M2M transmission with uplink channels in LTE-A network. We formulate it into a jointed problem of Modulation and-Coding Scheme (MCS) assignment, resource allocation and power control, which can be expressed as a NP-hard mixed-integer linear fractional programming problem. Then we propose a global optimization scheme with Charnes-Cooper transformation and Glover linearization. The numerical experiment results show that with limited resource blocks, our algorithm can maintain low data packets dropping ratios while achieving optimal energy efficiency for a large number of M2M nodes, comparing with other typical counterparts.

Supported in part by grants from the National Natural Science Foundation of China (51877060), Fundamental Research Funds for the Central Universities, and ANHUI Province Key Laboratory of Affective Computing & Advanced Intelligent Machine, Grant No. ACAIM180102.

V. C. M. Leung et al. (Eds.): 5GWN 2019, LNICST 278, pp. 124–140, 2019.
https://doi.org/10.1007/978-3-030-17513-9_9

Keywords: Energy efficiency ·
Machine-to-Machine (M2M) communication ·
Real-time data reporting · Resource allocation and scheduling

1 Introduction

Machine-to-Machine (M2M), also known as machine-type communication (MTC) technology, emerging as a new communication technology, has recently gained a great deal of attention [1]. It allows MTC devices (MTCDs) communicate with each other intelligently without or with very little human interventions. The technology has been utilized in a variety of M2M applications, such as smart grids (SG), intelligent transportation system (ITS), e-healthcare, industrial/home automation, and so on [2].

According to Cisco, it is predicted that M2M connections will increase to 12.2 billion by 2020, accounting for nearly half of the total global connections [3]. To take advantages of the opportunities created by a global M2M communications over cellular networks, the 3rd Generation Partnership Project (3GPP) Release 10 [4] first proposed service requirements for supporting MTC in LTE-A cellular networks. LTE-A networks can offer higher capacity and more flexible radio resource management (RRM) schemes than the existing packet access data technologies [5]. In LTE-A network, evolved universal terrestrial radio access (E-UTRA) NodeBs (eNBs), home eNBs (HeNBs), and relay nodes (RNs) can be deployed to provide general wireless access in outdoor and indoor environments.

In LTE-A cellular networks, Orthogonal Frequency Division Multiple Access (OFDMA) is chosen for the LTE's downlink, while the Single-Carrier FDMA (SC-FDMA) is chosen for the uplink. Advantages of such multi-carrier access techniques include their robust communication and stable interference management [6]. However, the OFDMA technique also introduces considerable challenges when it comes to designing RRM functionalities such as resource allocation and packet scheduling. In LTE networks, the radio resources are distributed in both time and frequency domains. In the time domain, radio resources are allocated on every Transmission Time Interval (TTI), which consists of two time slots and has a duration of 1 ms. One LTE frame is composed by 20 slots or 10 TTIs. In the frequency domain, a full LTE system bandwidth (20 MHz) is divided into 100 uplink sub-channel each including 12 subcarriers. Every sub-channel has a bandwidth of 180 kHz and 7 symbols in the time domain constitute a Resource Block (RB) as shown in Fig. 1.

Originally, LTE-A networks were designed for human-to-human (H2H) communications, where the amount of uplink traffic is normally lower than the downlink traffic. However in many M2M applications, data reporting with Quality of Service (QoS) constraints is a typical requirement. For example, in the e-healthcare application, each patient is equipped with smart device which can sample several types of health-related data, such as heart beat rate, body temperature, blood glucose levels and so on. The smart devices must upload data in real time to the healthcare provider via eNB. With the reported data,

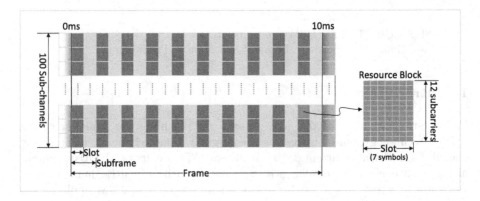

Fig. 1. The LTE-A frame structure and resource blocks.

the healthcare provider can assess each patient's health condition and react to an emergency situation immediately. In such applications, M2M traffic is distinct from the H2H traffic, in which more application data will be generated in uplink channels than that on downlink channels. Thus, congestion and packet drop would happen due to concurrent transmit messages from massive MTCDs, which leads to a low successful rate of random access (RA) [5,7]. Therefore, different M2M applications impose challenges to the designs of efficient radio resource allocation algorithms for M2M communications in LTE-A networks [8]. First, the radio resource allocation scheme should accommodate a large number of MTCDs with finite resources and diverse requirements. Second, it should have extreme low complexity to schedule the massive MTCDs efficiently. Finally, it should also maximize the energy efficiency to keep the M2M network alive for at least several years. In most of M2M application, usually an observation period is defined for each type of sensory data due to the real-time constraint. A MTCD must upload all the sampled data packets within the specified reporting period, otherwise the data will be dropped. On the other hand, if a MTCD is not allocated to transmit any data in a certain time slot, it can switch to sleep mode to reduce its energy consumption.

Some research efforts have been made to design effective resource allocation scheme [9]. [1, 10] design scheduling algorithms for M2M communications wherein devices report multiple types of real-time data. They investigated the energy minimized scheduling problem for real-time reporting of data critical M2M applications, and proposed heuristic energy efficient algorithms. However, the algorithms only considered the data packets scheduling problem, without the resource allocation and MCS selection, which are the important parts in LTE-A network. In [11], the authors proposed two uplink scheduling algorithms in a MTCD/UE hybrid network that schedule MTCD based on their delay tolerance. The algorithm first allocated UE traffic, then allocated the remaining RBs to MTCDs. In [12], a greedy algorithm for solving approximate optimal solution is proposed, which effectively solves the NP-hard problem. [13] studied the joint optimization problem including the quality of service (QoS)-driven resource allocation and the layer selection, and proposed a tabu search-based metaheuristic algorithm for resource allocation. The authors in [14] presented a clustering-based approach to scheduling devices in LTE-A network by clustering machines based on a their QoS requirements, with a scheduling period defined for each cluster and is adapted based on jitter of clusters. Similar to [11], the algorithms are designed to accommodate with a M2M/H2H hybrid network, is not suitable to a real-time M2M application. In [15], the authors formulated the energy-optimal routing and multiple-sink aggregation into a mixed-integer programming problem, and presented a throughput-optimal scheduling algorithm to allocate the resource blocks under physical interference model in the pure aggregation case. However, as mentioned above, usually several different types of sensors with different QoS constraints are equipped on the MTCDs, which are not considered in [15].

Besides, although 3GPP has introduced some new enhanced power modes and more energy efficient signaling techniques to better handel M2M communications based on the LTE infrastructure, the size of data packets is not considered in the Modulation and Coding Scheme (MCS) selection process. In general, MCS is controlled by channel quality (e.g., receive power, Signal-to-Interference-plus-Noise Ratio (SINR) and so on). Usually when the channel quality between MTCD and eNB is good, a higher MCS selection can be used, or vice versa. For a higher MCS selection, a larger transport block (TB) can be transmitted in LTE-A [16], leading to a higher data rate. Obviously as the restriction of receiver's SINR and data packet size, a higher MCS may be over-qualified to a certain MTCD, which would cause extra energy consumption. Therefore, the resource allocation scheme in uplink M2M communications based on SC-FDMA LTE-A network is a jointed problem of MCS assignment, resource allocation, data scheduling and power control.

To the best of our knowledge, prior works have not proposed a resource allocation scheme to jointly consider MCS assignment, resource allocation and power control. Therefore, we present a resource allocation and data scheduling scheme to maximize the overall energy efficiency which is defined by the ratio of total transmitted data to the energy consumed. In this paper, we formulate the joint allocation and scheduling scheme into a Mixed Integer Linear Programming (MILP) problem, and then reconstruct it Charnes-Cooper transformation and Glover linearization scheme to obtain the global optimum.

The remainder of this paper is organized as follows. Section 2 formulates the energy efficiency optimization scheduling problem. Then, Sect. 3 introduces the reconstruction method of the original NP-hard problem to obtain it's global optimum. In Sect. 4, we evaluate the performance of the proposed algorithm. Finally, this paper is concluded in Sect. 5.

2   Problem Formulation

In this paper, we consider a typical scenario that consists of only one eNB and a number of MTCDs, within the coverage area of the eNB. Different types of sensors are equipped on each MTCD, which can sample data with different fixed intervals. The eNB can perform a scheduling procedure to decide the transmission time of the sampled data. All the MTCDs will transmit data to eNB according to the scheduling decision.

2.1   Assumptions

Without losses of generality, we make some assumptions in this paper. The sampling time of each sensor is short and can be neglected compared with LTE time slot. And each type of sensors will generate constant small size of data, and can only be transmitted in one time slot. Due to different usages and applications of different sensors, we assume different data packets can not be aggregated and have to be transmitted separately.

2.2   Network Architecture and System Model

We consider the uplink channel in a single cell of a multiuser 3GPP LTE-A network with SC-FDMA channel access for sensor data reporting, and the network architecture is shown in Fig. 2.

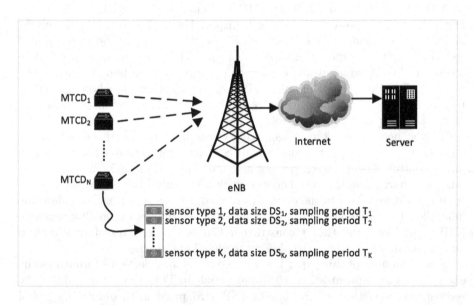

Fig. 2. Network architecture.

There are N MTCDs in the network, and all the MTCDs are equipped with K types of sensors and sample data. Let DS_k is data packet size sampled by sensor k, and T_k is sampling and reporting period of sensor k. Similar to [1], we also define a observation period T (time slots), which is the Least Common Multiple

(LCM) of the all the sampling periods of each sensor type in the networkwide. Obviously, the data reporting of all the N MTCDs will repeat every T time slots, thus eNB can perform a scheduling algorithm every T in a centralized manner. Let $d_{n,k,j}$ denote the jth data packet sampled by sensor K in MTCD n, Y the total RBs ready to allocate in every time slot, and M total MCS selections available for each MTCD.

2.3 Problem Statement

In this paper, we consider how to determine an efficient reporting schedule and resource allocation scheme which can maximize Energy Efficiency (EE) of all the N MTCDs, in which EE is defined as a ratio of all the data packets (bytes) transmitted to all the power (Joule) consumed. In a typical application all the MTCDs are used to monitor some certain physical values collaboratively, which makes EE a very important metric to evaluate the lifetime of the whole M2M network [17]. Thus this energy efficiency maximized scheduling problem can be formulated as follows:

$$(P0) \quad \max EE = \frac{\sum_{n=1}^{N} \sum_{k=1}^{K} \sum_{j=1}^{T/T_k} DS_k}{\sum_{n=1}^{N} \sum_{k=1}^{K} \sum_{j=1}^{T/T_k} \sum_{t=1}^{T} \sum_{b=1}^{Y} (\varphi_{n,k,j,t,b} \times P_{n,k,j,t,b})} \quad (1)$$

where $\varphi_{n,k,j,t,b}$ is a binary variable, $\varphi_{n,k,j,t,b} = 1$ when the RB b in time slot t is allocated to data $d_{n,k,j}$, otherwise $\varphi_{n,k,j,t,b} = 0$. $P_{n,k,j,t,b}$ is the consumed power when transmitting data $d_{n,k,j}$ on RB b time slot t.

The constraints are:

$$P_{n,k,j} \leq P_{max}, \forall n \in N, k \in K, j \in J \quad (2)$$

$$\varphi_{n,k,j,t,b_1} \times P_{n,k,j,t,b_1} = \varphi_{n,k,j,t,b_2} \times P_{n,k,j,t,b_2},$$
$$\forall n \in N, k \in K, j \in J, t \in T, b_1 \in Y, b_2 \in Y, and \ \varphi_{n,k,j,t,b_1} = \varphi_{n,k,j,t,b_2} \quad (3)$$

$$\sum_{b=1}^{Y} \varphi_{n,k,j,t,b} \times R(m_{n,k,j,t}) \geq DS_k, \forall n \in N, k \in K, j \in J, t \in T \quad (4)$$

$$P_{n,k,j,t,b} + 10 \times \log(\sum_{b=1}^{Y} \varphi_{n,k,j,t,b}) + (\alpha - 1) \times PL_n - IoT \geq SINR(m_{n,k,j,t}) \quad (5)$$

$$\sum_{n=1}^{N} \sum_{k=1}^{K} \sum_{j=1}^{T/T_k} \sum_{b=1}^{Y} \varphi_{n,k,j,t,b} \leq Y, \forall t \in T \quad (6)$$

$$\begin{cases} \varphi_{n,k,j,t}^{max} - \varphi_{n,k,j,t}^{min} = \sum_{b=1}^{Y} \varphi_{n,k,j,t,b} - 1 \\ \varphi_{n,k,j,t}^{max} = \max\{b | \varphi_{n,k,j,t,b} = 1\} \\ \varphi_{n,k,j,t}^{min} = \min\{b | \varphi_{n,k,j,t,b} = 1\} \end{cases} \quad (7)$$

$$\sum_{n=1}^{N}\sum_{k=1}^{K}\sum_{j=1}^{T/T_k} \varphi_{n,k,j,t,b} \leq 1, \ \forall t \in T, b \in Y \qquad (8)$$

Constraint 2 means the total transmission power of MTCD n can not exceed the maximum power P_{max}.

Constraint 3 means transmission power on all the RBs allocated to data $d_{n,k,j}$ should be equal, according to SC-FDMA uplink channel access protocol in 3GPP LTE-A network.

Constraint 4 means data rate $R(m)$ supported by MCS selection m should be greater than transmitted data packet size, in which $m_{n,k,j,t}$ is the MCS assigned to tranmsit data $d_{n,k,j}$ at time slot t.

Constraint 5 is the uplink channel power control model defined by 3GPP LTE-A protocol [18], in which α is the cell-specific path-loss compensation factor that can be set to 0.0 and from 0.4 to 1.0 in steps of 0.1. PL_n is the downlink path-loss measured by eNB, which can be considered as a constant value for each static MTCD n, and IoT is the Interference over Thermal, which should be equal to 0 in our single cell case. $SINR(m_{n,k,j,t})$ is the SINR requirement of MCS selection $m_{n,k,j,t}$.

Constraint 6 means total RBs allocated in one time slot can not exceed Y.

Constraint 7 is the contiguity constraint, means all the RBs allocated to one data packet should be adjacent, according to SC-FDMA uplink channel access model.

Constraint 8 means one RB can only be allocated to one MTCD.

It can be proved that energy efficiency maximized scheduling problem $P0$ is NP-hard with unlinear terms and constraints. Thus we can only perform exhaustive search algorithm with exponential complexity to obtain global optimum. However, with the rapidly development of IoT, the number of MTCDs could be enormous, and it is impossible for eNB to perform optimal scheduling with exhaustive search algorithm. Thus in this paper, we try to reformulate $P0$ into an equivalent two-dimensional knapsack problem, and then reconstruct it into a Mixed Integer Linear Programming (MILP) problem with Charnes-Cooper transformation and Glover linearization scheme [19], to find the global optimum.

3 Problem Reformulation and Proposed Algorithm

3.1 Problem Reformulation

Given the K types of sensors, each type of sensory data will be transmitted to the base-station $N \times DT_k$ times. Then the total amount of data times is $\sum_{k=1}^{K}(N \times DT_k)$. The total amount of wireless resource blocks is $T \times Y$, and there are M kinds of MCS selection methods to transmit data, which are mutual. Thus this problem can be reformulated into a two dimensional knapsack problem. We can consider the total resource blocks as a knapsack, and all the transmitted data as the items. Each item has some contribution to the EE object, and for each item there is only one method among M kinds organizations. Each data can only be inserted into the place t. If data $d_{n,k,j}$ is transmitted by m MCS at time slot t, then

1. It's capacity in the knapsack is $(1, \lceil \frac{DS_{n,k,j,m,t}}{R_{n,k,j,m,t}} \rceil)$

2. It's contribution to EE is $\frac{DS_{n,k,j,m,t}}{\lceil \frac{DS_{n,k,j,m,t}}{R_{n,k,j,m,t}} \rceil \times P_{n,k,j,m,t}}$

Thus, we can define a binary variable $x_{n,k,j,m,t}$. When the data $d_{n,k,j}$ is transmitted at time slot t with MCS selection m, $x_{n,k,j,m,t} = 1$, otherwise, $x_{n,k,j,m,t} = 0$.

Thus, the EE optimization can be reformulated into a two dimensional knapsack problem.

$$(P1) \quad \max \frac{\sum_{n=1}^{N} \sum_{k=1}^{K} \sum_{j=1}^{DT_k} \sum_{m=1}^{M} \sum_{t=1}^{T} x_{n,k,j,m,t} \times DS_{n,k,j,m,t}}{\sum_{n=1}^{N} \sum_{k=1}^{K} \sum_{j=1}^{DT_k} \sum_{m=1}^{M} \sum_{t=1}^{T} (x_{n,k,j,m,t} \times \lceil \frac{DS_{n,k,j,m,t}}{R_{n,k,j,m,t}} \rceil \times P_{n,k,j,m,t})} \tag{9}$$

s.t.

$$\sum_{n=1}^{N} \sum_{k=1}^{K} \sum_{j=1}^{DT_k} \sum_{m=1}^{M} (x_{n,k,j,m,t} \times \lceil \frac{DS_{n,k,j,m,t}}{R_{n,k,j,m,t}} \rceil) \leq Y, \ \forall t \in T \tag{10}$$

$$\sum_{t=1}^{T} x_{n,k,j,m,t} \leq 1, \ \forall n \in N, k \in K, j \in J, m \in M \tag{11}$$

$$P_{n,k,j,m,t} + 10 \times \log \lceil \frac{DS_{n,k,j,m,t}}{R_{n,k,j,m,t}} \rceil + (\alpha - 1) \times PL_n - IoT \geq SINR_{n,k,j,m,t} \tag{12}$$

$$P_{n,k,j,m,t} \times \lceil \frac{DS_{n,k,j,m,t}}{R_{n,k,j,m,t}} \rceil \leq P_{max} \tag{13}$$

$$\sum_{m=1}^{M} x_{n,k,j,m,t} \leq 1, \ \forall n \in N, k \in K, j \in J, t \in T \tag{14}$$

$$\sum_{m=1}^{M} \sum_{t=1}^{T} x_{n,k,j,m,t} \leq 1, \ \forall n \in N, k \in K, j \in J \tag{15}$$

$$x_{n,k,j,m,t} \in \{0,1\} \tag{16}$$

The constraint 10 means the resource blocks allocated in one time slot can not exceed Y. The constraint 11 means each item(data) can only be put in a single time slot. The constraint 12 means the power allocated to a single RB has to meet the MCS requirement. The constraint 13 means the total power allocated to all RBs can not exceed the maximum power of the device. The constraint 14 means one data packet can only be transmitted with one MCS selection. And the constraint 16 means $x_{n,k,j,m,t}$ is a binary variable.

3.2   Mixed-Integer Linear Fractional Programming Reconstruction

Regarding to the problem $(P1)$ defined in Eq. 9, first we can reconstruct the problem by simplifying the subscripts of parameters. Let $l_1 = \lceil \log_2 N \rceil$, $l_2 = \lceil \log_2 K \rceil$, $l_3 = \lceil \log_2 DT_{max} \rceil$, $l_4 = \lceil \log_2 M \rceil$, $l_5 = \lceil \log_2 T \rceil$. A, A_1, A_2, A_3, A_4, A_5 are binary numbers with length of $l_1 + l_2 + l_3 + l_4 + l_5$, among which the first l_1 bits in A_1, the $l_1 + 1$ to l_2 bits in A_2, the $l_2 + 1$ to l_3 bits in A_3, the $l_3 + 1$ to l_4 bits in A_4, the $L - 4 + 1$ to l_5 bits in A_5 are '1's, and the rest bits are '0's. Then the subscript n of $x_{n,k,j,m,t}$ can be placed at top l_1 bits of A with binary value. The subscript k of $x_{n,k,j,m,t}$ can be placed at $l_1 + 1$ to l_2 bits of A with binary value. The subscript j can be placed at $l_2 + 1$ to l_3 bits of A with binary value. The subscript m can be placed at $l_3 + 1$ to l_4 bits of A with binary value. The subscript m can be placed at $l_3 + 1$ to l_4 bits of A with binary value. The subscript t can be placed at $l_4 + 1$ to l_5 bits of A with binary value. Then we can reconstruct $(P1)$ into the following problem.

$$(P2) \quad \max \frac{\sum_{a=1}^{2^{l_1+l_2+l_3+l_4+l_5}} DS_a \times x_a}{\sum_{a=1}^{2^{l_1+l_2+l_3+l_4+l_5}} \left\lceil \frac{DS_a}{R_a} \right\rceil \times P_a \times x_a} \tag{17}$$

s.t.

$$\sum_{a=1+(i-1)\times 2^{l_1+l_2+l_3+l_4}}^{i\times 2^{l_1+l_2+l_3+l_4}} \left(\left\lceil \frac{DS_a}{R_a} \right\rceil \times x_a \right) \leq Y, \ \forall 1 \leq (A\&A_5) \leq T, \ i = 1, 2, 3, \cdots, 2^{l_5} \tag{18}$$

$$P_a + 10 \times \log\left(\left\lceil \frac{DS_a}{R_a} \right\rceil \right) + (\alpha - 1) \times PL_n - IOT \geq SINR_a \tag{19}$$

$$P_a \times \left\lceil \frac{DS_a}{R_a} \right\rceil \leq P_{max} \tag{20}$$

$$\sum_{j=1}^{2^{l_5}} x_{i+(j-1)\times 2^{l_1+l_2+l_3+l_4}} \leq 1, \quad i = 1, 2, 3, \cdots, 2^{l_1+l_2+l_3+l_4} \tag{21}$$

$$\forall n \in N, k \in K, j \in J, m \in M$$

$$\sum_{j=1}^{2^{l_4}} x_{i+(j-1)\times 2^{l_1+l_2+l_3}} \leq 1, \forall n \in N, k \in K, j \in J, t \in T$$

$$i = (h - 1) \times 2^{l_1+l_2+l_3+l_4} + 1, (h - 1) \times 2^{l_1+l_2+l_3+l_4} + 2, \cdots, \tag{22}$$

$$(h - 1) \times 2^{l_1+l_2+l_3+l_4} + 2^{l_1+l_2+l_3}, \ h = 1, 2, 3, \cdots, 2^{l_5}$$

$$\sum_{j=1}^{2^{l_4+l_5}} x_{i+(j-1)\times 2^{l_1+l_2+l_3}} \leq 1, \quad i = 1, 2, 3, \cdots, 2^{l_1+l_2+l_3}, \tag{23}$$

$$\forall n \in N, k \in K, j \in J$$

$$x_a \in \{0, 1\} \tag{24}$$

It can be seen that the objective function $P2$ is a ratio of two linear functions, and all the constraints are linear. Thus $P2$ is a mixed-integer linear fractional programming (MILFP) problem. Besides, it can be proven that $P2$ is a NP-hard MILFP problem with quasi-convex and quasi-concave property, thus the local optimal of $P2$ is the global optimal in feasible region.

3.3 The Proposed Algorithm

To obtain the global optimal in polynomial time, we propose a optimal algorithm based on Charnes-Cooper transformation and Glover linearization, the former of which can transform the original MILFP problem into a mixed-integer nonlinear programming (MINLP) problem, while the later can convert MINLP problem into an equivalent mixed-integer linear programming (MILP) problem.

First, we introduce a new positive variable u, and let

$$u = \frac{1}{\sum_{a=1}^{2^{l_1+l_2+l_3+l_4+l_5}} \times P_a \times x_a} \tag{25}$$

Obviously $u > 0$. Thus the fractional objective function in $P0$ can be transformed into a linear function, i.e.

$$\max \frac{\sum_{a=1}^{2^{l_1+l_2+l_3+l_4+l_5}} DS_a \times x_a}{\sum_{a=1}^{2^{l_1+l_2+l_3+l_4+l_5}} \left\lceil \frac{DS_a}{R_a} \right\rceil \times P_a \times x_a} = \max \sum_{a=1}^{2^{l_1+l_2+l_3+l_4+l_5}} DS_a \times (x_a \times u) \tag{26}$$

As u is positive, we can multiply by u on both sides of Eqs. 18, 21 and 23, and the following constraints can be obtained.

$$\sum_{a=1+(i-1)\times 2^{l_1+l_2+l_3+l_4}}^{i\times 2^{l_1+l_2+l_3+l_4}} \left(\left\lceil \frac{DS_a}{R_a} \right\rceil \times x_a \times u\right) \leq Y \times u, \ i = 1,2,3,\cdots,2^{l_5} \tag{27}$$

$$\sum_{j=1}^{2^{l_5}} x_{i+(j-1)\times 2^{l_1+l_2+l_3+l_4}} \times u \leq u, \quad i = 1,2,3,\cdots,2^{l_1+l_2+l_3+l_4}, \tag{28}$$

$$\forall n \in N, k \in K, j \in J, m \in M$$

$$\sum_{j=1}^{2^{l_4}} x_{i+(j-1)\times 2^{l_1+l_2+l_3}} \times u \leq u, \quad \forall n \in N, k \in K, j \in J, t \in T$$

$$i = (h-1) \times 2^{l_1+l_2+l_3+l_4} + 1, (h-1) \times 2^{l_1+l_2+l_3+l_4} + 2, \cdots, \tag{29}$$

$$(h-1) \times 2^{l_1+l_2+l_3+l_4} + 2^{l_1+l_2+l_3}, h = 1,2,3,\cdots,2^{l_5},$$

$$\sum_{j=1}^{2^{l_4+l_5}} x_{i+(j-1)\times 2^{l_1+l_2+l_3}} \times u \leq u, \quad i = 1,2,3,\cdots,2^{l_1+l_2+l_3}, \tag{30}$$

$$\forall n \in N, k \in K, j \in J$$

$$x_a \times u \in \{0, u\} \tag{31}$$

According to definition of u, Eq. 25 can be converted to

$$1 = u \times \sum_{a=1}^{2^{l_1+l_2+l_3+l_4+l_5}} \left\lceil \frac{DS_a}{R_a} \right\rceil \times P_a \times x_a$$

$$= \sum_{a=1}^{2^{l_1+l_2+l_3+l_4+l_5}} \left\lceil \frac{DS_a}{R_a} \right\rceil \times P_a \times (x_a \times u) \tag{32}$$

Thus, the MILFP problem $P2$ can be transformed to an equivalent MINLP problem $P3$.

$$(P3) \quad \max \sum_{a=1}^{2^{(l_1+l_2+l_3+l_4+l_5)}} DS_a \times (x_a \times u) \tag{33}$$

The constraints are illustrated as Eqs. 19, 20, 27, 28, 29, 31 and 32.

The only unlinear item in MINLP problem $P1$ is the bilinear one $x_a \times u$, which can be accuartely linearized by intro ducting some auxiliary variables and constraints using the Glover linearzation scheme. By introducing $w_a = x_a \times u$, the MINLP problem $P1$ can be linearized to a mix-integer linear programming (MILP) problem, i.e.

$$(PR) \quad \max Z = \sum_{a=1}^{2^{l_1+l_2+l_3+l_4+l_5}} DS_a \times w_a, \quad a \in B \tag{34}$$

s.t.

$$\sum_{a=1+(i-1)\times 2^{l_1+l_2+l_3+l_4}}^{i \times 2^{l_1+l_2+l_3+l_4}} \left(\left\lceil \frac{DS_a}{R_a} \right\rceil \times w_a \right) \leq Y \times u, \quad i = 1, 2, 3, \cdots, 2^{l_5} \tag{35}$$

$$\sum_{j=1}^{2^{l_5}} w_{i+(j-1)\times 2^{l_1+l_2+l_3+l_4}} \leq u, \quad i = 1, 2, 3, \cdots, 2^{l_1+l_2+l_3+l_4} \tag{36}$$

$$\sum_{j=1}^{2^{l_4}} w_{i+(j-1)\times 2^{l_1+l_2+l_3}} \leq u,$$

$$i = (h-1) \times 2^{l_1+l_2+l_3+l_4} + 1, (h-1) \times 2^{l_1+l_2+l_3+l_4} + 2, \cdots,$$
$$(h-1) \times 2^{l_1+l_2+l_3+l_4} + 2^{l_1+l_2+l_3}, h = 1, 2, 3, \cdots, 2^{l_5} \tag{37}$$

$$\sum_{j=1}^{2^{l_4+l_5}} w_{i+(j-1)\times 2^{l_1+l_2+l_3}} \leq u, \quad i = 1, 2, 3, \cdots, 2^{l_1+l_2+l_3} \tag{38}$$

$$P_a + 10 \times \log\left(\left\lceil \frac{DS_a}{R_a} \right\rceil \right) + (\alpha - 1) \times PL_n - IOT \geq SINR_a \tag{39}$$

$$1 = \sum_{a=1}^{2^{l_1+l_2+l_3+l_4+l_5}} \left\lceil \frac{DS_a}{R_a} \right\rceil \times P_a \times w_a \tag{40}$$

$$w_a \in \{0, u\} \tag{41}$$

$$P_a \times \left\lceil \frac{DS_a}{R_a} \right\rceil \leq P_{max} \tag{42}$$

Obviously PR is a MILP problem equivalent to the original MILFP problem $P0$, and it can be easily solved by the commercial linear programming toolbox.

4   Simulation and Performance Analysis

In this section, we evaluate the performance achieved by our scheduling and allocation algorithm. The experiments are conducted using discrete-event simulations, where the M2M communication network is considered to consist of one eNB and N MTCDs, without considerable inter-cell interference. The position of MTCDs are randomly generated in the range of [20, 300] to eNB. Table 1 lists the detailed parameters used to evaluate the network performance. The parameter values comply with the 3GPP TS25.104 and TR36.814 standards [20]. The channel gains for uplink and downlink are included in the transmit power and receiver sensitivity, respectively. According to [16], there are 28 MCS selections in physical uplink shared channel (PUSCH), and a sample of the data rate in bits and SINR requirement defined is illustrated in Table 2.

For the sensory data, we assume there as many as 10 types of sensors equipped on each MTCD. Obviously, the results of resource allocation and data scheduling are dependent on data packet size and sampling periods. Thus we randomly generate the data packet size of each type of sensor in the range of [10, 500] bytes, and sampling periods in the range of [1, 120] s, which are practical in typical M2M applications. Then the simulation is repeated for 100 times and the results are averaged.

In the simulation, we use the open source lp_solve toolbox to solve the MILP problem PR.

To evaluate our proposed algorithm, we compare two classic resource allocation and scheduling algorithms: Energy-Efficient Scheduling algorithm (EES) [1], and Greedy algorithm as provided in [9]. The Greedy algorithm determines the optimal pair of MCS and number of RBs, at which the transport block size is sufficient to transmit sensing data within the minimum transmit power. In addition, it can utilize the optimal MCS selections as main criteria for spectrum allocation has been proposed for better adapting to the sensing node requirements. The EES algorithm is a heuristic one to schedule the transmissions of a MTCD in one time slot with energy efficiency, while maintaining fairness and low data dropping. The simulation results are presented in terms of EE and packet dropping rate of all the MTCDs. With these metrics, we investigate the impacts of the number of MTCDs and sensors.

Table 1. Simulation parameters

Parameters	Values
Network topology	Random deployment
Number of MTCDs	1–80
Maximum transmit power	23 dBm
MTCD's Receiver sensitivity	−100 dBm
Path loss model	3GPP outdoor: $PL(d) = 15.3 + 37.6 \times \log_{10}(d)$(dB)
Distances between MTCDs and eNB	20–300 m
Bandwidth	20 MHz
Number of RBs	100
α	0.9
Number of MCS selection	28
Number of sensor types on each MTCD	2–8
Sensory data size	10–500 bytes
Sampling period of each sensor	1–120 s

Table 2. A sample of supported data rate in bits defined in 3GPP TS 36.213 [16]

MCS selection	Number of RBs					
	1	2	3	4	5	...
...	...	...	...	...	...	...
7	104	224	328	472	584	...
8	120	256	392	536	680	...
9	136	296	456	616	776	...
10	144	296	456	616	776	...
11	176	328	504	680	872	...
...	...	...	...	...	...	...
27	616	1256	1864	2536	3112	...
28	712	1480	2216	2984	3752	...

Figures 3, 4 and 5 show that our algorithm performs better than Greedy in terms of energy efficiency with different number of sensor types. First, we can observe that when N increases, the EE values of both the Greedy and our proposed methods increase and then decrease. When N increases, the data transmissions from the same MTCD are scattered over more time slots, causing higher energy consumption. Then as N keeps increasing, the available RBs is insufficient to transmit all the sensory data and some will be dropped. However, our algorithm can effectively schedule data packets and allocate resources optimally to all the MTCDs. Thus our algorithm can achieve higher energy efficiency, and have less impact of resource insufficiency on energy consumption. However, it can be seen that EES causes higher energy efficiency than ours. It is understandable as only data scheduling is considered in EES, without resource allocations. Thus although some data packets are scheduled at certain time slots, there is no sufficient RBs to transmit, leading to many infeasible scheduling.

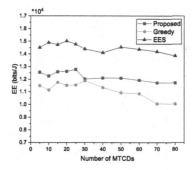

Fig. 3. Energy efficiency (K = 2) with different number of MTCDs.

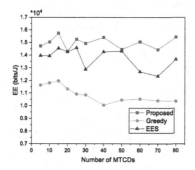

Fig. 4. Energy efficiency (K = 4) with different number of MTCDs.

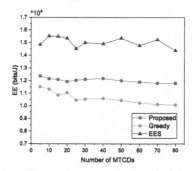

Fig. 5. Energy efficiency (K = 8) with different number of MTCDs.

Figures 6, 7 and 8 show the data packets dropping ratio of our algorithm and the counterparts. Obviously, when the number of MTCDs is small, all the sensory data can be transmitted. However, there will be no enough RBs to support the enormous data packets generated by a larger number of M2M devices. Similar to *EE*, without resource allocation EES can achieve slightly better in terms of data dropping ratio.

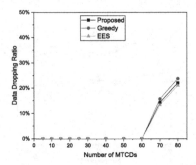

Fig. 6. Data dropping ratio (K = 2) with different number of MTCDs.

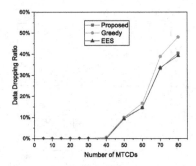

Fig. 7. Data dropping ratio (K = 4) with different number of MTCDs.

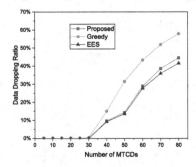

Fig. 8. Data dropping ratio (K = 8) with different number of MTCDs.

5 Conclusion

Although the LTE-A infrastructure introduces many benefits for the applications of M2M communication sensing platforms, the challenges are also considerable, especially in terms of energy efficiency of whole M2M network. In this paper, we formulate the energy efficient M2M communications in SC-FDMA based LTE-A networks into a jointed problem of MCS assignment, resource allocation, data scheduling and power control, which can be expressed as a NP-hard MILP problem.

Then we reconstruct it with Charnes-Cooper transformation and Glover linearization scheme to obtain the global optimum. Based on the optimal MCS, transmission power and resource planning scheme, the sampled data packets can be
reported to eNB with maximum energy efficiency. We also compare the performance of our scheme with other typical counterparts. The numerical experiment
results show that with limited resource blocks, our algorithm can maintain low
data packets dropping ratios while achieving optimal energy efficiency for a large
number of M2M nodes.

References

1. Chen, Y., Yang, S., Hwang, J., Wu, M.: An energy-efficient scheduling algorithm
   for real-time machine-to-machine (M2M) data reporting. In: 2014 IEEE Global
   Communications Conference, pp. 4442–4447, December 2014
2. Rajandekar, A., Sikdar, B.: A survey of MAC layer issues and protocols for
   machine-to-machine communications. IEEE Internet of Things J. 2(2), 175–186
   (2015)
3. Cisco. Cisco visual networking index (VNI) complete forecast for 2015 to 2020.
   Technical report, Cisco, San Jose, CA, USA (2017)
4. 3GPP. Service requirements for machine-type communications (MTC); stage 1.
   Technical report, 3GPP Standard TS 22.368 V10.0.0, March 2010
5. Ghavimi, F., Chen, H.: M2M communications in 3GPP LTE/LTE-A networks:
   architectures, service requirements, challenges, and applications. IEEE Commun.
   Surv. Tutorials 17(2), 525–549 (2015). Secondquarter
6. Abu-Ali, N., Taha, A.M., Salah, M., Hassanein, H.: Uplink scheduling in LTE and
   LTE-advanced: tutorial, survey and evaluation framework. IEEE Commun. Surv.
   Tutorials 16(3), 1239–1265 (2014). Third
7. Hasan, M., Hossain, E., Niyato, D.: Random access for machine-to-machine communication in LTE-advanced networks: issues and approaches. IEEE Commun.
   Mag. 51(6), 86–93 (2013)
8. Tefek, U., Lim, T.J.: Relaying and radio resource partitioning for machine-type
   communications in cellular networks. IEEE Trans. Wirel. Commun. 16(2), 1344–
   1356 (2017)
9. Wong, I.C., Oteri, O., Mccoy, W.: Optimal resource allocation in uplink SC-FDMA
   systems. IEEE Trans. Wirel. Commun. 8(5), 2161–2165 (2009)
10. Fu, H., Chen, H.-C., Lin, P., Fang, Y.: Energy-efficient reporting mechanisms for
    multi-type real-time monitoring in machine-to-machine communications networks.
    In: 2012 Proceedings IEEE INFOCOM, pp. 136–144, March 2012
11. Lioumpas, A.S., Alexiou, A.: Uplink scheduling for machine-to-machine commu-
    nications in LTE-based cellular systems. In: 2011 IEEE GLOBECOM Workshops
    (GC Workshop), pp. 353–357, December 2011
12. Guo, C., Cui, Y., Ng, D.W.K., Liu, Z.: Multi-quality multicast beamforming with
    scalable video coding. IEEE Trans. Commun. 66(11), 5662–5677 (2018)
13. Zhou, H., Wang, X., Liu, Z., Ji, Y., Yamada, S.: Resource allocation for SVC
    streaming over cooperative vehicular networks. IEEE Trans. Veh. Technol. 67(9),
    7924–7936 (2018)
14. Lien, S., Chen, K., Lin, Y.: Toward ubiquitous massive accesses in 3GPP machine-
    to-machine communications. IEEE Commun. Mag. 49(4), 66–74 (2011)

15. Fitzgerald, E., Pióro, M., Tomaszewski, A.: Energy-optimal data aggregation and dissemination for the Internet of Things. IEEE Internet of Things J. **5**(2), 955–969 (2018)
16. 3GPP. Evolved universal terrestrial radio access (E-UTRA); physical layer procedures (release 13). Technical report, 3GPP TS 36.213 Technical specification v13.0.0, March 2015
17. Zhang, P., Miao, G.: Energy-efficient clustering design for M2M communications. In: 2014 IEEE Global Conference on Signal and Information Processing (GlobalSIP), pp. 163–167, December 2014
18. Ubeda Castellanos, C., et al.: Performance of uplink fractional power control in UTRAN LTE. In: VTC Spring 2008 - IEEE Vehicular Technology Conference, pp. 2517–2521, May 2008
19. Chen, J.C., Lai, H.C., Schaible, S.: Complex fractional programming and the Charnes-Cooper transformation. J. Optim. Theory Appl. **126**(1), 203–213 (2005)
20. 3GPP. Base station (BS) radio transmission and reception (FDD) (release 13). Technical report, 3GPP TS 36.814 Technical specification v13.1.0, March 2016

Energy Efficient Resource Allocation in Small Cells with WiFi Unlicensed Bands Sharing

Lei Zhu[1]([✉]), Haijun Zhang[2], and Xuebin Li[1]

[1] Beijing University of Chemical Technology, Beijing, China
zhuleibuct@126.com
[2] Beijing Advanced Innovation Center for Materials Genome Engineering,
Beijing Engineering and Technology Research Center for Convergence
Networks and Ubiquitous Services, Institute of Artificial Intelligence,
University of Science and Technology Beijing, Beijing, China
haijunzhang@ieee.org

Abstract. Unlicensed spectrum has long been considered a powerful candidate for addressing spectrum resource shortages. The emergence of small cells makes network coverage more seamless, switching, and a better user experience. This paper introduces small base station (SBS) to enable not only the information transmission on the WLAN unlicensed spectrum, but also the communication with connected terminals through the licensed spectrum. The energy efficiency (EE) in small cells with WiFi unlicensed band sharing is studied. We first build a two-layer network model containing small cells and macro cells. In particular, the subchannel allocation and power optimization problems are jointly studied using the alternative direction method of multipliers (ADMM) algorithm. Then, to obtain an optimization scheme, a radio resource scheduling strategy is proposed, taking into account Quality of Service (QoS) requirements, maximum transmit power, and same layer interference. The effectiveness and optimal solution of the method are shown by simulation results.

Keywords: Energy efficiency · Small cells · Unlicensed band · ADMM

1 Introduction

Recently, with the explosive development of data service, data traffic has increased dramatically, and the contradiction between high-bandwidth wireless services and shortage of spectrum resources has become prominent. Unlicensed band is widely regarded by industry and researchers as a promising technology. The 2.4 GHz and 5 GHz unlicensed bands used by WiFi as the main candidate for cellular network are getting more and more attention [1]. Signal transmission on the WLAN unlicensed frequency band in the cellular network can effectively

© ICST Institute for Computer Sciences, Social Informatics and Telecommunications Engineering 2019
Published by Springer Nature Switzerland AG 2019. All Rights Reserved
V. C. M. Leung et al. (Eds.): 5GWN 2019, LNICST 278, pp. 141–151, 2019.
https://doi.org/10.1007/978-3-030-17513-9_10

alleviate the information congestion problem caused by the shortage of licensed spectrum. Considering the application of unlicensed frequency bands in WiFi systems, it is necessary to not affect the performance of WiFi systems when studying the maximum system capacity under cellular networks over unlicensed spectrum.

Although the unlicensed band has the advantages of strong anti-interference performance and fast transmission speed, the 5 GHz unlicensed band has short wavelength, fast attenuation and short transmission distance. In view of this, the wireless researchers are investigating a promising solution for small cells that combines with unlicensed band to provide ubiquitous networking and seamless switching for mobile users. As an important part of heterogeneous networks, small cells are considered to be effective techniques for increasing system capacity and expanding coverage of cellular networks [2]. Especially in the indoor environment, relevant scholars have done a lot of research work to transfer the traffic of the macro cells to the small cells.

The combination of small cells and unlicensed band in cellular networks has been of concern to the research community for a long time. An unlicensed spectrum partitioning strategy based on Quality of Service (QoS) is proposed in [3]. Although the coexistence of the WiFi and the cellular network is guaranteed, at the cost of system capacity. In [4], the author uses the method of transmitting blank subframes by the base station (BS) at low power for unlicensed spectrum sharing. In [5], an integrated femto-WiFi (IFW) device was introduced that can be applied in both licensed and unlicensed spectrum. Currently LTE-Unlicensed (LTE-U) has also been proposed as a promising technology. The above work is on account of the fair use of unlicensed band by the WiFi system and the cellular network. According to the author's understanding, there is currently no joint use of licensed band and unlicensed band to achieve system energy efficiency maximization via the alternative direction method of multipliers (ADMM) research.

In this paper, the energy efficiency (EE) in small cells with WiFi unlicensed band sharing is studied. We have developed a system model, then the system EE is formulated into a convex function, and constraints such as QoS requirements and maximum transmit power are considered. A radio resource scheduling scheme based on ADMM is given and verified by simulation.

The following is the organizational structure of this paper. System model and problem modeling for sharing unlicensed bands between small cells and WiFi systems are presented in the Sect. 2. In Sect. 3, the ADMM algorithm is introduced and the optimization problem in Sect. 2 is solved by ADMM. In Sect. 4, the tendency and effectiveness of the proposed radio resource scheduling strategy are verified by simulation, followed by conclusion in Sect. 5.

2   System Model

We assume a downlink transmission in a multi-small cell network. In Fig. 1, under the macro base station, the WiFi system coexists with a small cell that can occupy both the licensed band and the unlicensed band. Then we envisioned a two-tier network, the cellular network terminal can be connected to the small cell, and can perform information transmission on the licensed band communication as well as on the unlicensed band of the WLAN. Let $K = \{1, 2, 3, ..., k, ..., K\}$ and $S = \{1, 2, 3, ..., s, ..., S\}$ denote the SBSs set and the small cell users set respectively. Macro users are represented by $M = \{1, 2, 3, ..., m, ..., M\}$. The bandwidth of this two-layer network is assumed as W, which is divided into N subchannels. And we assume that each channel fading is the same.

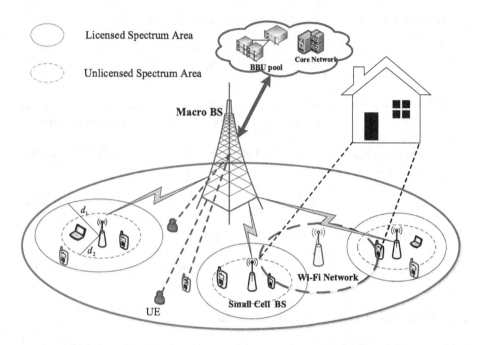

Fig. 1. Network architecture of small cells and WiFi coexistence.

In our architecture, each SBS has two coverage areas with radius d_1 and d_2 respectively. d_1 indicates the SBS users associated with a SBS in a licensed frequency band. Similarly, d_2 is the area covered by the unlicensed band under the SBS. Within this range, SBS can occupy unlicensed bands for information transmission. To guarantee the QoS of SBS and alleviate the interference of WiFi system on SBS under unlicensed band, d_1 and d_2, and the power of WiFi system must meet the following conditions, given by [9]

$$P_0 \times G(d_1 - d_2) \leq \xi \tag{1}$$

where the P_0 is the transmission power of the WiFi system, which is a fixed value, $G(d)$ is large-scale fading (path loss) over unlicensed frequency band, and ξ is the interference threshold of the WiFi system.

We assume that one channel can only be assigned to one user in a communication connection, and $a_{k,s,n} \in \{0, 1\}, \forall k, s, n$ represents the channel status.

2.1 Licensed Frequency Band Area

Let $g^1_{k,s,n}$ be the channel gain between terminal s and SBS k on subchannel n. $p_{k,s,n}$ denotes transmit power on subchannel n between SBS terminal s and small cell k. The SINR from SBS k is received on channel n on SBS user s is given by:

$$\gamma^1_{k,s,n} = \frac{p_{k,s,n}g^1_{k,s,n}}{I_1 + \delta^2} \tag{2}$$

At the same time, we also consider the same layer interference:

$$I_1 = \sum_{l,l\neq k}^{K} p_{l,s,n}g^1_{l,s,n} \tag{3}$$

I_1 indicates same layer interference (generated when the same channel is occupied by other small base stations). δ^2 denotes the system additive white Gaussian noise (AWGN) power at SBS k.

The data transmission rate on subchannel n between the kth SBS and the terminal s can be defined as:

$$C^1_{k,s,n} = \frac{W}{N}\log_2(1 + \gamma^l_{k,s,n}) \tag{4}$$

Therefore the total capacity under the licensed band is

$$C^1 = \sum_k \sum_s \sum_n C^1_{k,s,n} \times a_{k,s,n} \tag{5}$$

2.2 Unlicensed Frequency Band Area

Let $g^2_{k,s,n}$ denote the channel gain from base station k to terminal s on subchannel n in the unlicensed band. I_2 indicates interference from other WiFi systems on the same subchannel. If the subchannel of the unlicensed band is not occupied, $I_2 = 0$. The SINR on the unlicensed band subchannel n from the SBS k to the user s is thus given

$$\gamma^2_{k,s,n} = \frac{p_{k,s,n}g^2_{k,s,n}}{I_2 + \delta^2} \tag{6}$$

In the unlicensed band, the rate from k SBS to user s on channel n can also be defined as

$$C^2_{k,s,n} = \frac{W}{N}\log_2(1 + \gamma^2_{k,s,n}) \tag{7}$$

Then the total capacity under the licensed band is

$$C^2 = \sum_k \sum_s \sum_n C^2_{k,s,n} \times a_{k,s,n} \tag{8}$$

2.3   Problem Formulation

So the total capacity of the entire system is given:

$$C_T = C^1 + C^2 \tag{9}$$

And the total energy consumption of the system is expressed as

$$P_T = \sum_k p_{C,k} + \sum_k \sum_s \sum_n a_{k,s,n} p_{k,s,n} \tag{10}$$

where $p_{C,k}$ is the circuit power consumed by the SBS k, and $\sum_k \sum_s \sum_n a_{k,s,n} p_{k,s,n}$ is the total transmit power consumed by the SBSs.

Our objective function is to maximize system EE (the ratio of total system capacity and total energy consumption) on the premise of guaranteeing the QoS, so we get the following optimization problem:

$$\max_{a_{k,s,n}, p_{k,s,n}} \frac{C_T}{P_T}$$
$$s.t.$$
$$C1 : \sum_k a_{k,s,n} \leq 1, \forall s, n$$
$$C2 : a_{k,s,n} \in \{0,1\}, \forall k, s, n \tag{11}$$
$$C3 : \sum_n a_{k,s,n} p_{k,s,n} \leq p_{\max}, \forall s, k$$
$$C4 : \sum_n a_{k,s,n} C_{k,s,n} \geq R_s, \forall s, k$$
$$C5 : P_0 \times G(d_1 - d_2) \leq \xi.$$

where constraints C1 and C2 represent subchannel allocation constraints, limiting each channel to only one user per communication connection. While constraint C3 represents the total power constraint, and $p_{\max}$ indicates the maximum value of each SBS transmit power. The C3 limits that the total transmit power of subchannel must be lower than the maximum value of the SBS. C4 is the system QoS guarantee, the sth user capacity must be greater than the QoS minimum requirement R_s. Constraint C5 is designed to alleviate interference from the WiFi system after the SBS occupies the unlicensed band.

3   Energy Efficient Optimization Using ADMM

In this section, the ADMM algorithm is introduced, the principle of the algorithm is briefly introduced, and the optimization problem obtained hereinbefore is transformed into a convex optimization that can be solved by the ADMM algorithm. A radio resource allocation scheduling scheme based on ADMM is proposed.

3.1   Principle of the ADMM

The ADMM algorithm [11] is a simple and effective method, which is very suitable for solving distributed convex optimization problems, especially large-scale problems in related fields.

The ADMM algorithm solves functions in the form:

$$\min_{x_1,x_2} f_1(x_1) + f_2(x_2)$$

$$\text{s.t.} Ax_1 + Bx_2 = c$$

(12)

where variables $x_1 \in R^{m \times 1}$ and $x_2 \in R^{r \times 1}$, where $A \in R^{p \times m}$, $B \in R^{p \times r}$, and $c \in R^{p \times 1}$. The augmented Lagrangian is given as:

$$L_\rho(x_1, x_2, y) = f(x_1) + g(x_2) + y^T(Ax_1 + Bx_2 - c)$$

$$+ \tfrac{\rho}{2}\|Ax_1 + Bx_2 - c\|_2^2$$

(13)

After scaling the augmented Lagrangian dual variable and combining the quadratic terms, the ADMM can be slightly modified to become scaled form. At this time, the augmented Lagrangian:

$$L_\rho(x_1, x_2, \mu) = f_1(x_1) + f_2(x_2)$$

$$- \tfrac{\rho}{2}\|\mu\|_2^2 + \tfrac{\rho}{2}\|x_1 - x_2 + \mu\|_2^2$$

(14)

where $\mu = \frac{1}{\rho}y$ denotes the scaled-dual variable. In this case, according to parameters μ, ADMM is further expanded as:

$$x_1^{t+1} := \arg\min_{x_1}(f_1(x_1) + \tfrac{\rho}{2}\|Ax_1 + Bx_2^t - c + \mu^t\|_2^2)$$

$$x_2^{t+1} := \arg\min_{x_2}(f_2(x_2) + \tfrac{\rho}{2}\|Ax_1^{t+1} + Bx_2 - c + \mu^t\|_2^2)$$

$$\mu^{t+1} := \mu^t + Ax_1^{t+1} + Bx_2^{t+1} - c$$

(15)

There is no essential difference between the scaled form and the previous form, while the scaled form is more efficient and convenient to use and will be used in this paper.

3.2   Problem Soving via ADMM

Before using the ADMM algorithm to solve the optimization problem, Eq. (11) can be rewritten as:

$$\min_{a_{k,s,n}, p_{k,s,n}} -G(\tilde{A}, \tilde{P})$$

$$\text{s.t.}$$

$$C1, C2, C3, C4, C5$$

(16)

Algorithm 1. Radio resource scheduling according to ADMM.

1: Initialization: Initialize the value of matrix A and matrix B; each SBS k gets the channel state information of all terminals; then initialize $\mathbf{x}^0$, $\mathbf{z}^0$, μ^0 and $\rho > 0$;
2: **for** $t = 0, 1, 2, ...,$ **do**
3:    **while** $F(A, P) > \xi$ (stop criterion threshold) **do**
4:       1) calculate $\mathbf{x}^{t+1}$ according to formula (20)
5:       2) take $\mathbf{x}^{t+1}$ and μ^t into the formula (21), update $\mathbf{z}^{t+1}$;
6:       3) update μ^{t+1} via (22);
7:    **end while**
8:    if $F(A, P) > \xi$;
9:    To the last step;
10: **end for**
11: Output optimized subchannel matrix A and power matrix P;

where $-G(\tilde{A}, \tilde{P}) = \lambda P_T - C_T$. According to [12] the formula can be expressed as:

$$\lambda P_T - C_T = \lambda(\sum_k p_{C,k} + \sum_k \sum_s \sum_n a_{k,s,n} p_{k,s,n})$$

$$\tag{17}$$

$$-a_{k,s,n} \sum_k \sum_s \sum_n (C^1_{k,s,n} + C^2_{k,s,n})$$

Then an indicator function $f(z)$ is given, when $z \in \Psi$ ($\Psi = C1 \cap C2 \cap C3 \cap C4 \cap C5$), $f(z) = 0$; otherwise, $f(z) = +\infty$. The optimization problem (16) can be rewritten as

$$\min_{a_{k,s,n}, p_{k,s,n}} -G(\tilde{A}, \tilde{P}) + f(z)$$

$$\tag{18}$$

$$s.t. X - z = 0$$

where X is a variable vector containing substitution variables $\{a_{k,s,n}, p_{k,s,n}\}$; The same factor z is an auxiliary vector, including auxiliary variables $\{z_a, z_p\}$. We can get the augmented Lagrangian in scaled form:

$$L_\rho(X, z, \mu) = -G(\tilde{A}, \tilde{P}) + f(z)$$

$$-\frac{\rho}{2}\|\mu\|_2^2 + \frac{\rho}{2}\|X - z + \mu\|_2^2$$

$$\tag{19}$$

where μ denotes the scaled dual-variable vector, including scaled dual-variables $\{\mu_a, \mu_p\}$, and ρ denotes a constant penalty parameter. The iterations of scaled form can be formulated as

$$X^{t+1} := \arg\min_x \{-G(\tilde{A}, \tilde{P})$$

$$+\frac{\rho}{2}\sum_k \sum_s \sum_n [(a_{k,s,n} - z_a^t + \mu_a^t)^2$$

$$\tag{20}$$

$$+(p_{k,s,n} - z_p^t + \mu_p^t)^2]\}$$

$$z^{t+1} := \arg\min_{z}\{\frac{\varrho}{2}\sum_{k}\sum_{s}\sum_{n}[(a_{k,s,n}^{t+1} - z_a + \mu_a^t)^2$$

$$+(p_{k,s,n}^{t+1} - z_p + \mu_p^t)^2]\} \tag{21}$$

$$\mu^{t+1} := \mu^t + \mathrm{x}^{t+1} - z^{t+1} \tag{22}$$

Based on the above analysis, we can summarize Algorithm 1. The convergence and effectiveness of the radio resource scheduling according to ADMM will be discussed in the next section.

4   Simulation Results

In this section, we prove the tendency and effectiveness of the proposed radio resource allocation scheduling scheme by giving simulation results. WiFi system is randomly distributed in the macro cell. Single SBS coverage radius d_1 and d_2 are 200 m and 20 m. The maximum transmit power of the macro BS is 8.91 mW, and maximum transmit power of the small BS is 2.95 mW. The AWGN power is 3.98 W. The unlicensed band path loss calculation formula is $G(d) = 15.3 + 50\log_2(d)$ [15]. The interference threshold ξ of the WiFi system is -77 dB.

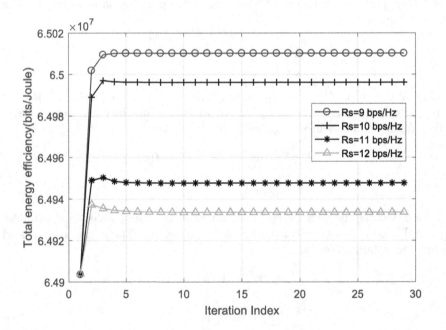

Fig. 2. Total energy efficiency versus iteration index with different QoS demands.

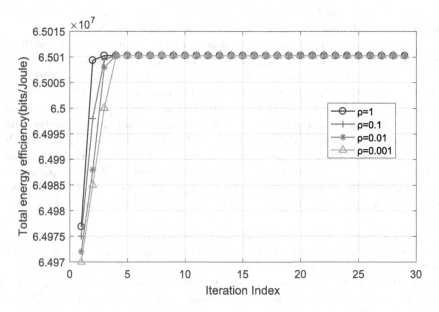

Fig. 3. Convergence of the algorithm versus iteration index with different ρ.

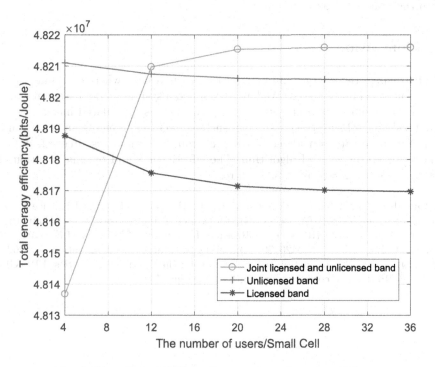

Fig. 4. The effect of SBS small users on total energy efficiency.

In Fig. 2, the total EE versus the number of iteration with different size QoS demands is illustrated. As shown in Fig. 2, the smaller the QoS requirement is, the faster the curve converges under the same number of iterations. In addition, we can find that after multiple iterations, the curve value with small QoS requirement is outperform than the QoS requirement. The change in QoS requirements does not affect the convergence iterations of the proposed algorithm.

In Fig. 3, we want to verify the action of Lagrangian parameter ρ on the curve tendency rate. Through observation, we can see that the parameter ρ has a significant influence on the tendency speed of the proposed algorithm. The larger the ρ value, the faster the convergence speed. The smaller the ρ value, the more iterations are needed. It can be seen that the selection of the parameter ρ value is directly related to the performance of the algorithm. This effect will be more obvious in the scenario where large-scale small cells and WiFi systems coexist.

Figure 4 shows the effect of SBS small users on total energy efficiency. For ease of comparison, the system EE in the licensed band scenario and the system energy efficiency in the unlicensed band scenario are also listed. From Fig. 4, we can see that when the number of users per SBS reaches a threshold, the total EE of the system is higher than that of the other two scenarios in joint licensed frequency band and unlicensed frequency band. Due to the greater bandwidth, the total EE of the network in the unlicensed band scenario is always higher than the unlicensed band scenario.

5   Conclusion

In this paper, the energy efficiency (EE) in small cells with WiFi unlicensed band sharing is investigated. We have developed a system model based on which the optimization system energy efficiency function is formulated into a convex optimization problem, the constraints such as QoS requirements and maximum transmit power are considered. Then we propose a radio resource scheduling scheme based on ADMM algorithm. The effectiveness and optimal solution of the method are shown by simulation results.

Acknowledgment. This work is supported by the National Natural Science Foundation of China (61822104, 61771044), the Young Elite Scientist Sponsorship Program by CAST (2016QNRC001), the Research Foundation of Ministry of Education of China & China Mobile (MCM20170108), Beijing Natural Science Foundation (L172025, L172049), and the Fundamental Research Funds for the Central Universities (FRF-GF-17-A6, RC1631). The corresponding author is Haijun Zhang.

References

1. Zhang, H., Chu, X., Guo, W., Wang, S.: Coexistence of Wi-Fi and heterogeneous small cell networks sharing unlicensed spectrum. IEEE Commun. Mag. **53**(3), 158–164 (2015)
2. Hwang, I., Song, B., Soliman, S.S.: A holistic view on hyper-dense heterogeneous and small cell networks. IEEE Commun. Mag. **51**(6), 20–27 (2013)
3. Hajmohammad, S., Elbiaze, H.: Unlicensed spectrum splitting between femtocell and Wi-Fi. In: IEEE International Conference on Communications (ICC), pp. 1883–88, June 2013
4. Zhang, R., Wang, M., Cai, L.X., Zheng, Z., Shen, X., Xie, L.-L.: LTE-unlicensed: the future of spectrum aggregation for cellular networks. IEEE Wirel. Commun. **22**(3), 150–159 (2015)
5. Small Cell Forum: Integrated femto-WiFi (IFW) networks. Whitepaper at smallcellforum.org, February 2012
6. Zhang, Y., Wang, H.M., Zheng, T.X., Yang, Q.: Energy-efficient transmission design in non-orthogonal multiple access. IEEE Trans. Veh. Technol. **PP**(99), 1 (2016)
7. Fang, F., Zhang, H., Cheng, J., Leung, V.C.M.: Energy-efficient resource allocation for downlink non-orthogonal multiple access network. IEEE Trans. Commun. **64**(9), 3722–3732 (2016)
8. Dong, Y., Zhang, H., Hossain, M.J., Cheng, J., Leung, V.C.M.: Energy efficient resource allocation for OFDMA full duplex distributed antenna systems with energy recycling. In: 2015 IEEE Global Communications Conference (GLOBECOM), San Diego, CA, pp. 1-6 (2015)
9. Mollanoori, M., Ghaderi, M.: Uplink scheduling in wireless networks with successive interference cancellation. IEEE Trans. Mob. Comput. **13**(5), 1132–1144 (2014)
10. Zhang, H., Huang, S., Jiang, C., Long, K., Leung, V.C.M., Poor, H.V.: Energy efficient user association and power allocation in millimeter-wave-based ultra dense networks with energy harvesting base stations. IEEE J. Sel. Areas Commun. **35**(9), 1936–1947 (2017)
11. Eckstein, J.: Augmented Lagrangian and alternating direction methods for convex optimization: a tutorial and some illustrative computational results. Rutgers University, Piscataway, NJ, USA, Technical report, December 2012
12. Yu, Y., Peng, M., Li, J., Cheng, A., Wang, C.: Resource allocation optimization for hybrid access mode in heterogeneous networks. In: IEEE Wireless Communications and Networking Conference (WCNC), pp. 1243–1248, March 2015
13. Liang, C., Yu, F.R., Yao, H., Han, Z.: Virtual resource allocation in information-centric wireless networks with virtualization. IEEE Trans. Veh. Technol. **65**(12), 9902–9914 (2016)
14. Liu, F., Erkip, E., Beluri, M., Yang, R., Bala, E.: Dual-band femtocell traffic balancing over licensed and unlicensed bands. In: Proceedings of the IEEE ICC, Ottawa, ON, Canada, pp. 6809–6814, 10–15 June 2012
15. Liu, F., Bala, E., Erkip, E., Beluri, M.C., Yang, R.: Small-cell traffic balancing over licensed and unlicensedbands. IEEE Trans. Veh. Technol. **64**(12), 5850–5865 (2015)

Security and Privacy in Emerging 5G Applications

TME²R: Trust Management-Based Energy Efficient Routing Scheme in Fog-Assisted Industrial Wireless Sensor Network

Weidong Fang[1,2], Wuxiong Zhang[1,2], Wei Chen[3(✉)], Yang Liu[1,2], and Chaogang Tang[3]

[1] Key Laboratory of Wireless Sensor Network and Communication, Shanghai Institute of Microsystem and Information Technology, Chinese Academy of Sciences, Shanghai 200051, China
[2] Shanghai Research Center for Wireless Communication, Shanghai 201210, China
[3] School of Computer Science and Technology, China University of Mining and Technology, Xuzhou 221116, Jiangsu, China
chenw@cumt.edu.cn

Abstract. Fog-assisted Industrial Wireless Sensor Network (F-IWSN) is a novel wireless sensor network (WSN) in the industry. It not only can more efficiently reduce information transmission latency, but also can more conducively achieve real-time control and rapid resource scheduling. However, similar to other distributed networks, it also faces enormous security challenges, especially from internal attacks. The differences from those traditional security schemes are that, one is the trade-off between security, transmission performance and energy consumption to meet the requirements of information convergence and control, the other constructs a multi-dimensional selective forwarding scheme to achieve the real time transmission. In this paper, we propose a Gaussian distribution-based comprehensive trust management system (GDTMS) for F-IWSN. Furthermore, in its trust decision, the analytic hierarchy process is introduced to achieve the trade-off between security, transmission performance and energy consumption. The proposed trade-off can effectively select the secure and robust relay node. Namely, Trust Management-based Energy Efficient Routing Scheme (TME²R). In addition, GDTMS is also applicable to defending against bad mouthing attacks. Simulation results show that, the comprehensive performance of GDTMS is better than other similar algorithms, it can effectively prevent the appearance of network holes, and balance the network load, promote the survivability of the network.

Keywords: 5G · Industrial wireless sensor network · Fog computing · Secure routing protocol · Trust management

1 Introduction

As the next-generation broadband communication network, the main goal of 5G networks is to keep end users connected. The devices that 5G networks will support in the future are much more than just smartphones - it also supports a variety of smart

© ICST Institute for Computer Sciences, Social Informatics and Telecommunications Engineering 2019
Published by Springer Nature Switzerland AG 2019. All Rights Reserved
V. C. M. Leung et al. (Eds.): 5GWN 2019, LNICST 278, pp. 155–173, 2019.
https://doi.org/10.1007/978-3-030-17513-9_11

terminals. In the past few years, with the 5G networks development, industrial wireless sensor network (IWSN) have been successfully deployed in industrial fields, such for safety protection, production supervision, data acquisition, and control etc. The sensed information can communicate from the nodes to the supervisory control and data acquisition systems for processing and controlling purposes. Based on these observations, the central manager can control the producing processes, or directly command a mobile worker at the plant. Hence, the risk of equipment damage is reduced, and efficiency and productivity are increased. IWSN bring several advantages over conventional wired industrial networks in terms of infrastructure (no long cable runs), ease of troubleshooting, and rapid deployment [1, 2]. Furthermore, combined with cloud computing, IWSNs can offer more economical solutions in many harsh environments where it is difficult to deploy wires.

The cloud computing has inherent advantages: elasticity and scalability, and three key facts, including IssS (Infrastructure as a Service), PaaS (Platform as a Service), SaaS (Software as a Service). It has provided many opportunities and conveniences for the manufacturing industry. However, it is limited by the distance between the terminal devices and the cloud, which will cause significant latency, and bring many issues for latency-sensitive applications (i.e. real-time control, field parameters). Currently, the cloud computing paradigm can hardly meet the requirements regarding to the mobility support, the location awareness and the low latency. In addition, it alone does not support 5G and AI (Artificial Intelligence). Benefiting from distributed computing, the emerging fog computing [3] can tackle the above issues. Fog is "cloud closer to ground". it is a novel paradigm extending traditional cloud computing and services to the edge of the network. Similar to Cloud, Fog provides computational, networking and storage services to terminal-users. In a sense, fog computing is also a paradigm of 5G flat management. However, different from Cloud, the fog provides additional advantages such as distributed characters, which is the key feature of the fog computing.

Due to its distributed feature, fog computing enable providing services outside the cloud, at the edge of the network and closer to terminal devices., It has several technical innovations with the following aspects: (1) Storage, (2) Communication, (3) Control, configuration, measurement and management. Compared with some previous technologies, such as storing data primarily in cloud data centers, routing over the internet backbone, controlling primarily by network gateways (i.e. those gateways in the LTE core network), fog computing can use one or more collaborative terminal-user clients or near-user edge devices to carry out a substantial amount of storage, communication, control, configuration, measurement and management. Hence, it can provide low latency, location awareness, and improved quality-of-services (QoS) for streaming and real time applications, as well as the real time big data analytics. It also supports densely distributed data collection. Fog computing is well positioned for many application scenarios: it is strongly useful in connecting vehicle, smart grid and wireless sensor and actuator networks (WSAN) [3]; it has great potential in smart building and software-defined networking (SDN) [4]. Moreover, the augmented reality (AR) and real-time video analytics, the content delivery and caching, and the mobile big data analytics also benefit from concept of fog computing [5]. In a word, the fog computing is introduced into IWSN, namely fog-assisted Industrial Wireless Sensor Network (F-IWSN). A typical architecture of F-IWSN is shown in Fig. 1.

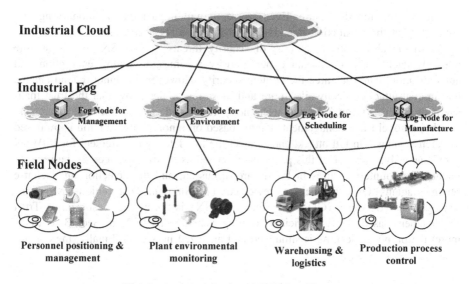

Fig. 1. A typical fog-based IWSN architecture

Practically, just as classical IWSN, F-IWSN is more preferred in harsh industrial environments, which involve high temperatures, high humidity, stronger noise, and so on. These extreme conditions can cause unpredictable interference on wireless channels. Moreover, the monitoring and controlling process with maximum accuracy is required in industry, which also reduce the risk of equipment damage. Some critical industrial applications need the real-time communication, that is, a task must be done within a specific time interval. These features demand the reliability, latency and real-time communication of IWSN. Many technologies are researched to meet the above requirements of IWSN. Currently, there are three accepted standards: Wireless HART [6], International Society of Automation (ISA) 100.11a [7], and WIA-PA [8]. The Wireless HART is a mesh network which utilizes the time-division multiple access (TDMA) to transmit data packets and route them by using graph routing. The ISA100.11a uses TDMA with variable time-slot, and transmitted paths are made by the graph routing and source routing. The 6LoWPAN is utilized to provide the advantage of Internet protocol (IP) into the wireless system. The WIA-PA supports the hybrid topology of star and mesh, and it exploits hybrid mode of CDMA and CSMA. All of them use IEEE 802.15.4 standard at PHY and MAC layer under the 2.4-GHz frequency spectrum.

Compared with the wireless sensor network (WSN), F-IWSN not only has stronger security requirements, but also face more security challenges. F-IWSN needs to detect the malicious nodes quickly, and defend against it effectively, when the network is invaded or attacked. The harsh deployed environments lead to the obvious degradation of the wireless channel quality, which increases the packet loss rate. Hence, it is very difficult to distinguish between the normal noise and the jamming attacks [9], especially, those internal attacks (i.e. Black hole attack, selective forwarding attack, and tampering attack). In addition, once these unauthorized nodes access F-IWSN, it will lead to information disclosure. Even worse, it will impact on the monitoring and controlling of the production line, and result in the safety accidents.

From the above analysis, most of security threats in F-IWSN come from the internal attacks. The traditional cyber security schemes, involving encryption and authentication, can guarantee the content security. However, it cannot defend against the internal attacks. Meanwhile, more and more researches show that the trust management scheme is an effective technology to defend against the internal attack. Hereby, a novel trust management scheme based on binomial distribution is proposed to defend against On-Off attack, and to meet the low latency requirement for F-IWSN simultaneously. The rest of this paper is organized as follows. In Sect. 2, the security threats and countermeasures in IWSN are discussed, and the detection and defense schemes against On-Off attack are reviewed. The Binomial Distribution-based Trust Management Scheme (GDTMS) for F-IWSN is proposed, especially Trust Management-based Energy Efficient Routing Scheme (TME^{2}R) in Sect. 3. Furthermore, the proposed scheme is simulated and analyzed in Sect. 4. Finally, the conclusion is given in Sect. 5.

2   Related Works

In this section, we will investigate the security threats and countermeasures in IWSN in terms of internal attacks and external attacks. Moreover, we will review and analyze the trust management.

2.1   Security Threats and Countermeasures in IWSN

1. SECURITY THREATS

For IWSN, the security threats come from the security attacks, which are classified as external attacks and internal attacks.

(a) *External attacks*

Under external attacks, the malicious nodes are usually unauthorized or Illegal. The external attacks consist of passive attacks and active attacks. For passive attacks, the attacker can 'listen' and analyze sensed information without interference, including eavesdropping and traffic analysis. In contrast, the active attacks that the attacker launch disrupts network functionality by introducing just as jamming attacks and power exhaustion attacks.

(1) *Passive attacks*

Eavesdropping attack: an attacker wiretaps network to obtain information in illegal ways [10]. This is due to that the broadcast characteristic and openness of the wireless medium, IWSN is vulnerable to be eavesdropped [9].

Traffic Analysis: an attacker can obtain the source and destination node addresses and route by monitoring and analyzing PDUs, and further deduce the network topology and routing algorithm to launch the tamper attack. Also because of the openness nature of wireless channels, the attacker does not need a physical link to analyze traffic actually.

(2) *Active attacks*

Jamming attack: an attacker intentionally transmits wireless signals for disrupting the data communications between the sensor node and sink nodes in IWSN. Since 2.4 GHz is usually facilitated in IWSN, the attacker can launch this attack to interference the network using Wi-Fi or Bluetooth devices which are under the same frequency spectrum.

Power exhaustion attack [11]: The lifetime of the network depends on the battery power of the node, so an attack can make the node to consume its battery power with transmitting unnecessary signals rapidly. This attack is unique for resource-constrained nodes as it is performed by utilizing vulnerabilities of wireless networks.

(b) *Internal attacks*

The internal attacks are mainly launched by the compromised nodes. Compared with disabled nodes, compromised nodes actively seek to paralyze the network. They can achieve to modify the traffic flow and disrupt services by selective forwarding, tampering, or replaying.

Modifying the traffic flow: The selective forwarding attack: refers to the malicious node selectively to discard some received packets or completely discard the received packets without forwarding. The tamper attack can maliciously modify the transmitting data packet via the network. In wormhole attack, an attacker establishes a hypothetical tunnel with two ends through the wireless link. Multi-hop routing nodes think that there is a single hop between them. Thereby, the malicious node attracts nearby nodes to transmit data packets via this wrong path, and achieve to destroy the network. An attacker that launched Sybil attack masquerades as nodes which have multiple identities, to destroy the reputation system of peer-to-peer (P2P) network.

Disrupting service: any DoS attacks can cause IWSN not to provide services properly. There are two DoS attacks in IWSN. The former is a malicious node acting as the proxy node to deny the Access-Request of normal nodes. The latter is an attacker tampering the DLPDU (Data Link Protocol Data Unit), recalculating CRC, and transmits these packets continuously. The receiver always checks the integrity of packets, which are transmitted by malicious nodes. By checking the wrong MIC (Message Integrity Code), the receiver discards the wrong packets and requests for the packet retransmission.

(1) *Countermeasures*

In this part, we review the security services that are provided by IEEE STD 802.15.4, and then discuss the corresponding countermeasures for each attack mentioned above.

(a) *Basic security service by IEEE STD 802.15.4*

IEEE STD 802.15.4, utilized by the above mentioned three standards, provides two security services: point-to-point security and end to-end security.

(1) Point-to-point transmission security

In the data-link layer, the data encryption and MIC are deployed to guarantee the point-to-point data security using AES-CCM mode (Counter with CBC-MAC). This mode involves two parts: in Cipher Block Chaining-Message Authentication Code (CBC-MAC) mode, the string that includes key, DLPDU header, DLPDU payload and nonce is divided into several 16-byte sub-strings. One of the 16-byte sub-strings are set to calculate MIC by using the key and AES in order to provide the integrity check, meanwhile, the nonce is introduced to defend against the replay attack. In counter mode, the 16-byte sub-string in CBC-MAC mode and the encrypted counter are taken as the input to calculate the cipher text to achieve the confidentiality of the information. The point-to-point transportation security can detect the unidentified devices, which try to access the network without authentication, and defend against eavesdropping attacks for transmitting data in wireless medium.

(2) End-to-end transmission security

In the application layer (AL), the data encryption and MIC are used to ensure the communication security between the source node and the destination node. Similarly, the AES-CCM mode as above mentioned can be deployed. MIC is calculated over AL key and AL payload to implement the integrity check.

(b) *Countermeasures*

Eavesdropping: two above security services can defend against the eavesdropping attacks. Regularly updating key can make that it is difficult for an attacker to obtain it. In addition, a key can be also generated based on stochastic physical characteristics of the wireless propagation [9]. The other idea is that make the signal difficult to be captured for an attacker. For example, the frequency-hopping scheme is used in WIA-PA [10]. Besides, the specifically-designed noise may be generated to interfere with the eavesdropper without impacting on the receiving of the sink node. In addition, the beam-forming technology may be exploited to transmit the signal in a specific direction, so that the sink node receives the constructive interference signal, whereas the eavesdropper receives the destructive interference signal. However, both of them consume additional energy for generating the artificial noise, or exhibit a high computational complexity with the beam-forming design. Therefore, the diversity technology can be used to solve these issues. Currently, the diversity technology is commonly used to improve the security. They include multi-user diversity, multi-antenna diversity, and cooperative diversity [12]. Sun et al. [13] applied fountain coding to achieve secure cooperative transmission in IWSN.

Traffic analysis: point-to-point security mechanism can defend against traffic analysis effectively. However, the intermediate routing node must decrypt the data packets to obtain the destination address and the routing information, and transmits them to the destination node after they have been encrypted. It can bring additional time overhead.

Jamming and power exhaustion attack: the jamming or interference signal will result in abnormal changes of the received signal strength (RSS) and packet error rate (PER) in IWSN [14], then further these two measurements could be used to detect the jamming power exhaustion attack. Frequency hopping is an effective anti-interference paradigm. The carrier frequency of wireless signal can be changed by a known pseudo-random sequence in the sink node. In addition, the direct sequence spread spectrum (DSSS) technology can spread a transmit signal over an extremely wide frequency bandwidth. In this way, the transmit signal will have a very low power spectral density. It is difficult to demodulate the DSSS modulated signal from the background interference for the jamming attackers, so that they cannot track and interfere with the information transmission between sensor nodes and sink nodes. Chiwewe et al. [15] proposed and integrated cognitive radio technique into IWSNs to enhance the detection and defense ability for the interference. Zhang et al. [16] considered the resulting optimization problem is nonconvex for the scenario with cooperative jamming, and then proposed a heuristic algorithm based on alternating optimization.

Selective forwarding and tempering: malicious nodes can be removed by authorization and authentication. The security administrator has been set up to implement this work in the above three standards [17]. The network administrator is responsible for regularly collecting device status to evaluate and diagnose the network performance. This approach can detect and mitigate this attack to some extent. In addition, the check for MIC could guarantee the data integrity, and effectively defend against data tampering. In case of no access to key information, it is very difficult to launch a tampering attack for an attacker. Besides, the authorization and authentication for all nodes can defend against wormhole attacks and Sybil attacks.

DoS attack: authentication for nodes can defend against DoS attack in some extent. Lee et al. proposed FlexiCast [18], which presents an energy-efficient method to check the integrity of software objects being installed by reprogrammable sensor nodes in industrial wireless active sensor networks.

From the above analysis, the security guarantee in IWSN mainly comes from encryption, authorization, authentication, signal processing, as well as some management regulations. Admittedly, these approaches can improve the content security of IWSN. However, they are suitable for defending against external attacks, and seem powerless for internal attacks. This is due to the fact that the internal attacks are launched by compromised nodes [19], which can steal secrets from the encrypted data passed them, report other normal nodes as compromised nodes, and breach routing by introducing many routing attacks. Meanwhile, the encryption, authorization and authentication are deployed to require more computing and storage resources, this is an enormous challenge for the resource-constrained IWSN.

More and more researches show that the trust management technology is a better approach to defend against the internal attacks. In next sub-section, we will discuss a typical internal attack – On-Off attack, and analyze various defense schemes (including trust management) against it.

2.2 Trust Management

Currently, one of the effective ways to defend against internal attack is trust management technologies, which are involved trust model, trust management scheme, and protocol optimization.

1. TRUST MODEL

Ganeriwal et al. proposed the reputation-based framework for high integrity sensor networks (RFSN) [20]. Then, based on Beta distribution and Bayesian formula, the Beta reputation system for sensor networks (BRSN) was proposed. BRSN is a simple trust evaluation system and it has been widely studied and used. Firoozi et al. still follows the classical trust model Beta reputation, use time windows to subdivide time slot in a hierarchical network, and the trust values of different clusters are averaged and normalized. [21]. Sinha proposed the Gaussian trust and reputation for fading MIMO WSNs [22]. Based on multivariate Gaussian distribution and Bayesian theorem, they considered the impact of the MIMO wireless fading channel, furthermore, they combined the reputation information on direct and indirect. The reputation and trust value are also calculated. This method can effectively isolate the malicious node, but the calculation process is too complex for energy-limited WSNs. There are other representative researches. Janani et, al. presents an efficient distributed trust computation with Bayesian and Evidence theorem, on hexagonally clustered MANET [23]. Mahmud et al., proposed TMM to utilize both node behavioral trust and data trust, which are estimated using ANFIS including the Beta reputation, and weighted additive methods respectively, to assess the nodes trustworthiness [24]. In addition, Wang et al. used a popular light-weight trust management mechanism–Bayesian trust model [25]. Zhu et al. [26] put forward a rank-based application-driven resilient reputation framework model for wireless sensor networks (RARRM). The model is based on application-driven. The different requirements could rank trust values.

Umarani et al. established enhanced beta trust model (EBTM) to detect malicious attacks [27]. In this model, the neighbor node was selected by the sensor node based on trust information in the course of communication. Moreover, the state of neighbor node is periodically updated. The recovery procedure is incorporated to raise the throughput of the network.

2. TRUST MANAGEMENT SCHEME/SYSTEM

Recently, many researches on trust management schemes are emerging. Within the hierarchical network the cells were divided evenly by grid in plane space, and the data in the cell were processed [21]. Cell distance and number of non-empty cells were defined for processing. And special situations into consideration, such as, the level of trustworthiness about nodes and sleep mode. This mechanism efficiently assesses reliability of nodes based on the received observations, while DiSLIP provides efficient performance in detecting nodes that report different events. A secured PKI system [23] is designed in the paper by applying the proposed trust management scheme in terms of certificate revocation. By evaluating the hybrid trust value with the trust evaluation vector method, this mechanism is effectively integrated into the hexagonal clusters to secure the PKI framework and detects and classifies the misbehavior, either selfishness or malicious, to take revocation actions on those nodes. Mahmud [24] et al. introduced an adaptive neuro-fuzzy inference system (ANFIS). Brain-inspired trust management model (TMM) to secure IoT devices and relay nodes, and to ensure data reliability. The proposed TMM ensures the function of identifying malicious nodes in the communication network. ETMRM [25] firstly extend the Sensor Flow tables to realize a lightweight trust monitoring and evaluation scheme at the node level and propose a centralized trust management scheme to detect and isolate the malicious nodes based on the trust information collected from sensor nodes. Based on game theory, Duan [28] proposed the trust derivation scheme. In this scheme, they analyzed the network security requirements and secure scheme. Then, they established a risk model to stimulate the cooperation of WSNs node to derive an optimal number of cooperating nodes. Finally, the game theoretic approach was applied to the trust scheme derivation process to reduce the overhead of the process. Fang et al. Beta-based Trust and Reputation Evaluation System (BTRES) [29], Simulation results show that the use of BTRES could effectively maximize the defense of internal attacks from compromised nodes to improve the WSN information security. Li et al. [30] presented a data-centric trust evaluation mechanism in WSNs (DTSN). They pointed out that WSN was a data-centric network, and the traditional trust evaluation based on entities could not suitable for WSNs. Zia et al. [31] proposed a solution based on communal reputation and individual trust (CRIT) for WSNs. By using watch dog, the nodes' behaviors were monitored, and each node had a trust table and a reputation table for its neighbor nodes.

Fang et al. proposed a trust management scheme to defend against On-Off attack based on BETA distribution [32]. In this scheme, a control factor was introduced to prevent trust value increasing so fast for the malicious node, in order to mitigate the damage of On-Off attack, In Addition, they h proposed a time-window-based resilient trust management scheme (TRTMS) to defend against the type of attacks [33].

3. TRUST-BASED ROUTING

Wang proposed - An Energy-efficient Trust Management and Routing Mechanism (ETMRM) [25] for SDWSNs proposed the ETMRM-An Energy-efficient Trust Routing Mechanism for SDWSNs, considering the node's residual energy and trust level to guarantee the transmission of data traffic, detecting the internal network attacks, such as Greyhole attacks, Blackhole attacks, new-flow attacks, efficiently. ETMRM improves the packet delivery ratio, reduces and balances the energy consumption, prolongs the network lifetime, and suffers lower control overhead.

Based on intrusion detection, Gheorghe carried out an adaptive trust management protocol (ATMP) [34], which is applied in TinyOS system, and it can defend against many kinds of attacks Fang et al. represented a reputation management scheme [35]. The proposed scheme described the initialization, updating, and storage for the reputation value, as well as the punishment and redemption of malicious nodes. This proposed scheme could apply to the Security Privacy In Sensor Network (SPIN) protocol, therefore a novel trust enhanced routing protocol was proposed based on reputation. The simulation indicated that the trust enhanced routing protocol could enhance the security, improve the data forwarding rate and delivery success rate in distrusted environment. Tajeddine et al. put forward a centralized TRust And Competence-based Energy-efficient routing scheme for wireless sensor networks (TRACE) [36]. In this scheme, they used centralized management of sinks to make routing more efficient and secure. Subsequently, they proposed a centralized trust-based efficient routing protocol for wireless sensor networks (CENTER) [37]. In the proposed protocol, the BS (Base Station) calculates different quality metrics - namely the maliciousness, cooperation, compatibility and approximates the battery life, which can evaluate the data trust and forwarding trust values of each node. Then, the BS used an effective technique to isolate all "bad" nodes, which is misbehaving or malicious based on their history. At last, the BS uses an efficient method to disseminate updated routing information, indicating the uplinks and the next hop downlink for every node. In addition, Li proposed a novel authentication protocol for healthcare applications using wireless medical sensor networks with user anonymity [38]. Gerrigagoitia proposed a new IDS design based on reputation and trust of the different nodes of a network for decision-making and analysis of possible sources of malicious attacks [39]. Arijit put forward a trust and reputation based collaborating computing model. The detection of malicious nodes along with trust and reputation analysis of WSN makes this model robust and secure.

The trust management technology had been researched for many years. In distributed networks, the trust generally refers to the trustworthiness of entity. The trust value is unusually a variable. It determines two nodes interact or not. Currently, many scholars focus on how to establish a trust management system, or how to defend against malicious attacks. Unfortunately, they rarely pay attention to the study of trust decision. Moreover, we argue that trust value is a few measurable metric of security.

Otherwise, joint fog computer and industrial WSN provide a novel applied architecture. This characteristic of application is lower energy, stronger security and higher transmission performance. Hence, we first propose a Gaussian distribution-based comprehensive trust management system (GDTMS), and then give a trust management-based energy efficient routing (TME^{2}R) scheme in Fog-assisted Industrial Wireless Sensor Network.

3 TME^{2}R for Fog-Assisted Industrial Wireless Sensor Network

Assume there is an interaction between node i and node j in the current sensor network environment; Node i calculates the trust value of node j. and then decides whether to interact with it. First, the node i calculates a direct trust value based on historical interaction information with node j. The neighbor node of node j is then queried for the trust value of node j to obtain the indirect trust value of node j and this information is used for trust value integration.

3.1 Initial

The current sensor network environment is assumed that, if there is an interaction between node i and node j. First of all, node i calculate the trust value of node j and then decides whether to interact with it. Moreover, the node i calculates a direct trust value based on historical interaction information with node j. Furthermore, it query the common neighbor node of node j to gain the trust value of node j. In order to obtain the indirect trust value of node j and this information is used for trust value integration.

$(a + b)$ times interact between node i and node j, where, a represents the number of successful interactions, and b represents the number of unsuccessful, and obey the Gaussian distribution as follows:

$$N\left(\frac{a}{a+b}, \frac{ab}{(a+b)^2}\right) \tag{1}$$

3.2 Modelling and Updating Direct Reputation

Based on a known set of interactive information, we model Gaussian distribution. The variance is $u^2 = \frac{ab}{(a+b)^2}$ is expectation is given by $v = \frac{a}{(a+b)}$. Assume that the reputation distribution of node i relative to node j is $R_{ij} \sim N(\mu_j, \sigma_j^2)$, $(R_{ij})1, (R_{ij})2, \ldots, (R_{ij})t$ is the sample of R_{ij} and the parameter of the prior distribution $\mu_{ij} \sim N(v, u^2)$. It is assumed that the reputation is initialized with a Gaussian distribution of $N(0.5, 0.25)$.

3.3 Trust Transfer

During the time period t, node i and node j interact $a + b$ times, where a and b are the number of cooperation and non-cooperation, respectively. The conditional density of the parameter μ_j is:

$$p((X_{ij})_1, (X_{ij})_2, \cdots (X_{ij})_t | \mu_j) = \frac{1}{(2\pi)^{\frac{t}{2}} \sigma_j^t} \exp\left(-\frac{\sum_{n=1}^{t}((X_{ij})_n - \mu_j)^2}{2\sigma_j^2}\right) \tag{2}$$

μ_j prior distribution is:

$$\pi(\mu_j) = \frac{1}{\sqrt{2\pi}u} \exp\left(-\frac{(\mu_j - v)^2}{2u^2}\right) \tag{3}$$

Posterior probability density:

$$
\begin{aligned}
&\pi(\mu_j | (X_{ij})_1, (X_{ij})_2, \cdots, (X_{ij})_t) \\
&= \frac{p((X_{ij})_1, (X_{ij})_2, \cdots, (X_{ij})_t | \mu_j)\pi(\mu_j)}{\int_{-\infty}^{+\infty} p((X_{ij})_1, (X_{ij})_2, \cdots, (X_{ij})_t | \mu_j)\pi(\mu_j)d\mu_j} \\
&= C \exp\left(-\frac{(\mu_j - s)^2}{2\eta^2}\right)
\end{aligned}
\tag{4}
$$

$$s = \frac{\frac{t}{\delta_j^2}\overline{X} + \frac{v}{u^2}}{\frac{t}{\delta_j^2} + \frac{v}{u^2}} \tag{5}$$

$$\eta = \frac{1}{\frac{t}{\delta_j^2} + \frac{1}{u^2}} \tag{6}$$

where, C is a constant independent of μ_j. It can be seen that the posterior distribution of μ_j is a Gaussian distribution, so the posterior distribution of the reputation obeys the Gaussian distribution.

3.4   Slot

We assume an average time slot, such as $t = 1, 2, 3, 4, 5, 6\ldots$ When the initial setting is $t = 1$, the number of success or failures is 1, $\mu j = 0.5$, $\sigma j = 0.25$, obeying normal distribution of $N(0.5, 0.25)$.

$$A = \frac{t}{0.25}$$
$$B = \frac{(a+b)}{b} \tag{7}$$
$$C = \frac{(a+b)^2}{ab}$$

$\overline{X}$ is ratio, which is the average number of successful interactions for the previous t slots to the total number.

$$DT = s = \frac{A\overline{X} + B}{A + C} \tag{8}$$

For example, when t is 2, $X1$ is (1, 0), then $\overline{X} = \frac{1+1}{1+1} = 1$, yet A = 8, B = 2, C = 9/2, then, DT = 14/17.

3.5   Direct Trust

Here, we define the trust value based on the established mathematical model, that is, the mathematical model established based on the number of interactions at the previous moment - the expectation of the Gaussian distribution:

$$DT_{ij} = \text{expectation}(\mu_j) = s \tag{9}$$

3.6   Aging Weight

Historic observations & Aging weight in Direct information collected

$$S_{ij}^{new} = \alpha S_{ij} + 1$$
$$U_{ij}^{new} = \beta U_{ij} + 1 \tag{10}$$

where, S_{ij} and U_{ij} are the number of successful and failed interactions, respectively. α and β are aging weights. Here, the number of successful interactions and the number of failed interactions between Sij^{new} and Uij^{new} at the current moment, Historic observations correspond to Sij and Uij, plus 1 indicates that the size of the slot is 1 observation.

3.7 Trust Decision

As the only security quantitative indicator, Trust value can have multiple security purposes, such as removing malicious nodes out of trusted table, or canceling it convergence role. However, for Industrial WSN, especially Fog-assisted Industrial WSN, they need secure and efficient transmission, meanwhile, reduce energy consumption.

Hence, based on our previous research, we introduce the multi-dimensions Analytic Hierarchy Process (AHP)

AHP <Trust Value, Energy, Hops, QoS, ToS)>

Where, QoS (Quality of Service) involves more data metric of the transmission layer, such as packet loss rate, and latency. ToS (type of service): in the network layer, the data types transmitted are divided into three categories: text, audio, and video, which are assigned three different priorities of low, medium, and high. All above, full consideration of the actual needs of network transmission represents (Fig. 2).

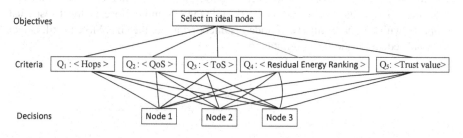

Fig. 2. A trust-based AHP

4 Simulation and Analysis

In this section, we first compare our proposed GDTMS with RFSN (reputation Beta distribution), then we discuss the TME²R routing scheme.

4.1 Gaussian Distribution-Based Trust Management Scheme

We assume that initial Gaussian reputation distribution is N(0.5, 0.25), α and β are both 0.8, the number of interactions is 30, as each interaction continues successfully or unsuccessfully, then we use MATLAB to simulate, the trust value changes as shown: For continuous cooperation and non-cooperation nodes, the changes of trust values completely different. They can reflect the trend of change in a timely manner. Comparing with RFSN, the change of trust value for GDTMS tends to highlight the nodes' behavior, hence, GDTMS can applied in the trusted scheme effectively.

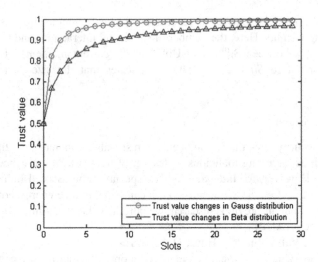

Fig. 3. Comparison of trust value under continuous cooperation

From Figs. 3 and 4, if node j and node i continue to cooperate, the trust value continues to rise steadily. Compared with RFSN, The trust value of the Gaussian distribution is stable at around 0.95 after 5 periods, and the former stabilizes at around 0.95 after 25 periods. For a new network, GDTMS is more close to the latest trust compared with RFSN. Similarly, if node j is uncooperative, the GDTMS can still detect them and reduce to the latest reputation.

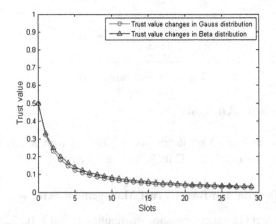

Fig. 4. Comparison of trust value under continuous noncooperation

4.2 Trust Management-Based Energy Efficient Routing Scheme

By using NS2, the improved AHP-based protocol based on the AODV protocol is simulated, in which a certain transmission node A is set to send data to the node B, and each type of data packet is counted according to the Trace record file within a certain period of time. The specific parameters are set as follows.

The above parameters, the abscissa is the network running time, its unit is s (seconds), the ordinate is the network throughput, its unit is b/s (bits per second), and the network transmission rate is set to 500 bits/s. In the proposed AHP-based AODV in this paper, the content of the data packet of the set data packet is reserved for 3 Bytes * 5 = 120 bits as the storage trust value, the current remaining energy of the node, and the destination node. The shortest hop count, end-to-end delay, network transmission data type and other five parameters of the memory space, respectively, is 3 bytes (Fig. 5).

$$Throughput = \frac{actual\_transimission\_data}{overall\_transimission\_data\_packet} \times transimission\_rate \quad (11)$$

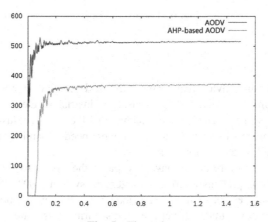

Fig. 5. Throughput

Here, the throughput simulation removes those data packet, which involve the routing establishment and routing maintains, and the routing overhead. Meanwhile, this simulation also removes the five parameters of the AHP-based routing protocol, including storing the trust value, the node's current remaining energy, the required reach of the destination node, as well as actual effective data transmission rate under the condition of the shortest hop count, end-to-end latency. Finally, it represents the network transmission data type (Fig. 6).

$$Energy\_efficiency = \frac{actual\_transimission\_data\_per\_packet}{overall\_transimission\_data\_per\_packet} \quad (12)$$

Similarly, energy efficiency simulation, statistics for each transmitted packet, assuming that each bit of actual transmission consumes a certain amount of energy, then the actual effective energy ratio can be obtained according to the ratio of the effective data size of the transmission to the total transmission data size. To reflect the effectiveness of energy.

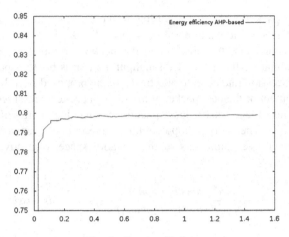

Fig. 6. Energy efficiency.

5   Conclusions

The fog computer can provide real time control and schedule, for industrial wireless sensor network. Unfortunately, the fog-assisted industrial wireless sensor network is still facing many security challenges. Meanwhile, the harsh industrial applications require not only enhanced security, but also higher speed transmission performance of information, as well as energy efficiency.

In this paper, our contributions have two parts, the first is to propose a Gaussian distribution-based comprehensive trust management system (GDTMS). The proposed system could quickly establish the trust management system for normal nodes. The second is to construct the trade-off between the security (trust value), energy (residual energy) and transmission (transmission performance). The trade-off can meet the security requirement for industrial wireless sensor network.

Acknowledgment. Part of this work has been presented at IEEE 18th International Conference on Computer and Information Technology (CIT-2018), July 30 - Aug 03, 2018, Halifax, Canada, [41] This work is partially supported by the National Natural Science Foundation of China (61571004), the Shanghai Natural Science Foundation (No. 17ZR1429100), the Science and Technology Innovation Program of Shanghai (No. 115DZ1100400, No. 17511105903, No. 17DZ1200302), the Scientific Instrument Developing Project of the Chinese Academy of Sciences (No. YJKYYQ20170074) and Fujian Science and Technology Plan STS Program (2017T3009).

References

1. Gungor, V.C., Hancke, G.P.: Industrial wireless sensor networks: challenges, design principles, and technical approaches. IEEE Trans. Ind. Electron. **56**(10), 4258–4265 (2009)
2. Salam, H.A., Khan, B.M.: IWSN - standards, challenges and future. IEEE Potentials **35**(2), 9–16 (2016)

3. Bonomi, F., Milito, R., Zhu, J., Addepalli, S.: Fog computing and its role in the internet of things. In: Proceedings of the 1st Edition the MCC Workshop on Mobile Cloud Computing, pp. 13–16 (2012)
4. Stojmenovic, I., Wen, S.: The fog computing paradigm: scenarios and security issues. Comput. Sci. Inf. Syst. 2, 1–8 (2014)
5. Mouradian, C., Naboulsi, D., Yangui, S., Glitho, R.H., Morrow, M.J., Polakos, P.A.: A Comprehensive Survey on Fog Computing: State-of-the-art and Research Challenges. arXiv preprint arXiv: 1710.11001 (2017)
6. Song, J., Han, S., Mok, A.K., Chen, D., Lucas, M., Nixon, M.: WirelessHART: applying wireless technology in real-time industrial process control. In: Proceedings of Real-Time and Embedded Technology and Applications Symposium, pp. 377–386. IEEE (2008)
7. Rezha, F.P., Shin, S.Y.: Performance analysis of ISA100.11a under interference from an IEEE 802.11b wireless network. IEEE Trans. Ind. Electron. 10(2), 919–927 (2014)
8. Liang, W., Zhang, X., Xiao, Y., Wang, F., Zeng, P., Yu, H.: Survey and experiments of WIA-PA specification of industrial wireless network. Wirel. Commun. Mob. Comput. 11(8), 1197–1212 (2011)
9. Zhu, J., Zou, Y., Zheng, B.: Physical-layer security and reliability challenges for industrial wireless sensor networks. IEEE Access. 5, 5313–5320 (2017)
10. Qi, Y., Li, W., Luo, X., Wang, Q.: Security analysis of WIA-PA protocol. In: Wang, X., Cui, L., Guo, Z. (eds.) Advanced Technologies in Ad Hoc and Sensor Networks. LNEE, vol. 295, pp. 287–298. Springer, Heidelberg (2014). https://doi.org/10.1007/978-3-642-54174-2_26
11. Mollah, M.B., Azad, M.A.K., Vasilakos, A.: Security and privacy challenges in mobile cloud computing: survey and way ahead. J. Netw. Comput. Appl. 84, 34–54 (2017)
12. Zou, Y., Zhu, J., Wang, X., Leung, V.: Improving physical-layer security in wireless communications using diversity techniques. IEEE Network 29(1), 42–48 (2014)
13. Sun, L., Ren, P., Du, Q., Wang, Y.: Fountain-coding aided strategy for secure cooperative transmission in industrial wireless sensor networks. IEEE Trans. Ind. Electron. 12(1), 291–300 (2016)
14. Pelechrinis, K., Iliofotou, M., Krishnamurthy, S.V.: Denial of service attacks in wireless networks: the case of jammers. IEEE Commun. Sur. 13(2), 245–257 (2011)
15. Chiwewe, T.M., Mbuya, C.F., Hancke, G.P.: Using cognitive radio for interference-resistant industrial wireless sensor networks: an overview. IEEE Trans. Ind. Electron. 11(6), 1466–1481 (2015)
16. Zhang, H.J., Xing, H., Cheng, J., Nallanathan, A., Leung, V.C.M.: Secure resource allocation for OFDMA two-way relay wireless sensor networks without and with cooperative jamming. IEEE Trans. Ind. Inform. 12(10), 1714–1725 (2016)
17. Wei, M., Kim, K., Wang, P., Choe, J.: Research and implementation on the security scheme of industrial wireless network. In: Proceedings of International Conference on Information Networking, pp. 37–42 (2011)
18. Lee, J., Kim, L., Kwon, T.: FlexiCast: energy-efficient software integrity checks to build secure industrial wireless active sensor networks. IEEE Trans. Ind. Inform. 12(1), 6–14 (2016)
19. Chen, X., Makki, K., Kang, Y., Pissinou, N.: Sensor network security: a survey. IEEE Commun. Sur. 11(2), 52–73 (2009)
20. Ganeriwal, S., Srivastava, M.B.: Reputation-based framework for high integrity sensor networks. In: Proceedings of the 2nd ACM workshop on Security of ad Hoc and Sensor Networks (SASN 2004), pp. 66–77. ACM, Washington, D.C. (2004)
21. Firoozi, F., Zadorozhny, V.I., Li, F.Y.: Subjective logic-based in-network data processing for trust management in collocated and distributed wireless sensor networks. IEEE Sens. J. 18(15), 6446–6460 (2018)

22. Sinha, R.K., Jagannatham, A.K.: Gaussian trust and reputation for fading MIMO wireless sensor networks. In: Proceedings of IEEE International Conference on IEEE Electronics, Computing and Communication Technologies (CONECCT) pp. 1–6 (2014)
23. Janani, V.S., Manikandan, M.S.K.: Efficient trust management with Bayesian-Evidence theorem to secure public key infrastructure-based mobile ad hoc networks. Eurasip J. Wirel. Commun. Networking 1, 25 (2018)
24. Mahmud, M., Kaiser, M.S., Rahman, M.M., et al.: A brain-inspired trust management model to assure security in a cloud based IoT framework for neuroscience applications. Cogn. Comput. (9), 1–10 (2018)
25. Wang, R., Zhang, Z., Zhang, Z., Jia, Z.: ETMRM: an energy-efficient trust management and routing mechanism for SDWSNs. Comput. Netw. 139, 119–135 (2018)
26. Zhu, M., Chen, H., Wu, H.: A rank-based application-driven resilient reputation framework model for wireless sensor networks. In: Proceedings of International Conference on IEEE Computer Application and System Modeling (ICCASM), vol. 9, pp. V9-125–V9-129 (2010)
27. Labraoui, N.: A reliable trust management scheme in wireless sensor networks. In: IEEE International Symposium Programming System, pp. 1–6 (2015)
28. Duan, J., Gao, D., Yang, D., et al.: An energy-aware trust derivation scheme with game theoretic approach in wireless sensor networks for IoT applications. IEEE Internet Things J. 1(1), 58–69 (2014)
29. Fang, W., Zhang, C., Shi, Z., Zhao, Q., Shan, L.: BTRES: beta-based trust and reputation evaluation system for wireless sensor networks. J. Network Comput. Appl. 59(1), 88–94 (2017)
30. Li, M., Hu, J., Du, J.: A data-centric trust evaluation mechanism in wireless sensor networks. In: 2010 Ninth International Symposium on Distributed Computing and Applications to Business Engineering and Science (DCABES), pp. 466–470. IEEE (2010)
31. Zia, T.A., Islam, M.Z.: Communal reputation and individual trust (CRIT) in wireless sensor networks. In: Proceedings of IEEE International Conference on Availability, Reliability, and Security (ARES 2010), pp. 347–352 (2010)
32. Fang, W., Shi, Z., Shan, L., Li, F., Wang, X.: Trusted scheme for defending on-off attack based on BETA distribution. J. Syst. Simul. 27(11), 2722–2728 (2015)
33. Fang, W., Zhang, W., Yang, Y., Liu, Y., Chen, W.: A resilient trust management scheme for defending against reputation time-varying attacks based on BETA distribution. Sci. Chin. Inform. Sci. 60(4), 040305 (2017)
34. Gheorghe, L., Rughinis, R., Tataroiu, R.: Adaptive trust management protocol based on intrusion detection for wireless sensor networks. In: 2013 RoEduNet International Conference 12th Edition Proceedings of Networking in Education and Research, pp. 1–7. IEEE (2013)
35. Fang, F., Li, J., Li, J.: A reputation management scheme based on multi-factor in WSNs. In: Proceedings of IEEE International Conference on Mechatronic Sciences, Electric Engineering and Computer, pp. 3843–3848 (2013)
36. Tajeddine, A., Kayssi, A., Chehab, A.: TRACE: a centralized trust and competence-based energy-efficient routing scheme for wireless sensor networks. In: Proceedings of the 7th IEEE International Wireless Communications and Mobile Computing Conference (IWCMC), pp. 953–958 (2011)
37. Tajeddine, A., Kayssi, A., Chehab, A.: CENTER: a centralized trust-based efficient routing protocol for wireless sensor networks. In: Proceedings of IEEE Tenth Annual International Conference on Privacy, Security and Trust, pp. 195–202 (2012)
38. Li, X., Niu, J., Kumari, S., Liao, J., Liang, W., Khan, M.K.: A new authentication protocol for healthcare applications using wireless medical sensor networks with user anonymity. Secur. Commun. Networks 9(15), 2643–2655 (2016)

39. Gerrigagoitia, K., Uribeetxeberria, R., Zurutuza, U., et al.: Reputation-based intrusion detection system for wireless sensor networks. In: Proceedings of IEEE Complexity in Engineering, pp. 1–5 (2012)
40. Arijit, U.: Trust and reputation based collaborating computing in wireless sensor networks. In: Proc of the Second IEEE International Conference on Computational Intelligence, Modelling and Simulation, pp. 464–469 (2010)
41. Zhou, N., Fang, W., Zhang, W., Lv, X., Huang, J.: A novel trust management scheme for defending against On-off attack based on Gaussian distribution. In: Proceedings of IEEE 18th International Conference on Computer and Information Technology (CIT-2018), July 30 - Aug 03, 2018, Halifax, Canada, to be published

Security Risk Assessment for Miniature Internet of Thing Systems with 5G

Wei Chen[1,2], Lei Wang[1,2], Fangming Bi[1,2(✉)], Chaogang Tang[1,2], and Senyu Li[1,2]

[1] School of Computer Science and Technology,
China University of Mining and Technology, Xuzhou 221116, Jiangsu, China
bfm@cumt.edu.cn
[2] Mine Digitization Engineering Research Center of the Ministry of Education,
China University of Mining and Technology,
Xuzhou 221116, Jiangsu, China

Abstract. In order to improve the traditional analytic hierarchy process method, information entropy and interval fuzzy number are introduced to AHP respectively on the weight of the hierarchy and the weight of the index. The effectiveness of the improved method is tested by a Simulation example which is based on risk assessment index system of miniature Internet of things system. Meanwhile, 5G as the fifth generation of mobile communication technology, will be widely used in entertainment, health care, education and autonomous driving. It will extend the capabilities of various applications on our personal devices and wearable devices will fill every corner of our lives by the application with miniature Internet of thing systems. At the same time, 5G also faces the threat of information security risk, which is our paper concerned.

Keywords: Security risk assessment · Analytic hierarchy process · Information entropy · Interval fuzzy number · 5G

1 Introduction

The Internet of things emerged as the times require which makes the new forms of network combined with various traditional and new industry applications, by using Internet platform as the backbone. Trust-based communication can greatly enhance the performance of sensor-cloud for Internet of things [1]. There is an essential difference between the Internet of things with the existing Internet and mobile communication network [2, 3]. Nowadays, the security problem has become an important problem that hinders the further development of the Internet of things [4]. How to extend the information security protection to the extension of the Internet of things system and how to protect the privacy information while sharing data in the Internet of things are the most significant problems need to be solved in the current research on the security of the Internet of things [5]. Meanwhile, 5G as the next generation of wireless technologies will bring our society into a new statement. 5G wireless networks with big-data-driven and big-data-assisted can be widely used. Another promising application scenario of fifth generation (5G) wireless communications is vehicle-to-everything (V2X).

V. C. M. Leung et al. (Eds.): 5GWN 2019, LNICST 278, pp. 174–181, 2019.
https://doi.org/10.1007/978-3-030-17513-9_12

It also can be used to meet the demand of explosive mobile data. Ultra sense network is a solution for the 5G networks. It seems that 5G has a bright future, but some risks cannot be ignored. Information security risk assessment is one of the necessary things that should be emphasized.

In this paper, we present an information security risk assessment method based on improved analytic hierarchy process. The paper is organized as follows. Firstly,the theoretical background is briefly introduced in Sect. 2. Secondly, Sect. 3 presents the information security risk assessment model based on improved AHP. Thirdly, Sect. 4 presents the illustrative example. Finally, Sect. 5 contains the conclusions.

2 Related Works

2.1 IOT Security

The Internet of things market develops rapidly, the number of terminals increases sharply, and there are big security risks. The proportion of security links in the industrial chain of the Internet of things is low. The Internet of things has gone deep into many industries and affected people's lives in an all-round way. The main contents of IOT security include: data security, network security and node security.

(1) Data security

Due to the fierce growth of IOT devices and IOT data, the large amount of data generated by IOT systems poses a serious threat to people's privacy. In response to this threat, Toch et al. [6] proposed a classification method for information security and privacy risk assessment based on data exposure level, individual user identification level, data sensitivity, user control over monitoring and data collection and analysis. In addition to risk assessment of IOT data, Radanliev and Liu et al. [7], [8] predicted the future risk of IOT network based on test and verification of real data.

(2) Network security

Advanced persistent threats (APTs), combined with many different forms of attack, are becoming a major threat to network security. Existing security protections typically focus either on one-off situations or on weaknesses that separate detection from response decisions. Li et al. [9] proposed a security perception defense mechanism based on threat intelligence support, which introduced priority perception virtual queue to make robust defense strategies based on acquired heterogeneous knowledge. Likewise, the nature of industrial networks often impedes the adoption of classic security approaches, especially popular solutions based primarily on a philosophy of detection and patching. Cheminod et al. [10] evaluated the status quo of a class of industrial distributed computing systems from the perspective of security, and analyzed the characteristics of the system, the artistic standardization of the current state and the adoption of appropriate control (countermeasures), which can help reduce the security risk below a predefined and acceptable threshold.

(3) Node security

Node security is becoming a promising example of protecting wireless communications from eavesdropping between legitimate users because the primary link from source to destination has better propagation conditions than the eavesdropping link from source to eavesdropper. Codetta-Raiteri et al. [11] used decision network (DN) to analyze attack/defense scenarios in critical infrastructure, and they could directly use reasoning algorithm to carry out probability analysis on the risk and importance of attack. In order to reduce interrupt probability (OP), Zou et al. [12] proposed opportunity relay selection (ORS) and quantified the improvement of SRT while increasing the number of relays.

2.2 Security Target System of the Internet of Things

'EPCGlobal' Internet of things architecture is currently one of the most representative architecture of the Internet of things [13]. The architecture divides the Internet of things into three levels: the perception layer, the network layer and the application layer.

(1) Perceptual layer
   The perception layer of Internet of things is the foundation of data acquisition by Internet of things. It mainly uses video recognition, wireless terminals, sensors and other data acquisition devices to realize real-time perception and collect basic data. At the same time, the trust-based sensors also have an executive control system to perform simple control operations [1].
(2) Network layer
   The network layer of the Internet of things is usually based on the existing mobile communication network or the Internet. It mainly realizes the function of information transmission and aggregation, and transmits, integrates and spreads large scale information through the network [14]. At the same time, the network layer also contains certain functions of managing and processing the acquired perceptual data. Using Cloud computing as a platform for data storage and analysis of the Internet of things is the key to connect the Internet layer and application layer. The researchers developed a complex formal mathematical decision model to support the selection of cloud computing services in multi-source scenarios [1, 15].
(3) Application layer
   The application layer of the Internet of things acquires perceptual information from the supporting platform such as the Internet of things data center, and provides various services for users by using the acquired information. At present, there are more and more applications of Internet of things including public management, intelligent transportation, smart home [16], medical and health, public safety and other fields, but the whole system is not sound enough. The common Internet of things applications includes monitoring applications, payment applications, query applications, and so on. Android has emerged as the widest-used operating system for smartphones and mobile devices. Security of this platform mainly relies on applications (apps) installed by the device owner since permissions [17].

2.3 Analytic Hierarchy Process

Risk assessment may be a necessary process in Internet of things network security, and one deliverable can be used to deal with threats, thus promoting the formulation of security strategy [18]. Analytic hierarchy process (AHP) is often used as a qualitative and quantitative analysis method in the process of risk assessment [19]. The first task of using analytic hierarchy process to evaluate a system is to build a hierarchical model. Then some qualitative and unquantifiable factors are quantified on the basis of the hierarchical model, and some quantitative data are obtained through processing and analysis to help decision-makers to make decisions [8].

Traditional AHP method for information security risk assessment can be generally divided into four steps:

Step 1. Hierarchical structure model of the system
This step aims to analyze the relevant elements of the system. Then stratify the system according to a certain standard. We usually divide the system into three layers: the target layer, the criterion layer and the scheme layer.
Step 2. Structure judgment matrix
Judgment matrix is formed to calculate the weight of criteria. To compare in a more efficient way, nine point scales have been proposed as is shown in Table 1.

Table 1. The numerical scale in AHP used in the paired-comparison.

Significance	Description
1	Two elements are equally important
3	One element is weakly important than another
5	One element is important than another
7	One element is strongly important than another
9	One element is absolutely important than another
2, 4, 6, 8	These are intermediate values of decision

Step 3. Calculating the relative weight of the single layer
Calculating the characteristic vector of the judgment matrix and then normalize the characteristic vector to get the weight of the single layer.
Step 4. Calculating the final combination weights of each layer element.

3   Information Security Risk Assessment Model

In the evaluation process of AHP, the accuracy of the hierarchy weight depends on the construction of the judgment matrix. When the traditional analytic hierarchy process (AHP) is used to integrate the different evaluation results of the same scheme, a simple method of calculating the average value is often used, and the information behind the difference is ignored. Therefore, the concept of entropy and entropy method is introduced. With entropy method, weight is adjusted according to the difference of evaluation.

After optimization, the process of AHP risk assessment model can be express six steps as Fig. 1.

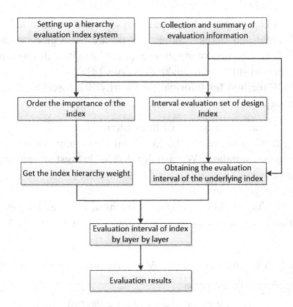

Fig. 1. Structure chart of improved AHP risk assessment model

Firstly, establish the hierarchy index system. According to the actual risk status of the system, the risk factors of the system are identified by risk identification, and the corresponding evaluation index is constructed. According to the common character-istics of the indicators, it is rationally designed into a hierarchical index system structure.

Secondly, obtaining the importance order of each layer. Through the assessment of the system security experts or senior managers, the importance of the indicators in the risk assessment index system is classified according to the 1–9 scale method inde-pendently. The corresponding judgment matrix is constructed according to the ranking results.

Thirdly, calculating the weight of the index. For different experts or executives, the weight matrix is calculated by AHP and the consistency test is carried out. After passing the test, it is merged into index weight matrix. Then entropy weight is used to solve the entropy weight of the index weight matrix, and the weight of index level is adjusted by entropy weight.

Fourthly, constructing interval evaluation set of index evaluation value. According to the actual situation of the risk assessment, a reasonable interval evaluation set is designed. The evaluation set should be as concise and reasonable as possible so that the investigator can understand the meaning of the evaluation clearly, and the manager can also determine the risk condition according to the result of the evaluation.

Fifthly, getting the evaluation value interval of the lowest index. According to the results of the risk assessment, the evaluation value interval of each lowest evaluation index is solved. In order to ensure the rationality of the evaluation results, the method of removing the extremes at the both ends can be taken to get the interval vector of the lowest index evaluation value.

Sixthly, combining the index hierarchy weight and index evaluation value interval, the evaluation value interval corresponding to the last layer of index is solved from bottom to top, and the comprehensive evaluation result of the whole evaluation system is finally obtained.

4 Simulation Experiment

In order to verify the correctness of the improved AHP risk assessment model, this chapter takes a miniature Internet of things system as an example to study the risk assessment model proposed above.

The risk assessment questionnaire is built on the basis of the four level evaluation index in the risk assessment system. 30 survey results were randomly selected as the basis for evaluating the importance of indicators. The distribution of evaluation results is shown in the following Table 2.

Table 2. Evaluation results of index importance

Forth level index	Very high	High	Medium	Low	Very low
Physical environment of outdoor equipment (X_{111})	2	7	17	4	0
Physical environment of internal equipment (X_{112})	0	4	9	14	3
Maintenance degree of hardware operation management (X_{113})	1	3	7	11	8
Degree of completeness of information security software (X_{121})	0	2	11	14	3
System security log (X_{122})	4	11	11	3	1
System access control (X_{123})	3	14	7	4	2
System update maintenance (X_{124})	1	7	14	6	2
Degree of completeness of database management (X_{131})	0	3	5	17	5
Data access control (X_{132})	6	10	7	6	1
Data secrecy (X_{133})	4	9	8	6	3
Influence of internal factors (X_{141})	0	2	4	11	13
Influence of external factors (X_{142})	1	0	5	10	14
Communication encryption (X_{211})	2	2	9	11	6
Communication access control and authentication (X_{212})	4	3	16	5	2
Attack protection (X_{213})	1	4	12	7	6
Security of communication platform (X_{214})	0	1	15	10	4
Information flow control (X_{221})	2	4	17	4	3
Environmental awareness and protection (X_{222})	0	3	12	14	1
Security level division (X_{223})	3	2	9	9	7
Technical level of staff (X_{311})	1	1	11	14	3
Staff safety awareness level (X_{312})	4	4	7	9	6
Staff supervision and management system (X_{313})	2	5	14	8	1
User operation specification (X_{321})	6	4	12	5	3
User safety awareness and attitude (X_{322})	4	7	8	10	1

With this evaluation method, when setting the risk response strategy, we can evaluate the specific details by combining the interval of index evaluation value and the hierarchy weight. For example, it can be seen from the evaluation value of the fourth level index that the system has loopholes in the authority management, which needs to be further improved, as well as the second level index from the level weight. The risk of data communication in the system has the highest weight, and the risk should be increased in the process of risk management and control. The risk control and management measures of information security are reasonably set up through comprehensive index weight and risk value interval.

5   Conclusion

Risk assessment is the cornerstone of information system security. After intensive study of relevant standards and methods in this field, comprehensive understanding of relevant theories and investigation and evaluation of the implementation process this paper deeply studies the risk assessment method based on hierarchical analysis and neural network, and establishes an index body of information security risk assessment based on the miniature Internet of things system. Furthermore, we put forward the improved AHP risk assessment model. Meanwhile, we emphasized the importance of information security risk assessment as a solution for the 5G networks. The effectiveness of the simulation test is tested. However, there are still some subjective factors in the evaluation process, and the information entropy cannot deal with the situation that only a few experts give the correct evaluation results. These problems remain to be solved further.

Acknowledgement. The research is supported by National Natural Science Foundation of China (Grant No. 51874300), the National Natural Science Foundation of China and Shanxi Provincial People's Government Jointly Funded Project of China for Coal Base and Low Carbon (Grant No. U1510115), National Natural Science Foundation of China (Grant Nos. 51874299, 51104157), the Qing Lan Project, the China Postdoctoral Science Foundation (Grant No. 2013T60574), the Ph.D. Programs Foundation of Ministry of Education of China (Grant No. 20110095120008) and the China Postdoctoral Science Foundation (Grant No. 20100481181).

References

1. Feng, J.Y., Liu, Z., Wu, C., Ji, Y.S.: Mobile edge computing for internet of vehicles: offloading framework and job scheduling. IEEE Veh. Technol. Mag. **14**(1), 28–36 (2019)
2. Perera, C., Zaslavsky, A., Christen, P., Georgakopoulos, D.: Sensing as a service model for smart cities supported by Internet of Things. Trans. Emerg. Telecommun. Technol. **25**(1), 81–93 (2014)
3. Wang, X., Liu, Z., Gao, Y., Zheng, X., Chen, X., Wu, C.: Near-optimal data structure for approximate range emptiness problem in information-centric Internet of Things. IEEE Access **7**, 21857–21869 (2019)
4. Marett, K., Vedadi, A., Durcikova, A.: A quantitative textual analysis of three types of threat communication and subsequent maladaptive responses. Comput. Secur. **80**, 25–35 (2019)

Security Risk Assessment for Miniature Internet of Thing Systems 181

5. Mohsin, M., Sardar, M.U., Hasan, O., Anwar, Z.: IoTRiskAnalyzer: a probabilistic model checking based framework for formal risk analytics of the Internet of Things. IEEE Access 5, 5494–5505 (2017)
6. Toch, E., et al.: The privacy implications of cyber security systems: a technological survey. ACM Comput. Surv. 51(2), 36:1–27 (2018)
7. Radanliev, P., et al.: Future developments in cyber risk assessment for the internet of things. Comput. Ind. 102, 14–22 (2018)
8. Wu, C., Liu, Z., Zhang, D., Yoshinaga, T., Ji, Y.S.: Spatial intelligence toward trustworthy vehicular IoT. IEEE Commun. Mag. 56(10), 22–27 (2018)
9. Li, Y.Q., Dai, W.K., Bai, J., Gan, X.Y., Wang, J.C., Wang, X.B.: An intelligence-driven security-aware defense mechanism for advanced persistent threats. IEEE Trans. Inf. Forensics Secur. 14(3), 646–661 (2019)
10. Cheminod, M., Durante, L., Valenzano, A.: Review of security issues in industrial networks. IEEE Trans. Industr. Inf. 9(1), 277–293 (2013)
11. Codetta-Raiteri, D., Portinale, L.: Decision networks for security risk assessment of critical infrastructures. ACM Trans. Internet Technol. 18(3), 29:1–22 (2018)
12. Zou, Y.L., Wang, X.B., Shen, W.M., Hanzo, L.: Security versus reliability analysis of opportunistic relaying. IEEE Trans. Veh. Technol. 63(6), 2653–2661 (2014)
13. Bandyopadhyay, D., Sen, J.: Internet of Things: applications and challenges in technology and standardization. Wirel. Pers. Commun. 58(1), 49–69 (2011)
14. Xu, D.Y., Ren, P.Y., Ritcey, J.A.: Independence-checking coding for OFDM channel training authentication: protocol design, security, stability, and tradeoff analysis. IEEE Trans. Inf. Forensics Secur. 14(2), 387–402 (2019)
15. Martens, B., Teuteberg, F.: Decision-making in cloud computing environments: a cost and risk based approach. Inf. Syst. Front. 14(4), 871–893 (2012)
16. Jacobsson, A., Boldt, M., Carlsson, B.: A risk analysis of a smart home automation system. Future Gener. Comput. Syst. Int. J. Escience 56, 719–733 (2016)
17. Deypir, M., Horri, A.: Instance based security risk value estimation for Android applications. J. Inf. Secur. Appl. 40, 20–30 (2018)
18. Gritzalis, D., Iseppi, G., Mylonas, A., Stavrou, V.: Exiting the risk assessment maze: a meta-survey. ACM Comput. Surv. 51(1), 11:1–30 (2018)
19. Xu, N., Zhao, D.M.: the research of information security risk assessment method based on AHP. In: Wu, Y.W. (ed.) Sports Materials, Modelling and Simulation, vol. 187, pp. 575–580. Trans Tech Publications Ltd., Stafa-Zurich (2011)

Improved Flow Awareness by Intelligent Collaborative Sampling in Software Defined Networks

Jun Deng, He Cai, and Xiaofei Wang($^{\boxtimes}$)

Tianjin Key Laboratory of Advanced Networking,
College of Intelligence and Computing, Tianjin University, Tianjin, China
xiaofeiwang@tju.edu.cn

Abstract. To improve the specific quality of service, internal network management and security analysis in the future mobile network, accurate flow-awareness in the global network through packet sampling has been a viable solution. However, the current traffic measurement method with the five tuples cannot recognize the deep information of flows, and the Deep Packet Inspection (DPI) deployed at the gateways or access points is lack of traffic going through the internal nodes (e.g., base station, edge server). In this paper, by means of Deep Q-Network (DQN) and Software-Defined Networking (SDN) technique, we propose a flow-level sampling framework for edge devices in the Mobile Edge Computing (MEC) system. In the framework, an original learning-based sampling strategy considering the iterative influences of nodes is used for maximizing the long-term sampling accuracy of both mice and elephant flows. We present an approach to effectively collect traffic packets generated from base stations and edge servers in two steps: (1) adaptive node selection, and (2) dynamic sampling duration allocation by Deep Q-Learning. The results show that the approach can improve the sampling accuracy, especially for mice flows.

Keywords: Edge Computing · Deep Q-Learning · SDN · Flow-awareness · Resource allocation

1 Introduction

With the increase of wireless access devices and traffic load in 5G networks, many traffic flows will not pass through the backbone or gateway, but only exist among the base stations (BSs) and the edge servers, such as cooperative caching, content sharing and intensive-computation offloading. Therefore, global accurate flow awareness in Mobile Edge Computing (MEC) system is an urgent need for fine-grained quality of service guarantee, security analysis, content awareness, internal network management and so on. These applications in MEC business model requires more flows, with their deep information (e.g., security, application type, flow behavior) which is brought by the payload of sampled packets.

© ICST Institute for Computer Sciences, Social Informatics and Telecommunications Engineering 2019
Published by Springer Nature Switzerland AG 2019. All Rights Reserved
V. C. M. Leung et al. (Eds.): 5GWN 2019, LNICST 278, pp. 182–194, 2019.
https://doi.org/10.1007/978-3-030-17513-9_13

Especially for security of network edge devices, DOS attacks could be packet-based with only a small amount packets and hide in short-life **mice flows** [1,2], which makes themselves hard to capture.

It is challenging to deeply obtain flow information while sampling network-wise flows accurately under DPI technology [3] or statistics-based reports created by other measurements based on telemetry or sketch [4-6]. DPI is used to inspect packet payload at the gateways or access points, which is, however, hard to be deployed on all nodes [7]. This leads to a lack of the global detailed flow information. Meanwhile, statistics-based reports are short of payload and flow-level recognition of internal traffic. In addition, sFlow-based solutions can capture the packet with payload in a probability [8,9]. However, the sampled packets of the same flow is non-consecutive, which is useless for recognizing the flow-level deep information. Fortunately, systematic packet sampling (SPS) which samples within a certain duration can capture consecutive packets [10,11]. The SDN with SPS is conducive to the global and cyclical sampling, which can achieve high-accuracy flow-level sampling. Besides, the MEC concept along with SDN can enable more applications requiring computing and storage resources [12].

However, due to restrictions on the resources (e,g., the processing capacity of collector) of MEC system, the selected sampling nodes should not be too many and the sampling duration cannot be assigned unlimitedly. Existing studies [10,11,13] have proposed different approaches by SPS to select the sampling nodes or allocate the resource in a real network, but they are limited to a certain extent. For example, study [10] selects K nodes with the most active flows currently passing through the node as the sampling nodes, and then assigns a equal sampling rate to the K nodes. However, the fixed K nodes are not guaranteed to cover all the flows in the network, and the decision of sampling rate cannot change dynamically according to the active flows covered by the nodes. In addition, study [13] selects sampling nodes based on a greedy strategy which can cover all the active flows, and it proposes a adaptive scheme to adjust the sampling rate considering the bandwidth resource. But its algorithm results in a reduced accuracy. Fortunately, a new technology, namely deep reinforcement learning (DRL), has an advantage to obtain the resource allocation policy for solving the complexity problem in real wireless environment [14,15].

In this paper, we focus on adaptively selecting sampling nodes and dynamically setting sampling strategies for each sampling period, aiming to improve network-wise flow-level sampling accuracy by SPS.

For this purpose, based on DRL and SDN, we propose a framework considering the iterative influences of global nodes and the dynamic allocation of sampling duration. The influence which is decided by the current active flows covered by each node can be used to measure the importance of a node and determine the sampling nodes. The allocation is decided by the centrally controlled learning-based strategy, which can allocate appropriate sampling duration to selected nodes, and finally lead to a great advantage in capturing mice flows. Our main contributions are summarized as follows:

- we propose a learning-based flow-level sampling strategy with SPS, which can cover all the active flows in the network and guarantee data integrity for training process of artificial neural network.
- we model flow-level sampling and the resource allocation as a Markov Decision Process (MDP) and propose a framework based on SDN and Deep Q-Network (DQN) for centrally controlled learning-based sampling strategy among BSs and edge servers.
- We evaluate the method by a relatively realistic topology and a real trace. Finally the results show that our learning-based method can improve the sampling accuracy by 5.9% and the accuracy of mice flows by 8.1%.

The remainder of this paper is organized as follows: The system model and problem formulation is discussed in Sect. 2. Then the learning-based sampling strategy and the resource allocation algorithm will be discussed in Sect. 3 in detail along with experiments in Sect. 4. Finally, conclusions are given in Sect. 5.

2   System Model and Problem Formulation

2.1   Flow-Awareness Architecture Based on SDN in MEC

The flow-awareness architecture based on SDN in MEC is illustrated in Fig. 1. In MEC environment, users receive services by sending requests to a base station with a fixed radio coverage, where each base station is linked to only an edge server. In our flow-awareness architecture, any base station and edge server can be selected as a sampling node. Besides, the SDN controller gathers and sends the flow information generated by these nodes to the learning-based neural network, after which the controller can receive a feedback about sampling duration allocation. Another component, traffic collector is responsible for collecting the sampled packets and informing the controller of the number of flows.

2.2   Sampling Modeling and Objective

First, we quantify the influence and the cost of each node in the unit sampling time. And next, the objective is given in detail.

Quantification of the Influence and Cost. The quantization of influence is based on the Flow Betweenness Centrality (FBC) [10,16], and we extended it. We define the set R including all nodes, so the number of nodes is $n = |R|$. Let F_i^c be the set including all active flows currently passing through R_i, and F^c is the set including all current active flows in the network, and $F^c = \bigcup_{i=1}^{n} F_i^c$. For each $f_k \in F_i^c$, suppose f_k transmits packets as a Poisson process with a rate λ_k in a unit time t [17], and λ_k is independent of the other flows. Thus, the probability that f_k is captured by R_i within t is

$$P\{N_k(t) > 0\} = 1 - P\{N_k(t) = 0\} = 1 - \frac{1}{e^{\lambda_k \cdot t}}. \tag{1}$$

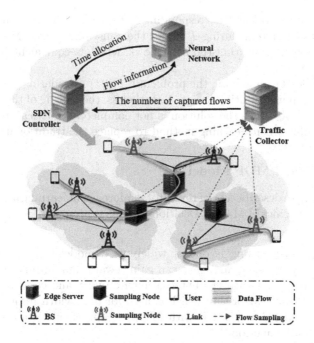

Fig. 1. Illustration of flow-awareness architecture in SDN.

and the expected number of active flows captured by R_i is $\sum_{f_k \in F_i^c} P\{N_k(t) > 0\}$. The influence of R_i within t can be quantified as (2), which describes the rate of the number of flows that a node can capture within t to the number of network-wise current active flows.

$$I_i(t) = \sum_{f_k \in F_i^c} P\{N_k(t) > 0\}/|F^c|. \tag{2}$$

Cost w_i is the total number of packets captured from R_i during t, which can be expressed as $w_i = \frac{v_i}{T/t}$, where v_i is the current packet speed (packets/T) during the sampling period T.

Objective. We formulate the influence-based sampling model in (3), with the constraints (4) and (5), where $\widehat{t_i}$ is the sampling duration allocated to R_i, and C is the capacity of collector (packets/T).

$$\max \sum_{i=1}^{n} I_i(\widehat{t_i}). \tag{3}$$

$$\text{s.t. } \sum_{i}^{n} w_i \cdot (\widehat{t_i}/t) \leq C. \tag{4}$$

$$0 \leq \widehat{t_i} \leq T. \tag{5}$$

The goal is to work out corresponding $\hat{t}_i$ for each R_i to maximize the total influences of the system during T under the constraints of C. Maximizing the value of (3) means capturing the most flows, which is equivalent to optimizing sampling accuracy.

The complexity for solving the problem is $O(2^n)$ considering whether a node is assigned sampling duration or not. Nonetheless, the lacking of the exact packet arrival strength λ_k make the solution is not completely practical. In this paper, we find a reinforcement learning method to replace the traditional solution.

2.3   Specifics of MDP Model

In this section, we describe a brief review of reinforcement learning and Q-learning, and then the specifics of Markov Decision Process is presented.

Q-Learning. Q-Learning is one of widely-used model free method in Reinforcement learning, where an agent can gain reward and automatically learn to behave by interacting with the external environment and constantly trying to act. The Q-Learning algorithm which is used for bandwidth resource allocation here can be modeled as a MDP with followed components: state space, action space and reward function.

State Space. We regard the whole of network nodes in the sampling environment as an agent. The sampling process is periodic, and state changes periodically with decision epoch. Therefore, for the agent in sampling environment, the j-th sampling period is equivalent to decision epoch. Let q_i^j is the number of the flows covered by any node R_i, and each node is assigned a ratio of sampling duration r_i^j. Under the constraints of node's packet speed and collector's processing capacity, r_i^j is used to calculate the unit sampling duration, and then the sampling duration of each node $\widehat{t_i^j}$ is also calculated. As shown below, during the j-th period, the packet speed of R_i is v_i^j, so the unit sampling duration $\widehat{t^j}$ can be expressed as

$$\widehat{t^j} = \frac{C \cdot T}{\sum_i^n r_i^j \cdot v_i^j}, \quad i, j \in \mathbb{Z}, \tag{6}$$

then,

$$\widehat{t_i^j} = r_i^j \cdot \widehat{t^j}. \tag{7}$$

Based on the above computing method, the state vector should include the vector of flow number q^j and the vector of sampling duration ratio r^j. Therefore, the observed state vector s_i during decision epoch j can be denoted as

$$s_j = [q^j, \quad r^j] \in S, \tag{8}$$

where S is the state space, and $q^j = [q_1^j, q_2^j, ..., q_n^j], r^j = [r_1^j, r_2^j, ..., r_n^j], q_i^j, r_i^j \in \mathbb{Z}$.

Action Space. The goal of one action is to allocate resources to one of the nodes in one of the three ways: increase, decrease and keep unchanged. When the agent is in the state s_j, it will decide which node to execute the action $\phi(s_j)$, and then r_i^j of the node will be changed. So the action space A is expressed as

$$A = [a_j^1, \ a_j^{-1}, \ a_j^0], \tag{9}$$

where a_j^1, a_j^{-1}, a_j^0 are defined as follow:

(1) The action vector $a_j^1 = [a_{j,1}^1, \ a_{j,2}^1 , ..., \ a_{j,n}^1]$, where any element $a_{j,i}^1 = 1$ represents increasing r_i^j by one.
(2) The action vector $a_j^{-1} = [a_{j,1}^{-1}, \ a_{j,2}^{-1} , ..., \ a_{j,n}^{-1}]$, where any element $a_{j,i}^{-1} = -1$ represents decreasing r_i^j by one.
(3) The action vector $a_j^0 = [0]$ means that any r_i^j remains unchanged.

Reward Function. The reward function needs to take into account the objectives of flow-awareness framework. As the (3) shows, the goal is to maximize the sampling accuracy of the whole sampling process by capturing the most flows in each sampling period. In order to achieve the goal through learning-based method, during the j-th period, we define F_j^s as the non redundant flows sampled by all the node in the network, and F_j^t is all flows covered by all the nodes. So the sampling accuracy in the j-th period is denoted as

$$\rho = \frac{F_j^s}{F_j^t}. \tag{10}$$

Then, in our flow-awareness architecture, reward function $R(s_j, \phi(s_j))$ is defined as

$$R(s_j, \phi(s_j)) = e^\rho, \tag{11}$$

when the agent perform the action $\phi(s_j)$ upon the state s_j.

2.4   Problem Formulation

Q-Learning solution is proposed here. Based on (11), taking into account the lone-term discount rewards, the expectation of maximizing objective upon the initial state $s_j = s$ is defined by a state value function, called Q-function:

$$Q(s,\varphi) = E\left[\sum_{j=1}^{J\to\infty} (\gamma)^{j-1} \cdot R(s,\varphi)|s_1 = s\right] \tag{12}$$

where $\gamma \in [0,1)$ is the discount factor, and $\varphi = \phi(s_j)$.

The Q-function obeys a Bellman criterion. Let the $s' = s_{j+1}$ is the next state after taking the action φ, so the (12) can be optimized as:

$$Q(s,\varphi) = R(s,\varphi) + \gamma \max_{\varphi'} Q(s',\varphi'). \tag{13}$$

After taking the optimal action, the iterative formula of Q-function can be obtained as:

$$Q^{j+1}(s,\varphi) = Q^j(s,\varphi) + \alpha \cdot \left(R(s,\varphi) + \gamma \max_{\varphi'} Q^j(s',\varphi') - Q^j(s,\varphi) \right), \quad (14)$$

where $\alpha \in [0,1]$ is the learning rate. The (14) expresses that after the agent performs the current optimal action $\phi(s_j)$, the state s_j turn to the state s_{j+1} and the corresponding reward is fed back.

Q-Learning use a Q-Table store the Q value of each state-action pair. However, in the real sampling environment, the state space and action space are huge. Thus, the approach based on Q-Learning will lead to a high-dimensional Q-Table, with which the learning process will be extremely slow. Here, a deep reinforcement learning method is used to solve this problem.

3   Sampling Strategy Based on DRL

In this section, we formulate the dynamic sampling duration allocation problem as a deep reinforcement learning process.

3.1   Double Deep Q-Learning for Resource Allocation

During the application of deep Q-learning, the state-action Q-function is replaced by a deep neural network, called Q-network. It have the possibility to generalize unseen states and narrow the state space, which is beneficial for accelerating the learning process. In the Q-network, the value in the Q-Table is replaced by multi-layer weight θ_j which will update after any policy decision j. Thus, the Q-function is changed as

$$Q(s,\varphi) = Q((s,\varphi);\theta_j). \quad (15)$$

In addition, the corresponding state transition $\widehat{T}_j = (s_j, \phi(s_j), R(s_j, \phi(s_j)), s_{j+1})$ will be stored in experience pool with a pre-defined capacity M at each training step. After the samples in the pool have accumulated to a certain number, the agent will sample the M_j batches (past experience) randomly for the reflective learning, which is what we called experience replay.

In our model, a more reliable algorithm Double Deep Q-Network (Double DQN) [18] is used for training to achieve appropriate resource allocation, which can address the issue of over-estimation Q-value in DQN, and then accelerate convergence velocity of iteration. It is because Double DQN use different Q-network, known as main network $Q(s,\varphi;\theta_j)$ and target network $\widehat{Q}(s,\varphi;\widehat{\theta}_j)$ respectively, to select action and evaluate action.

Then at the training process, the network Q will approximate gradually to the network $\widehat{Q}$ by the Stochastic Gradient Descent (SGD) algorithm with the objective of minimizing the loss function as follow:

$$L(\theta_j) = E_{(s,\varphi,R(s,\varphi),s') \in M_j} \left[(\widehat{y}_j - Q(s,\varphi;\theta_j))^2 \right], \quad (16)$$

where $\widehat{y}_j = R(s,\varphi) + \gamma \cdot \widehat{Q}(s^{'},\arg\max_{\varphi^{'}} Q(s^{'},\varphi^{'};\theta_j);\widehat{\theta}_j)$ is the target value. Algorithm 1 shows the details of training process based on Double DQN.

Algorithm 1 Double DQN-based Sampling Resource Allocation Algorithm

---

Initialization:
    Initialize action space A.
    Initialize experience replay memory M.
    Initialize main network Q with random weights θ.
    Initialize target network $\widehat{Q}$ with $\widehat{\theta} = \theta$.

Iteration:
1: The learning system receives the flow number q^1 from SDN controller, then combines q^1 and the initial ratio of resource allocation r^1 into the first observed state s_1.
2: **for** episode $j = 1$ **to** J **do**
3:     Generate a random number g
4:     if $g \leq \varepsilon$
5:         randomly choose an action $\phi(s_j)$
6:     else
7:         choose action $\arg\max_{\phi(s_j)} Q(s_j, \phi(s_j); \theta_j)$
8:     Execute action $\phi(s_j)$, gain the reward $R(s_j, \phi(s_j))$, and the new observation s_{j+1}.
9:     Construct the transition $\widehat{T_j} = (s_j, \phi(s_j), R(s_j, \phi(s_j)), s_{j+1})$, and store $\widehat{T_j}$ in M.
10:    Sample M_j mini-batch of transitions from M randomly.
11:    Update θ_j by minimizing loss with partial derivative $\frac{\partial L(\theta_j)}{\partial \theta_j}$.
12:    Every κ update $\widehat{\theta}_j = \theta_j$.

---

4 Trace-Driven Evaluation and Results

4.1 Experiment Settings

To verify the performance of learning-based method, we built a experimental bed based on Floodlight controller, Tensorflow, OpenVswitch and Mininet. The test bed contains 6 Dell servers, and each server has a 20-core CPU and runs Ubuntu 16.06.2 LTS. One of the servers runs the Floodlight which is mainly responsible for the statistics of flow information of nodes. Another one performs the Double DQN-based algorithm with TensorFlow and the collector runs on another different ones. With respect to the parameter settings on neural network, the two fully-connected hidden layers with the first-layer 128 neurons and the second-layer 64 neurons is used to serve as the eval and target Q network. Table 1 gives the remaining parameter setting.

    The network topology we deploy on the remaining 3 servers comes from the open dataset provided by Shanghai Telecom[1] [19]. In order to simulate data

---

[1] http://sguangwang.com/TelecomDataset.html.

Table 1. Parameter setting

Symbol	Range	Description
M	2000	Experience pool capacity
M_j	128	Minibatch size
γ	0.9	Discount factor
ϵ	0.1	Final exploration probability
α	0.05	Learning rate
κ	250	The period of replacing target Q network

packet transmission, virtual switches are used to replace base stations and edge servers. This is equivalent to deploying a switch upon each base station or edge server. As shown in Fig. 2, a grey node is regarded as a base station and a blue one is an edge server, and a host is mounted to each base station node. In the experiments, we let $T = 1$ s. The real trace collected by "the WIDE Project"[2] in 2018/09/27 is used. We reserve the TCP and UDP flows, and select up to 13000 flows from the trace for different sets of experiments. The radio of elephant flows to mices flow obeys the 2–8 principle [1].

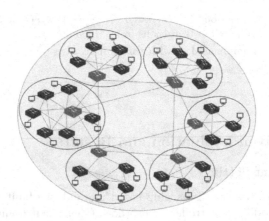

Fig. 2. Experimental topology.

4.2   Results and Analysis

We implement three algorithms for selecting nodes.

(1) Top-k based on Flow Betweenness Centrality (FBC) [10]: Select the fixed K sampling nodes covering the most current active flows.

---

[2] http://mawi.wide.ad.jp/mawi/.

(2) Random-k: Select K nodes randomly.

(3) Adaptive selection based on the extend FBC: Select the sampling nodes by an iterative computing method. In the first iteration, the node with the most current active flow is selected, which is the same as Top-k based on FBC. But at the subsequent iteration, the flows covered by the selected nodes is no longer considered when the remaining nodes calculate the number of flows covered by their own. The iterative selection rounds will not stop until the number of flows at a node is calculated to zero. This original method can ensure coverage of all the flows in the network while reducing sampling nodes.

Then, the SDN controller will send the flow number of selected nodes to the neural network. For evaluating the sampling accuracy through a complete experiments, the three node selection algorithms should be combined with equal sampling duration or dynamic learning-based sampling duration respectively. The flow-level sampling accuracy is expressed as the rate of the number of captured flows to that of the total flows in the network throughout the experiment.

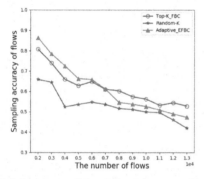 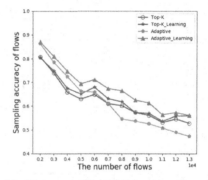

(a) Accuracy of total flows in a equal sampling duration

(b) Accuracy of total flows in a learning-based duration allocation

Fig. 3. Comparison with respect to different algorithms.

Figures 3 and 4 show the performance comparison after applying multiple approaches with different flow number at the same time of packet transmission when $K = 6$ and the collector's capacity C is 2000 packets/s. Obviously, as shown in Fig. 3(a), the sampling accuracy is in a downward trend. Besides, the adaptive method has the highest accuracy when the flow number is no more than 6000 compared with the other three traditional algorithms. However, the accuracy of Top-k based on FBC becomes higher with the increase of flow number. For example, when flow number rises to 8000, the accuracy of adaptive method decreases significantly. It's probable because many low-impact nodes are born in the network, even through iterative computing. In this way, the method of equal sampling duration we use here wastes the finite sampling resource, which leads to a low accuracy.

Hence, for addressing the issue, a Double DQN-based resource allocation algorithm is introduced, with an appropriate training episodes after multiple offline testing. We choose the two best algorithms in Fig. 3(a) to combine with the learning-based method.

Figure 3(b) shows that the adaptive learning-based method increases the accuracy by around 5.9%, 4.2% and 11.4%, compared with the basic Top-K, learning-based Top-k and basic adaptive method when the flow number is 8000. It is quiet possible that the adaptive learning-based method precisely identifies the nodes that actually covers more flows without the interference of redundant flows, and allocates more sampling resource to these nodes. However, the learning-based Top-k has only a few improvements in accuracy, which indicates the learning-based method does not work when the K is too small, e.g. K = 6. Meanwhile, the learning-based adaptive method can improve the accuracy of mice flows by 8.1% while maintaining the accuracy of elephant flows, which can be observed from the Fig. 4(a) and (b). In fact, the raises of total sampling accuracy mainly due to that of mice flows.

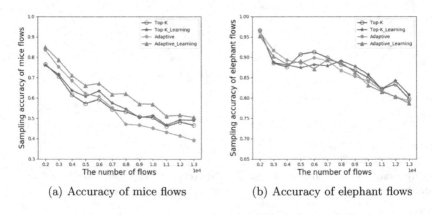

(a) Accuracy of mice flows   (b) Accuracy of elephant flows

Fig. 4. Comparison with respect to different algorithms.

Also, we compare the sampling accuracy at different K for each algorithm when flow number is 8000. As Fig. 5(a) shows, for the traditional algorithm, many flows cannot be sampled when K is too small. On the contrary, the sampling resources allocated to each node will be relatively limited, which also results in a lower accuracy. The basic adaptive method has no relation to K, and its performance is inferior to the others sometimes. However, through a reformed learning way, the accuracy can be improved obviously and keep a stable value, as shown in Fig. 5(b). Moreover, when $K = 9$, the accuracy of learning-based Top-k reaches a maximum but is still less than the learning-based adaptive method, from which we can infer that the iterative selection can indeed distribute resources more centrally to high-impact sampling nodes.

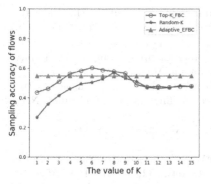

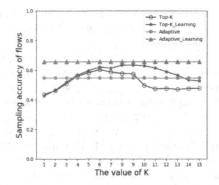

(a) Accuracy of total flows in a equal sampling duration

(b) Accuracy of total flows in a learning -based duration allocation

Fig. 5. Effect of K.

5   Conclusion

In this article, we proposed a flow-awareness framework based Double DQN and SDN techniques among MEC nodes, with a learning-based sampling strategy, for adaptively selecting sampling nodes and dynamically allocating sampling resource. We carried out the detailed experiments based on realistic traffic traces. Finally, compared with two traditional algorithms, our proposed approach can achieve excellent performance in terms of the flow-level sampling accuracy, especially for mice flows.

References

1. Benson, T., Akella, A., Maltz, D.A.: Network traffic characteristics of data centers in the wild. In: ACM SIGCOMM Conference on Internet Measurement, pp. 267–280, November 2010
2. Patel, M., et al.: Mobile-edge computing–introductory technical white paper. White Paper, Mobile-Edge Computing (MEC) Industry Initiative (2014)
3. Bremler-Barr, A., Harchol, Y., Hay, D., Koral, Y.: Deep packet inspection as a service. In: ACM CoNEXT, pp. 271–282, December 2014
4. Zhu, Y.B., Kang, N.X., Cao, J.X., Greenberg, A., Lu, G.H.: Packet-level telemetry in large datacenter networks. ACM SIGCOMM **45**(4), 479–491 (2015)
5. Su, Z.Y., Wang, T., Hamdi, M.: COSTA: cross-layer optimization for sketch-based software defined measurement task assignment. In: IEEE IWQoS, pp. 183–188, June 2015
6. Yu, M., Jose, L., Miao, R.: Software defined traffic measurement with OpenSketch. In: USENIX NSDI, pp. 29–42, April 2013
7. Bouet, M., Leguay, J., Conan, V.: Cost-based placement of virtualized deep packet inspection functions in SDN. In: IEEE MILCOM, pp. 992–997, February 2014
8. Suh, J., Kwon, T.T., Dixon, C., Felter, W., Carter, J.: OpenSample: a low-latency, sampling-based measurement platform for commodity SDN. In: IEEE ICDCS, pp. 228–237, July 2014

9. Xing, C.Y., Ding, K., Hu, C., Chen, M.: Sample and fetch-based large flow detection mechanism in software defined networks. IEEE Commun. Lett. **20**(9), 1764–1767 (2016)

10. Yoon, S., Ha, T., Kim, S., Lim, H.: Scalable traffic sampling using centrality measure on software-defined networks. IEEE Commun. Mag. **55**, 43–49 (2017)

11. Ha, T., Kim, S., An, N., Narantuya, J., Jeong, C., Kim, J.W.: Suspicious traffic sampling for intrusion detection in software-defined networks. Comput. Netw. **109**(2), 172–182 (2016)

12. Abbas, N., Zhang, Y., Taherkordi, A., Skeie, T.: Mobile edge computing: a survey. IEEE Internet Things J. **5**(1), 450–465 (2018)

13. Su, Z., Wang, T., Xia, Y., Hamdi, M.: CeMon: a cost-effective flow monitoring system in software defined networks. Comput. Netw. **92**(1), 101–115 (2015)

14. He, Y., Zhao, N., Yin, H.X.: Integrated networking, caching, and computing for connected vehicles: a deep reinforcement learning approach. IEEE Trans. Veh. Technol. **67**(1), 44–55 (2018)

15. Li, H., Gao, H., Lv, T.J., Lu, Y.: Deep Q-learning based dynamic resource allocation for self-powered ultra-dense networks. In: IEEE ICC, pp. 1–6, July 2018

16. Lu, L., Chen, D., Ren, X.L., Zhang, Q.M., Zhang, Y.C.: Vital nodes identification in complex networks. Phys. Rep. **65**, 1–63 (2016)

17. Vanini, E., Pan, R., Alizadeh, M., Taheri, P., Edsall, T.: Let it flow resilient asymmetric load balancing with flowlet switching. In: USENIX NSDI, pp. 407–420, May 2017

18. Van Hasselt, H., Guez, A., Silver, D.: Deep reinforcement learning with double Q-learning. In: Proceedings 30th AAAI Conference Artificial Intelligence, pp. 2094–2100 (2016)

19. Wang, S., Zhao, Y., Xu, J., Yuan, J., Hsu, C.H.: Edge server placement in mobile edge computing, June 2018. https://doi.org/10.1016/j.jpdc.2018.06.008

Author Index

Printed in the United States
By Bookmasters